FRANCIS POULENC
THE MAN AND HIS SONGS

An informal portrait of Pierre Bernac and
Francis Poulenc taken during the thirties

FRANCIS POULENC

THE MAN AND HIS SONGS

by

PIERRE BERNAC

Translated by
WINIFRED RADFORD
With a Foreword by Sir Lennox Berkeley

W · W · NORTON & COMPANY · INC ·
NEW YORK

Printed in Great Britain

To the memory of
Francis Poulenc

ACKNOWLEDGEMENTS

I wish to thank Éditions Bernard Grasset and Les Amis de Francis Poulenc for permission to quote from *Journal de mes mélodies* by Francis Poulenc, Henri Hell for allowing me to quote a few short passages from his book *Francis Poulenc* (Plon, 1958), Jean-Joel Barbier for one longer quotation from an article published in the journal *Disques* during the 1950s and Mme Jean Seringe, niece of Francis Poulenc, for the use of photographs which are all from her private collection, except the final one which is reproduced by courtesy of the photographer, Nancy Sorensen.

My thanks are also due to those mentioned below for permission to quote copyright song texts. The titles of some poems were changed when they appeared as song texts, but in these cases the original title of the poem has always been given. However, it has not been found practicable to print the few surrealist poems in their original layout.

All possible efforts have been made to reach copyright owners but in some cases these have been of no avail. The publishers would be glad to hear from any person(s) who can assist in tracing poems that are in copyright but not acknowledged.

Éditions Gallimard: Guillaume Apollinaire, poems from *Le bestiare, Il y a, Calligrammes* and *Alcools*; Paul Eluard, poems from *À toute épreuve, Les yeux fertiles, Chanson complète, Le livre ouvert I, Voir, La vie immédiate* and *Poésie et Vérité*; Louise de Vilmorin, poems from *Fiançailles pour rire*; Max Jacob, poems from *Chants Bretons* and *Le laboratoire central*; Robert Desnos, poems from *Le point du jour*; Jean Cocteau, poems from *Poésies 1916–1923*

Société Belge des Auteurs, Compositeurs et Éditeurs: Maurice Carême, poems from *La cage aux grillons* and *Le voleur d'étincelles*

Les Nouvelles Éditions Debresse: Maurice Fombeure, poems from *Chansons de la grande hune*

John Calder (Publishers) Ltd: Raymond Radiguet, 'Paul et Virginie' which appears in an English translation by Alan Stone in *Cheeks on Fire*

Mme Colette de Jouvenel: Colette, 'Le Portrait', copyright Colette de Jouvenel

Éditions Max Eschig: Laurence de Beylié, 'Nuage'

Les Éditions de la Table Ronde and Jean Anouilh: 'Les Chemins de l'Amour' © Jean Anouilh

New Directions Publishing Corporation, New York: Guillaume Apollinaire, 'Montparnasse' and '1904' from *Il y a*, published in the U.S.A. in *The Selected Writings of Guillaume Apollinaire*, all rights reserved, reprinted and published by permission.

CONTENTS

Illustrations follow pages 30 and 48

		page
	Foreword by Sir Lennox Berkeley	11
	Introduction	13
	List of Songs	15
I	Francis Poulenc, the Man	21
II	Francis Poulenc, Composer of Songs	37
III	Performance and Interpretation	42
IV	Guillaume Apollinaire	50
V	Paul Eluard	91
VI	Louise de Vilmorin	129
VII	Max Jacob	151
VIII	Maurice Carême	163
IX	Maurice Fombeure	170
X	Jean Cocteau—Raymond Radiguet	181
XI	Louis Aragon—Robert Desnos	186
XII	Colette—Laurence de Beylié—Jean Anouilh	193
XIII	Federico Garcia-Lorca	198
XIV	Jean Moréas	202
XV	Ronsard	207
XVI	Anonymous Texts of the Seventeenth Century	213
XVII	Malherbe—Racine—Charles d'Orléans	220
	Bibliographical Note	225
	Index of Titles	227
	Index of First Lines	230

FOREWORD

by Sir Lennox Berkeley

THAT PIERRE BERNAC was the supreme and unrivalled interpreter of Poulenc's songs is well known. In this book he tells us how he achieved his mastery of the composer's idiom by giving us detailed and lucid analyses of all the piano-accompanied songs. He has the unique advantage of a long association with Poulenc, who toured the world with him as his accompanist, thereby giving him an understanding of the songs that no one else could have.

Poulenc himself approached his task as a song writer by a minute examination of each poem, subjectively by a re-creation of its atmosphere, and objectively by a careful study of its prosody and vowel sounds. Pierre Bernac takes the reader through a similar process, showing that the text of the poem must be interpreted as accurately as the music. Those of us who were lucky enough to hear him sing them will realize that this principle was the basis of his performance. Indeed, his amazingly clear diction, allied to his purely vocal technique, was something quite unforgettable.

Poulenc's favourite poets, as far as providing texts for his music was concerned, were Apollinaire and Eluard. Apollinaire's poems drew from him a musical equivalent of the poet's prevailing mood of nostalgia; songs such as 'La Grenouillère', or 'Hôtel', are instances of this; nowhere is Poulenc's music more evocative or more completely individual. Eluard inspired him to seek a somewhat different style from that of his earlier songs; here he sometimes grouped poems together into a song-cycle such as *Tel jour telle nuit* or *Le travail du peintre*. Pierre Bernac provides us with a most valuable commentary on these later songs, showing how the composer reached in them another type of lyrical expression deriving directly from the poems.

Translation from French into English, and vice-versa, is notoriously difficult. Winifred Radford well deserves the gratitude that English readers will feel for her skill and knowledge in having made this book available to them in their own language. Certainly it is essential reading for singers who wish to include some Poulenc in their programmes. They will find the subtleties of French pronunciation discussed and unusual words explained. Nor is it only the vocal and literary aspects of the songs that are dealt with;

the author has much to tell us about the piano part. Poulenc was a very good pianist who had, as one often finds with composers, a somewhat idiosyncratic way of playing, and this is reflected in his piano-writing. Some of his accompaniments are real piano pieces needing separate study, so that here too is much valuable information for the accompanist. It is thought by many that Poulenc found his true musical personality most completely in his songs, and yet they are among the least well known of his works. This may well be because of the demands they make on both singer and pianist. Here, one is able to study the nature of these difficulties and to absorb some hints about how to tackle them. One may confidently hope that the book may do more than this, for the author writes with a love and enthusiasm that communicate themselves movingly to the reader.

INTRODUCTION

IT IS NOW some years since Francis Poulenc left us, and in duty to his memory I feel that I should attempt to communicate in a tangible way the understanding that I have of his songs, and also something of our mutual experience in interpreting and performing them. Therefore, prompted by this very valuable experience, I have written this book in the justifiable hope of passing on a little of my knowledge to singers and pianists who feel an interest in the songs and a wish to interpret them.

Two-thirds of the songs were written for the concerts given by Francis Poulenc and myself; we created them together and performed them many times during the 25 years of our collaboration. I often gave instruction on the songs composed for a woman's voice during Poulenc's own lifetime and at his request, since he himself had no love of coaching, even though the music was his own. He would frequently say to singers who sought his advice: 'Go and see Bernac, he will be able to tell you better than I what should be done.'

Francis Poulenc was, incontestably, the greatest composer of *mélodies* of his time. This has many times been affirmed by international critical opinion and is confirmed ever more strongly as the years pass. On his own admission his songs occupy a primal place in his work. I could wish for no better proof of this than the manuscript which he left to me: *Journal de mes mélodies (Diary of my Songs*—published in a limited edition by Bernard Grasset, and now unfortunately out of print). I shall quote from it frequently, and allow Poulenc himself to speak wherever possible.

I am not, alas, a writer, so the commentaries I shall make will be exempt from literary pretension. Neither am I a musicologist, therefore the songs will not be approached from the angle of musical analysis, but purely from the point of view of an interpreter who sang them many times and always loved them. Did Poulenc not say: 'Above all do not analyse my music—love it!'

A list of all the songs is given, classified in the order of their composition, with an indication of the range of voice to which each song is suited. The first chapter is a biography of Francis Poulenc, and includes a sketch of his personality, combined with some personal reminiscences. The two following chapters concern the composition of the songs, and general remarks on their performance and interpretation which will assuredly conform to the taste and wishes of Poulenc himself. The songs are briefly studied and grouped according to the poets who inspired them, preceded by a short biography of each poet.

The French poems of the songs are included, giving indications of the liaisons, the elisions, the breaths, etc. With these texts will be found literal line by line translations into English, all of which have been made by Winifred Radford.

Paris 1977   P. B.

KEY TO THE SIGNS IN THE FRENCH TEXTS

√	breath
(√)	breath, if unavoidable
│	break or no liaison
⌢	at the end of a line: no breath
‿	liaison or elision
s̲	consonant which should be pronounced
¢	consonant which should not be pronounced
m̲m̲	double consonant sounded
e̲n̲nui	expressive stress

LIST OF SONGS

The sign (W) indicates that these songs can be sung only by a woman's voice, the sign (M) only by a man's voice.

1918/19 *Le Bestiaire.* (G. Apollinaire) ESCHIG
    1. Le dromadaire 2. La chèvre du Thibet
    3. La sauterelle 4. Le dauphin
    5. L'écrevisse 6. La carpe

1919 *Cocardes.* (J. Cocteau) ESCHIG
    1. Miel de Narbonne 2. Bonne
    d'enfant 3. Enfant de troupe

1924/25 *Poèmes de Ronsard.* HEUGEL   (M)
    1. Attributs 2. Le tombeau 3. Ballet
    4. Je n'ai plus que les os 5. A son page

1926 *Chansons gaillardes.* (Textes anonymes du XVIIᵉ siècle) HEUGEL
    1. La maîtresse volage 2. Chanson à
    boire 3. Madrigal 4. Invocation aux
    Parques 5. Couplets bachiques
    6. L'offrande 7. La belle jeunesse
    8. Sérénade

1927/28 *Airs chantés.* (J. Moréas) SALABERT
    1. Air romantique 2. Air champêtre
    3. Air grave 4. Air vif

1930 *Epitaphe.* (Malherbe) SALABERT

1931 *Trois Poèmes de Louise Lalanne.* SALABERT   (W)
    1. Le présent 2. Chanson 3. Hier

1931 *Quatre Poèmes.* (G. Apollinaire) SALABERT
    1. L'anguille 2. Carte postale 3. Avant
    le cinéma 4. 1904

1931 *Cinq Poèmes.* (Max Jacob) SALABERT   (W)
    1. Chanson bretonne 2. Cimetière
    3. La petite servante 4. Berceuse
    5. Souric et Mouric

1935   *Cinq Poèmes.* (Paul Eluard) DURAND
          1. Peut-il se reposer   2. Il la prend dans
          ses bras   3. Plume d'eau claire
          4. Rôdeuse au front de verre
          5. Amoureuses

1935   *A sa guitare.* (Ronsard) DURAND

1937   *Tel jour telle nuit.* (P. Eluard) DURAND
          1. Bonne journée   2. Une ruine coquille
          vide   3. Le front comme un drapeau
          perdu   4. Une roulotte couverte en   (two keys)
          tuiles   5. A toutes brides   6. Une herbe
          pauvre   7. Je n'ai envie que de
          t'aimer   8. Figure de force brûlante et
          farouche   9. Nous avons fait la nuit

1937   *Trois Poèmes.* (L. de Vilmorin) DURAND   (W)
          1. Le garçon de Liège   2. Au-delà
          3. Aux officiers de la Garde Blanche

1938   *Deux Poèmes.* (G. Apollinaire) SALABERT
          1. Dans le jardin d'Anna   2. Allons plus
          vite

1938   *Miroirs brûlants.* (P. Eluard) SALABERT
          1. Tu vois le feu du soir   2. Je nommerai
          ton front

1938   *Le portrait.* (Colette) SALABERT

1938   *La grenouillière.* (G. Apollinaire) SALABERT

1938   *Priez pour paix.* (Ch. d'Orléans) SALABERT
                                        (two keys)

1938   *Ce doux petit visage.* (P. Eluard) SALABERT

1939   *Bleuet.* (G. Apollinaire) DURAND

1939   *Fiançailles pour rire.* (L. de Vilmorin)   (W)
     SALABERT
      1. La dame d'André   2. Dans l'herbe
      3. Il vole   4. Mon cadavre est doux
      comme un gant   5. Violon   6. Fleurs

1940   *Banalités.* (G. Apollinaire) ESCHIG
      1. Chanson d'Orkenise   2. Hôtel
      3. Fagnes de Wallonie   4. Voyage à
      Paris   5. Sanglots

1940   *Les chemins de l'amour.* (J. Anouilh) ESCHIG

1942   *Chansons villageoises.* (M. Fombeure)
     ESCHIG
      1. Chanson du clair tamis   2. Les gars qui
      vont à la fête   3. C'est le joli printemps
      4. Le mendiant   5. Chanson de la fille
      frivole   6. Le retour du sergent

1943   *Métamorphoses.* (L. de Vilmorin)
     SALABERT
      1. Reine des mouettes   2. C'est ainsi que
      tu es   3. Paganini

1943   *Deux Poèmes.* (L. Aragon) SALABERT
      1. 'C'   2. Fêtes galantes

1945   *Montparnasse.* (G. Apollinaire) ESCHIG

      Hyde Park. (G. Apollinaire) ESCHIG

1946   *Le pont.* (G. Apollinaire) ESCHIG

      Un poème. (G. Apollinaire) ESCHIG

1946   *Paul et Virginie.* (R. Radiguet) ESCHIG

1947   *Mais mourir.* (P. Eluard) HEUGEL   (M)

1947   *Hymne.* (Racine) SALABERT

1947   *Trois Chansons de F. Garcia-Lorca.* HEUGEL
        1. L'enfant muet   2. Adelina à la pro-
        menade   3. Chanson de l'oranger sec

1947   *Le disparu.* (R. Desnos) SALABERT   (M)

1947   *Main dominée par le coeur.* (P. Eluard)
        SALABERT

1948   *Calligrammes.* (G. Apollinaire) HEUGEL
        1. L'espionne   2. Mutation   3. Vers le
        Sud   4. Il pleut   5. La grâce exilée
        6. Aussi bien que les cigales   7. Voyage

1949   *Mazurka.* (L. de Vilmorin) (dans: (M)
        'Mouvements du coeur') HEUGEL

1950   *La Fraîcheur et le Feu.* (P. Eluard) ESCHIG
        1. Rayon des yeux . . .   2. Le matin les
        branches attisent . . .   3. Tout
        disparu . . .   4. Dana les ténèbres du
        jardin . . .   5. Unis la fraîcheur et le
        feu . . .   6. Homme au sourire
        tendre . . .   7. La grande rivière qui
        va . . .

1954   *Parisiana.* (Max Jacob) SALABERT
        1. Jouer du bugle   2. Vous n'écrivez
        plus?

1954   *Rosemonde.* (G. Apollinaire) ESCHIG

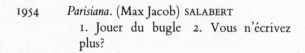
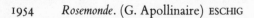

1956   *Le travail du peintre*. (P. Eluard) ESCHIG
      1. Pablo Picasso   2. Marc Chagall
      3. Georges Braque   4. Juan Gris   5. Paul
      Klee   6. Joan Miró   7. Jacques Villon

1956   *Deux mélodies 1956*. ESCHIG
      1. La souris (G. Apollinaire)   2. Nuage
      (L. de Beylié)

1956   *Dernier Poème*. (R. Desnos) ESCHIG   (M)

1958   *Une chanson de porcelaine*. (P. Eluard)
      ESCHIG

1960   *La courte paille*. (M. Carême) ESCHIG   (W)
      1. Le sommeil   2. Quelle aventure!
      3 La reine de coeur   4. Ba, be, bi, bo, bu
      5. Les anges musiciens   6. Le carafon
      7. Lune d'Avril

*   *   *

These 137 songs, which comprise the complete output of concert songs by
Francis Poulenc, will all be studied in the following chapters.

    The following works have not been included, because for various reasons
they cannot be considered as concert songs:

Vocalise, for voice and piano, 1927, Leduc.

Toréador, Spanish-Italian Song, text by Jean Cocteau, 1918, Salabert.

Four Songs for Children, text by Jaboune (alias Jean Nohain), 1934/35,
Enoch.
    1. La tragique histoire du petit René
    2. Nous voulons une petite sœur
    3. Le petit garçon trop bien portant
    4. Monsieur Sans-Souci

Huit chansons polonaises, harmonised by Francis Poulenc for the singer Marie
Modrakowska, 1939, Durand.

Fancy, a song for children on a text by Shakespeare, from *The Merchant of
Venice*, commissioned by the Countess of Harewood for a book, *Classical
Songs for Children*, 1962, Anthony Blond, London.

Colloque, duet for soprano and baritone, poem by Paul Valéry, 1940, shortly
to be published by Salabert.

Also the following are not included in the list of concert songs:

Le Bal Masqué, secular cantata, for baritone and chamber orchestra, on
poems by Max Jacob, 1932, Salabert.

La Dame de Monte-Carlo, monologue for soprano and orchestra, text by Jean
Cocteau, 1961, Ricordi.

CHAPTER I

Francis Poulenc, the Man

FRANCIS POULENC WAS born on January 7th 1899, in Paris, at number two, Place des Saussaies, a few steps from the Elysée Palace—residence of the Presidents of the Republic. His parents occupied an apartment, which, to judge by photographs, was large, comfortable, and lavishly furnished with upholstered suites, draped curtains and potted palms, according to the taste of the times. His father, Emile Poulenc, in association with his two brothers, directed a firm concerned with the manufacture of chemical products which, after great expansion, has now become the powerful Rhône-Poulenc Company, one of the biggest organizations in Europe.

The Poulencs originated from Aveyron, a strangely beautiful region in south-central France. In Espalion there is a 'rue Poulenc' which is not intended to perpetuate the memory of the musician, but one of his forefathers who was a local notability. The people of Aveyron, by very reason of the wild and rugged character of their land, are a serious, industrious race, very often adherent to the Roman Catholic faith. 'My father,' said Francis, 'had, without bigotry, superb religious belief.'

Emile Poulenc was a music lover, although he did not play any instrument; he was a loyal supporter of the *Concerts Colonne*, and never missed a first night at the Opéra or the Opéra-Comique. But his 'gods' were Beethoven, Berlioz, Franck, and so it can scarcely be said that he transmitted his musical tastes to his son.

It was Francis Poulenc's maternal heredity that was the predominant influence and from which he received, not only most of the traits of his character, but also his artistic gifts. His mother, Jenny Royer, came of a family that had been purely Parisian for a number of generations, which is quite unusual. The family consisted of craftsmen—tapestry makers, cabinet makers, bronze founders, etc. . . . who had always been lovers of the arts: literature, painting, drama, music.

The Royers were entirely hedonistic—not hostile to religion but totally indifferent to it. 'Uncle Papoum', brother of Madame Poulenc, was typical. He belonged to a race that has disappeared today, that of the 'man about town'. An execrable amateur painter (in the style of Toulouse-Lautrec), he was smitten with the theatre, haunted the wings and struck up friendships with several celebrated actors and singers. When he came to see his sister their conversation fascinated Francis who, pretending to play under the table with his mechanical railway, did not miss a word.

Holidays were spent on grandmother Royer's property at Nogent-sur-Marne, in the suburbs quite close to Paris, which for this family so purely Parisian represented the real countryside. The banks of the Marne were lined with pleasure gardens and popular dancing halls (*bals-musettes*) where, on fine Sundays, the good people of Paris came to dance to the sound of the accordion. Ever since his childhood Francis felt the specific poetry of this trivial gaiety and evoked it in many of his works.

Madame Poulenc played the piano with an amateur technique but 'she was gifted with impeccable musical sensibility and a delightful touch'. Her favourite composers were Mozart, Chopin, Schubert, Schumann. 'But being devoid of any artistic snobbery, she allowed herself at times to include what she called *her little fancies*, some pieces of Grieg or even the *Romance* of Rubinstein', which Francis called 'adorable bad music'.

She quickly realized that her son had one passion: that of playing the piano. From the age of four or five she began to teach him. Then he had as professor an assistant of Mademoiselle Boutet-de-Monval, a niece of César Franck. 'When I recall my childhood I see myself always sitting at a piano,' said Francis Poulenc, who in reading at sight and listening to music was seized with ever increasing amazement. 'One day I discovered *Die Winterreise* of Schubert and suddenly something very profound in my life was changed. Particularly the astonishing *Die Nebensonnen* which always keeps for me the same emotive power.'

He was overwhelmed by the revelation of Debussy when first hearing *Danse sacrée et Danse profane* for harp and string orchestra. On going home he tried to pick out on the piano the astonishing and subtle harmonies that he had heard.

It was doubtless about this time that the following scene took place: Francis and his mother happened to be in a shop in the *rue Tronchet*, at the corner of the *Place de la Madeleine*, when to their surprise they saw Debussy and his wife come in. They knew them by sight, having seen them in the distance at the rehearsals of the *Concerts Colonne*. Taking advantage of a moment of inattention, little Francis was able to touch Debussy's hat which had been put on a chair. 'If I had dared I would have kissed it,' he said in recounting this act of devotion.

During the years that followed he made another striking discovery—that of Stravinsky's works. *L'Oiseau de feu*; then *Petrouchka* and lastly *Le Sacre de Printemps*.

Little Francis tried his hand at composition: some *Préludes* for piano 'of unbelievable complexity' under the influence of Debussy. Also a certain *Processional pour la Crémation d'un Mandarin*, obviously inspired by the *Rossignol* of Stravinsky.

Madame Poulenc had hoped that her son would enter the Paris *Conservatoire*, but Emile Poulenc, as befits a good industrialist, insisted on the continuation of his classical education, and, the war having broken out while he was passing his first examinations, Francis soon found himself in uniform. It is to be regretted that he always lacked a certain basic training in composition. As a composer he was self-taught. When the war was over it was really too late for him to enter the *Conservatoire*, and it was only in 1921 to 1924, wishing to deepen his technical knowledge, that he worked under the direction of Charles Koechlin, who proved moreover to be an excellent and clear-sighted master for him.

          *   *   *

Happily, from the age of fourteen, Francis had been taught by the pianist Ricardo Viñes, admirable as an artist and as a man. He was the one great virtuoso who, at that period, played Debussy, Ravel, de Falla. The writer Léon-Paul Fargue, who knew him intimately, wrote: 'Three words seemed excluded for ever from his heart and his vocabulary; three ugly words that had no meaning at all for him: intrigue, push, concession.' And Francis described his dear Viñes thus:

> He was a remarkable man, a strange hidalgo with big moustachios, a large brown sombrero of purest Barcelona style on his head, fine buttoned boots with which he kicked my shins when my pedalling, an essential factor in modern music, was not good; and nobody knew better how to teach this than he did. He could play clearly in a flood of pedals. And what science of the *staccato* opposed to an absolute *legato*!

It was the instruction of Viñes that made of Poulenc the remarkable pianist that he became. But when Poulenc repeated incessantly, 'I owe him everything!', he meant also that he owed to him his emergence as a composer.

For not only was Viñes an excellent interpreter of his first works for piano, but it was through him that Poulenc came to know two artists, Erik Satie and Georges Auric, who in their different ways had an influence of prime importance on the beginnings of his career as a composer; and it was through them that he met other musicians of his epoch and his generation, notably those who with him formed the group which became known as *Les Six*: Darius Milhaud, Arthur Honegger, Georges Auric, Louis Durey, and

Germaine Tailleferre. This group was so named by the critic Henri Collet, because their works appeared at the same concerts, principally those organized by Felix Delgrange at *Lyre et Palette* and by Jane Bathori at *Le Vieux Colombier*. Bathori, a singer and a wonderful musician, was an ardent propagandist for new music. She was the first interpreter of Debussy, Ravel, Roussel, Satie, and many others also. She sang their works accompanying herself admirably on the piano. It is due to her that the first works of Poulenc were performed with an immediate and astonishing success. *La Rapsodie Nègre*, *Les Mouvements Perpetuels*, for instance.

But the group of Les Six was not in any sense a 'school' or a 'movement'. The six musicians were merely a group of friends and they always remained so. The very most that could be said is that they reacted against 'music to which one listens head in hand', against 'the Wagnerian clouds', against the 'mists of the Debussyists'. Jean Cocteau was their spokesman, their 'poetic chronicler', rather than their theoretician, notably in the ephemeral manifesto *Le Coq et l'Arlequin* which championed the aesthetic of Erik Satie. But if Poulenc, in all his earliest works was profoundly influenced by this aesthetic, the tastes and the musical tendencies of the six musicians remained very different. Their common reaction at that time was nevertheless salutary, since as a result, it allowed each one of them to develop his own personality.

An 'anti-Debussy' reaction on the part of Poulenc may seem surprising. He makes himself very clear on this subject:

> Despite an attack of anti-Debussyism out of self-defence at the time when I came to know Satie, in 1917, Debussy has always remained my favourite composer after Mozart. I could not do without his music. It is my oxygen. Moreover the reaction of Les Six was directed against the imitators of Debussy, not against Debussy himself. It is always necessary to repudiate for a time, at the age of twenty, those whom you have idolized, for fear of being overgrown with ivy.

*　　　　　*　　　　　*

From his childhood Francis had had, as a great friend, Raymonde Linossier, a young girl of exceptional intelligence and culture who unfortunately died very young. She was 'the true intellectual leaven of his adolescence' and she initiated him into the world of literature. With her he frequented the celebrated book-shop in the rue de l'Odéon: *Aux amis des livres*, run by Adrienne Monnier. All the writers and poets who were of importance between the two wars came there to talk and to read their works. It was there that Francis met Paul Valéry, André Gide, Paul Claudel, Valéry-

Larbaud, Léon-Paul Fargue, André Breton, Louis Aragon, Paul Eluard and others besides. Also the three astonishing American women, Gertrude Stein, Alice B. Toklas and Sylvia Beach who introduced James Joyce to these musical and literary circles. Here Francis also met painters such as Picasso, Juan Gris, Braque, Modigliani, Derain and Marie Laurencin. It was with the latter that he was soon to be associated in writing his first work for full orchestra.

At this time a very important event was about to take place. While he continued to compose chamber music—works of this period that do not add greatly to his fame—Poulenc had become sufficiently celebrated for that great discoverer of talent, Serge Diaghilev, to commission a ballet from him. Doubtless it is unnecessary to recall here that the Russian Ballet of Serge Diaghilev had a determining influence on the evolution of modern music. This impresario of flair and genius drew around him all those musicians and painters who had something new of value to offer. Diaghilev therefore suggested that Poulenc, in association with Marie Laurencin, should write 'a kind of modern *Sylphides*', and Poulenc made of this 'a kind of *Fêtes Galantes* 1923, in which, as in certain paintings by Watteau, nothing is actually seen but the worst can be imagined'. The French title of the ballet is *Les Biches*, playing on the double sense of this word, but in English it is *House Party*, which can be no less equivocal. At all events, the production in Monte Carlo, as well as the first performance in Paris, was an outstanding success.

*   *   *

I have mentioned many illustrious names of musicians, writers and painters, and the great Diaghilev. We can imagine how intoxicating it must have been for a young man, quite unprepared, to find himself suddenly involved in this most exciting period of artistic creation, thanks to the success of his first works. For it is difficult to realize in these days, after a war which has left the world more disturbed than ever, how great the outburst of exhilaration had been during the all too brief twenties following the First World War. It was thought, after that long, atrocious and appallingly murderous holocaust, that the world would at last know enduring peace. The extraordinary euphoria, the prodigious artistic vitality of Paris at this period which permitted all that was most daring, therefore remained for Poulenc the Golden Age, and Monte Carlo his Utopia. His artistic and musical tastes were indelibly marked and his creative talent influenced for a long time.

Among works in this vein are *Aubade*, concerto chorégraphique (1920), *Les Chansons Gaillardes* (1926) and *Le Bal Masqué*, secular cantata on poems by Max Jacob (1932). Much later came *Les Mamelles de Tirésias*, an opéra bouffe on the surrealist play by Guillaume Apollinaire (1944), and also, less than two years before his death, *La Dame de Monte Carlo*, a monologue for soprano and orchestra, on a text by Jean Cocteau (1961). This is a work which is not really worthy of him and which he would certainly never have written had it not been for his nostalgia for the dazzling, halcyon days of his youth, so well symbolized for him by Monte Carlo.

*   *   *

In his conversations with Stéphane Audel, Poulenc says:

> The three great encounters of my life, which have profoundly influenced my art, are those with Wanda Landowska, Pierre Bernac, and Paul Eluard.

The meeting with the great harpsichordist took place in 1923 at the home of Princess Edmond de Polignac. An American by birth, her maiden name was Winaretta Singer, and the fortune derived from the Singer Sewing Machine Company enabled her to become a generous and enlightened Maecenas. She commissioned works from Debussy, Fauré, Ravel, Stravinsky, from Poulenc himself (the Concerto for Two Pianos, 1932, and the Concerto for Organ, 1938), and from Manuel de Falla. It was at the first performance of *El Retablo de Maese Pedro* by de Falla, which took place in her salon under the direction of the composer himself, that Ricardo Viñes presented Poulenc to Wanda Landowska, who was playing the harpsichord part. 'I had as much artistic respect as human fondness for her,' said Poulenc. 'It was she who gave me the key to Bach's harpsichord works. It was she who taught me all that I know of the French composers for harpsichord.' She asked him to write a concerto for her, the *Concerto Champêtre*, but it did not appear until 1929.

I will speak of the meeting with Paul Eluard at the beginning of the chapter devoted to the songs inspired by his poems, so I must now come to the meeting between Poulenc and Bernac.

It was in 1926, when I was a young and still very little known singer, that one day on the telephone I heard a somewhat nasal voice telling me that the speaker was Francis Poulenc. He asked me to sing the first performance of a series of songs that he had just composed and which were called *Chansons Gaillardes*. The concert was to be of works by himself and Georges Auric. It attracted a big audience and was an astonishing success. But afterwards we were not very often in touch, only meeting occasionally in Parisian musical circles with no opportunity to collaborate. The circumstances which led to the formation of our ensemble are perhaps comic enough to merit description.

It was not until the spring of 1934, meeting again in the salon of a mutual friend (the sister of Edmond Rostand), where I had been singing some songs of Debussy, that Francis told me he would like to accompany me in these same songs and some of his own songs. I replied that it would be a joy, but for the moment I was about to leave for Salzburg where I was spending the summer working at my Lieder repertoire with my dear old master, Reinhold von Wahrlich. I suggested we could discuss it again in the autumn, but fate decreed otherwise.

That summer in Salzburg there was an American lady who had rented a superb house overlooking the Mirabell Gardens. She was extremely wealthy and, to say the least, original. Having been requested to call on her, I found her in bed, aiming a toy rifle at me. This lady wanted to organize an evening devoted to the music of Debussy, during the Festival, and she asked me to sing. By a coincidence, the newspaper *Le Figaro* had asked Poulenc to review the Festival. Knowing that he was coming, I left a note at his hotel asking him to accompany me.

What a strange event that Debussy evening was! . . . First there was an orchestral concert at the Mozarteum directed by a young conductor, for whom a brilliant future was predicted, Herbert von Karajan. After that the audience went to the Mirabell Gardens, where, in an open air theatre, Serge Lifar and the Ballet of the Vienna Opera danced *L'Après midi d'un faune*. Then the audience crossed the garden and climbed over a high wall by a wooden staircase which the American lady had had constructed, and which descended into her garden. There, under a big linden tree, stood a piano. At the stroke of midnight, it was there that Francis Poulenc and I gave a concert which was to be the first of a long series, for we found that our musical accord was such that we decided to form an association dedicated to the idea of bringing to the interpretation of the vocal concert repertoire a similar care and perfection of ensemble that is found in certain players of instrumental sonatas. From this moment our friendly collaboration began. Francis Poulenc and I were both thirty-five years old, for by a curious chance there was a difference of only five days between our ages. The collaboration was to last 25 years, until, on reaching our sixtieth birthday, I decided to retire from the concert platform.

Our association naturally encouraged Poulenc to write songs, for we always needed something fresh to renew the 'Poulenc group' of our programmes. Thus it was that we created together about 90 of his songs, specially written for our concerts. But Poulenc also said that it was through accompanying me in Schubert, Schumann, Fauré, Debussy, Ravel etc . . .

that he learned his art of song writing. In fact, it was for our first concert together in Paris that he undertook to set to music the poetry of Eluard. He wished to find for me a style that was both serious and profound and he was able to affirm later, 'At last I have found a lyric poet, a poet of love, be it human love or love of liberty.'

During the first years of our association, Francis and I passed our summer holidays together in order to prepare the works that we intended to include in our programmes for the following season. These periods of retreat also gave him the studious calm he found so necessary for composition. We chose beautiful regions in central France which, in those days, were still unknown to tourists, le Morvan or la Corrèze. So it was in 1936 we found ourselves in Uzerche. . . . But here I will allow Francis himself to describe, in his conversations with Claude Rostand, this event which was so important for his spiritual and artistic evolution:

I am religious by deepest instinct and by heredity. I feel myself incapable of ardent political conviction, but it seems quite natural to me to believe and to practise religion. I am a Catholic. It is my greatest freedom. Nevertheless the gentle indifference of the maternal side of my family had, quite naturally, led to a long fit of forgetfulness of religion. From 1920 to 1935 I was admittedly very little concerned regarding the faith.

In 1936, a date of primal importance in my life and my career, taking advantage of a period of work with Yvonne Gouverné and Bernac at Uzerche, I asked the latter to drive me in his car to Rocamadour, of which I had often heard my father speak. This place of pilgrimage is, in fact, quite close to the Aveyron.

I had just learned, a day or two before, of the tragic death of my colleague Pierre-Octave Ferroud.* The atrocious extinction of this musician so full of vigour had left me stupefied. Pondering on the fragility of our human frame, the life of the spirit attracted me anew.

Rocamadour led me back to the faith of my childhood. This sanctuary, certainly the most ancient in France, had everything to subjugate me. Clinging in full sunlight to a vertiginous craggy rock, Rocamadour is a place of extraordinary peace, accentuated by the very limited number of tourists.

With a courtyard in front, pink with oleanders in tubs, a very simple chapel, half hollowed into the rock, shelters a miraculous figure of the Virgin, carved, according to tradition, in black wood by Saint Amadour, the little Zacchaeus of the gospel who had to climb a tree to see the Christ.

---

* Pierre-Octave Ferroud born in 1900, composer and important promoter of the musical life in Paris between the two world wars. He died in 1935 in an automobile accident.

The evening of this same visit to Rocamadour, I began my *Litanies à la Vierge Noire* (Litanies to the Black Virgin) for women's voices and organ. In this work I have tried to express the feeling of 'peasant devotion' which had so strongly impressed me in that lofty place.

After this experience, a new artist coexisted in Poulenc, who, without abjuring the former, was to develop alongside it and assume his paternal heredity. He spoke the same musical language but was to achieve true greatness. In this spirit some of his abundant religious works should naturally be mentioned first: for *a cappella* choirs; Masses, Motets, *Lauds*, Prayers; for choirs with orchestra, *Stabat Mater*, *Gloria*, *Répons des Ténèbres*.

But some very different works, similar only in the gravity of their inspiration, should also be cited, such as the cycle of songs, *Tel jour telle nuit* (1937), the Concerto for Organ and Strings (1938), *Figure Humaine* on a poem by Paul Eluard, for double mixed choir *a cappella* (1943) and the Sonata for Two Pianos (1952); the opera *Dialogues des Carmelites* (*The Carmelites*) on the play by Bernanos (1953/56), and also *La Voix Humaine* (1958), lyrical scene on a text by Jean Cocteau.

I said earlier that before 1920 Poulenc had written some sonatas for wind instruments that did not add greatly to his fame. However, in 1926 he composed a Trio for Piano, Oboe and Bassoon, which was his first work of true chamber music and which had lacked nothing of his qualities of spontaneity, freshness and invention, and also a Sextet for Wind Instruments and Piano, dated 1932. In the nineteen-forties he wrote two sonatas, one for violin and piano, and one for cello and piano. But as he himself confessed, he was less at ease with strings, and in 1957 and 1962, he returned to wind instruments with three sonatas: for flute and piano, clarinet and piano, and oboe and piano. This last work ends with a noble and moving *Lament* which was to be Francis Poulenc's farewell to music. He died in Paris, on January 30th, 1963, suddenly and unexpectedly, leaving no unfinished work.

*　　*　　*

For all those who knew him even a little, Francis Poulenc was an unforgettable personality. His physical appearance alone was striking enough. Paul Guth compared him to the *Gilles* by Watteau with his hanging arms. He was tall and heavy with a strange walk, feet turned outwards. As a rule a coat hung loosely about him, for he felt the cold and travelled with a great profusion of woollens, shawls and rugs. His big face with its strong features, a large nose and enormous ears, was not handsome. His brown eyes were rather small and a little slanting, but their sweetness and intelligence were beyond description. His hands were very unusual—big, plump, with fingers like little sausages, and nails that he had bitten all his life. Astonishingly expressive hands, which he often held not normally straight, but turned outwards with the fingers spread. He used them a great deal when speaking, holding them stiffly, bending his wrists. They were a pianist's hands to an unparalleled degree. He had what seemed like a little cushion at the end of each finger and could easily stretch a tenth. One can despair of ever again hearing his music interpreted with a comparable sonority, either softly mellow, or violently percussive.

If his physical aspect was surprising enough, it was his extraordinary 'presence' which made Poulenc unforgettable. He was one of those exceptional people with a personality so strong that it left an indelible impression on all who came in contact with him: one of those who, although they have left us, seem always to be with us throughout our lives, so vividly does their presence remain. In the evening of a long life, I have known few others who, like Francis Poulenc, remain so intensely present. I always feel that if he were suddenly to open the door, I should not be surprised. It is impressive to find that every time his friends meet together, even after the fifteen years since his death, their conversation always returns unwittingly and inevitably to him, and he always seems to be with them.

Nevertheless it is very difficult to describe him adequately in a few pages, so complex was his personality and at times even contradictory. A surprising mixture of gaiety and melancholy, of profundity and futility, of triviality and nobility. At all events, none could remain unaffected by him. He could be the perfect type of 'bon vivant', loving life and all the good things it has to offer, but he could also sink into serious attacks of depression. His mood could vary from one day to another and even one moment to another, for he was extremely sensitive and emotional. At heart he was an anxious man.

Like many artists he was egocentric, but he was disinterested and generous. There was something of the 'spoilt child' about him, but this could be readily forgiven for he possessed great and genuine kindliness. He never lost his temper. He was the most natural and simple of men, the most direct and the least vain that it is possible to imagine. Nobody could be easier to approach, for he was cordial by nature. He was particularly kind to simple people; with his great intelligence and sensitivity he knew how to put them at their ease. In all social circles he had many faithful and affectionate friends.

Never having had any financial worries, he had always been able to do exactly as he wished in life. Attracted to Touraine by a dear old friend whom he called Aunt Liénard although she was not in any way related to him, he purchased, when he was twenty-nine years old, a beautiful

An early publicity photograph of
Francis Poulenc and Pierre Bernac

Poulenc at the piano at Noizay, 1955

Max Jacob

eighteenth-century house at Noizay, close to Amboise and Vouvray. He arranged it with perfect and very personal taste, with furniture and objects, which, without being very valuable, were beautiful and shown to great advantage. This house was extremely comfortable and pleasant to live in. In addition, he himself designed formal gardens, 'à la Française', on his terrace overlooking the Loire valley.

His ownership of this property has sometimes given rise to the idea that Poulenc was a musician from Touraine, but he denied it vehemently, maintaining that his roots stemmed entirely from Aveyron on his paternal side, and on his maternal side above all, from Paris.

When he was in this beautiful home, he never put a foot into the surrounding countryside, for he declared it depressed him. In actuality he detested the countryside. He was a true townsman, or rather a true Parisian.

> Paris takes me out of myself [he said], in a sense it is this that is one of its benefits; there are many days when I dislike myself! It is also the only place in the world where I can bear great sorrow, anguish, melancholy. I have only to take a walk in the *quartiers* that I love and life seems suddenly lighter.

I drove him back one day from Touraine to his apartment in Paris; on seeing the Luxembourg Gardens he exclaimed, 'That is the only countryside that I like!' This apartment, small as he wished it to be, was on the top floor of a house at number five *rue de Médicis*, and in fact overlooked the lovely Luxembourg Gardens. There also he knew how to create a beautiful abode, comfortable and strongly expressing his personality. In furnishing, his favourite colours were red, orange and brown.

These two homes were always admirably in order: his important musical and literary libraries, also his gramophone records were impeccably arranged and his papers filed; his flowers arranged by his own hand, for he adored flowers. Yet he detested occupying himself with material things, about which he was unbelievably inept. Equally, although a fastidious gourmet, he would have been incapable of boiling an egg. He dieted because he always feared for his liver, a typically French trait which causes amusement to foreigners.

'There are no eggs or cream in this cake?'

'Oh, no, Monsieur.'

The cake would be full of eggs and cream and he would eat a great deal of it and suffer no harm at all.

Although he had travelled often in his life, he did not like travelling except to the U.S.A. which, strangely enough, always amused him. It is true that he was extremely successful there and he knew that it was the country above all others where his music was best loved. But in distant lands he felt like a fish out of water. A tour in Egypt enchanted me by the beauty of all that we saw, but for him it was too exotic and he preferred to stay in his room rather than visit the Valley of the Kings or the temples at Luxor or Karnac.

Ultimately Francis lived rather seldom in his Touraine and Paris homes. He scarcely ever composed in Paris. It was for this reason that he bought his house in Touraine. He always rose very early there, and after a cup of tea with rusks and marmalade, he set to work until lunch time. He never composed during the afternoon or evening.

A considerable part of my music [he says], comes to my mind when I am walking,* it matters little where. But I need then to hear what I have imagined. This is where the piano is necessary. There are also ideas that I find directly at the piano, the fingers being the discoverers of which Stravinsky speaks. [He adds:] The story of Stravinsky and of Rimsky-Korsakov has consoled me once and for all. Stravinsky regretted using the piano so much. Rimsky said to him, 'There are great composers like Wagner who write without a piano, others like Moussorgsky who use a piano. You belong to those, that is all!'

In Paris he could never find his rhythm of work, he was too much disturbed by the telephone, there was too much distraction, he knew too many people and naturally went out every evening, to a concert, a theatre, or to visit friends. He could not bear an evening alone at home. For emotional and nervous as he was, he had two fears, solitude and boredom.

During the last years of his life he spent long periods of time in hotels—in Switzerland or on the Riviera. He had a piano taken to his room and there he worked and composed very well. Should he have difficulty with his work, or with himself . . . he felt that he could go down and find something going on around him and make contacts with new acquaintances, for he was very sociable.

Thus escaping solitude, he did not always escape boredom. For if he could have an extraordinary 'presence' which during an evening would hold the entire attention of an assembly of people, he could also have an extraordinary 'absence' and whatever was said to him would then seem to fall on completely deaf ears. I often saw him succumb to boredom in the middle of an assembly, even when it was convened in his honour. (I should say particularly in this case!) He would not make the slightest effort, even to

---

* He walked a great deal in cities, particularly in Paris.

put a good face on it. At the numerous receptions which belong, alas, to a life of concert tours, above all in foreign countries, I often found myself in a difficult situation! In fact, I must admit, he never could restrain himself in any way—he was capriciousness itself.

I could mention many occasions which would confirm this—here are two which are sufficiently typical and amusing.

Having one day invited some local notables to luncheon in his house in Touraine—the prefect, the mayor, etc.—he disappeared after the meal. The friend who was staying with him (due to his fear of solitude he always had a man or woman friend to stay) was anxious at his non-appearance and went to look for him. He was discovered peacefully drowsing on his terrace. 'I was too bored,' he said, 'and you entertain very well. Continue.'

At the Edinburgh Festival, during a year when we were giving one of our recitals, a 'French Week' was organized. There was an exhibition of paintings by Claude Monet at the Royal Scottish Academy, several French musicians participated in the concerts, and the Madeleine Renaud-Jean Louis Barraud Company gave performances. The French Ambassador came to Edinburgh for the occasion. After our concert there was a big official reception organized by the Lord Mayor and the Royal Scottish Academy. Having shaken hands with various official persons and finding the Monet exhibition badly hung and badly lighted, Francis said to me, 'I'm going.' 'But, Francis, that's impossible, this reception is in our honour.' Nevertheless he left. . . . But three-quarters of an hour later when I myself left, I found him sitting in the cloak room, muffled in his greatcoat with his hat on his head. He did not have the courage to take a taxi by himself to go back to the hotel.

Again it was his fear of boredom that made him dread anything resembling an official manifestation. He definitely decided never to submit his candidature to the Institut de France. All the same he was enchanted and flattered to go to Oxford to receive, at the same time as Shostakovich, the diploma of an Honorary Doctorate of the University. He was also very happy to be elected a member of the League of Composers of New York.

*   *   *

Having shown to what extent Francis could be sensitive, vulnerable, and easily overcome by anguish and melancholy, I do not want to give a false impression of him, for though several times he suffered terrible bouts of nervous depression, his nature was fundamentally gay and happy. He loved to laugh, and he himself could be highly amusing. When he was in a good mood and at the top of his form—this could happen when the atmosphere was truly amicable and stimulating—his conversation could be quite fascinating: the most brilliant, original, interesting and amusing that can be imagined. It is to be regretted that no written record exists of the many clever and irresistibly comic remarks he made. He had no fear of any subjects of conversation or any expressions used, however bawdy they might be. He was very witty, but not at the expense of others, for he never spoke ill of anyone. Malice and spitefulness were totally foreign to him.

Francis had numerous friends, and friendship meant a great deal to him; he felt the need of reciprocity and mutual confidence. That is why correspondence also held an important place in his life. He wrote with disconcerting speed, and his style was as alive, personal, unpredictable and spontaneous as his conversation. The many quotations that will be found in this book will without doubt give some idea of his facility.

He was not at all interested in discussing philosophy or politics, but on subjects that appealed to him—music, of course, or literature, and above all, painting—he could explain his very personal views with a zest, a spontaneity and a vitality all his own. He used to say that he liked painting as much as music, and his memory, not at all good musically, was infallible visually, especially for paintings. I had experience of this several times. During our tours we had many opportunities of visiting museums and galleries together, some of which were among the finest in the world. I remember one occasion, at the Phillips Collection in Washington, when he said to me: 'Do you see that the green of the dress in this portrait is exactly the same green as the costume of the soldier who holds the lance in the Mantegna of San Zenon in Verona?' And I could believe it. Did he not say to Claude Rostand: 'I could match from memory the colour of the velvet in *L'Enseigne de Gersaint* of Watteau.'

When he was asked if Watteau was for him the Mozart of painting, he gave this delightful reply:

> No, because there is only one Mozart as there is only one God . . . but there are many saints in painting that I revere: Titian, Tintoretto, Bellini, Raphael, Zurbaran, Goya, Chardin, Watteau, David, Corot, Degas, Cézanne, etc. . . . and among painters of the twentieth century: Matisse, Picasso, Braque, Bonnard and Paul Klee.

He often compared the painting of Dufy with his own music. There were also some painters whom he admired but did not like: El Greco, Van Gogh and Gauguin.

In music too, Poulenc could admire without liking. For instance, he had an 'indifferent veneration' for Bach. And after having listened to Wagner's music he felt the need 'to cleanse his spirit and his ears' by listening to

Mozart. Brahms 'had the defects of Schumann without his genius. Admittedly he had his own, but it is a genius that leaves me totally indifferent.' For Fauré he confessed to having an 'allergy', with the exception, nevertheless, of the songs and certain passages from *Penelope*. But of Roussel he liked neither 'the harmonic style nor the orchestral colour'.

Again it was to Claude Rostand that all these admissions were made. He also divulged to him:

> It was without doubt Debussy who awakened me to music, but it was Stravinsky who later served as my guide. On the harmonic plane I owe much to Ravel, enormously also to Satie, but more aesthetically than musically. And Chabrier is my grandfather!'

I should like to quote also the beautiful dedication of *Dialogues des Carmelites*:

> To the memory of my mother who revealed music to me, to Claude Debussy, who inspired me to compose, to Claudio Monteverdi, Giuseppe Verdi, Modeste Moussorgsky, who in this work were my models.

Again, Francis wrote: 'I shall never minimize these influences, not wishing to be the son of an unknown father.'

When Claude Rostand asked him to mention other musicians of the twentieth century whose work he liked, he added, 'The admirable Falla, Ravel, Prokofief, Bartòk', whom he admired as 'a prodigious inventor of forms', Richard Strauss, certain works of Hindemith 'with a lyricism both heavy and agile as mercury'. And questioned on the Viennese School, he replied, that he admired certain works of Schoenberg, Alban Berg 'of whom the fabulous craftsmanship never lacks humanity' and Webern, who 'delighted as a Mallarmé of music. . . But I admit I feel less at ease with them than with the others. I approach them more ceremoniously. Too much respect hinders intimacy!'

*   *   *

The several characteristics that I have described, the memories that I have evoked, together with my own observations, are inadequate to encompass the personality of a being whose nature had so many facets and whose moods were so changeable. Without doubt it is in listening to his music and in working at it, that it is possible to discover more deeply the man that he was. He said himself: 'My music is my portrait.' The man cannot be dissociated from his work. Francis in his unpredictable style wrote:

To a lady in Kamtchatka who would write to me to ask what I am like, I would send my portrait at the piano by Cocteau, my portrait by Bérard, *Le Bal Masqué*, and the *Motets pour un temps de pénitence*, I believe she would then have a very exact idea of Poulenc-Janus.

He advises a look at two of his portraits which seem to personify him best, and also to listen to two of his works which most clearly reveal his two-sided musical personality, 'ragamuffin' and 'monk', as Claude Rostand puts it.

In my opinion there are few composers whose music so faithfully reflects their personality. His music is the true expression of his being. The reason is that Poulenc never forced himself away from his natural bent, and this applies as much to his life as to his work. He always had the good fortune to be able to do what he wished, and only what he wished, in his existence as in his compositions. He followed the impulse of his sensibility and his heart, and gave himself up entirely to it.

But this is not to say that he ever lost his lucidity. He was far too French for that. He was very typically French, in the kind of man he was, in his way of living, in his tastes, his reactions, and also in his musical style.

Debussy speaks of 'the clarity of expression, the precision, the concentration in the French musical form' which can be contrasted with the Germanic genius which excels in long sentimental outpourings. Lyricism and even passion are not absent in French music, but reason and mind are always in control of the emotions. As Henri Hell put it, grief and sentiment are there, but under the veil of grace, clarity and proportion.

When Debussy wrote, 'Music must humbly seek to give pleasure', our thoughts turn to the music of Poulenc with its sonorous sensuousness, its subtle harmonies, the flexibility of its modulations and the play of the resulting colours, to the beauty and charm of its melodic lines. It can be that the art of our greatest musicians is an art of suggestion. Poulenc, with his great sensibility, undoubtedly excelled in the creation of a poetic climate.

As Paul Valéry, the great French poet and philosopher, said, 'He who would write his dream must be completely awake.' Poulenc was able to write his dream in a musical language that was his own and to which throughout his life he remained true, and he enjoyed the privilege of speaking this language with the pure accent of his native land.

CHAPTER II

Francis Poulenc, Composer of Songs

'Main dominée par le cœur'
—*Paul Eluard*

FRANCIS POULENC, WHEN asked by a musical review to define the 'rules' of his aesthetic, his principles of style, his system of composition and the part played by inspiration in the composing of music, responded in the following way: 'My "rules" are instinctive, I am not concerned with principles and I am proud of that; I have no system of writing (for me "system" means "tricks"); and as for inspiration, it is so mysterious that it is wiser not to try to explain it.' He thus defined extremely well his entire concept of his own music: the denial of abstract theories, of methods, of systems.

For Poulenc, writing music was not an intellectual exercise, but a means of expression. 'He was,' said the excellent English critic, Rollo Myers, 'that rare phenomenon: a born musician, for whom music was as natural a vehicle for the expression of his thoughts and feelings as speech is for ordinary men.' Yet towards the end of his life he would consider sympathetically the most recent theories of composition and think well of the young composers who adopted them, but he was too lucid concerning himself not to know that his path could not lie in that direction, for it would have been against his nature. And if these young composers could reproach him for lack of technique, the response could be that he had, nevertheless, sufficient technique to do extremely well all that he wanted to do. His harmonies were perhaps those of everyone, but in the use he made of them he resembled no one.

In speaking of Poulenc, the distinguished composer, Sir Lennox Berkeley, has said:

A composer who uses the traditional idiom in such an individual manner that you can recognise the music as his within the first few bars, may possess more true originality than one who adopts a startling and revolutionary language.

In fact, are there many other contemporary composers whose music, like Poulenc's, immediately discloses the name of its author? At all events, ever since his earliest works his music bears the stamp of his personality, and in growing older he remained true to himself and to his own concept of his music. 'There is more courage,' he wrote to the composer Henri Sauguet, 'in growing naturally as you are, than in forcing your flowers with a fashionable fertilizer.' He also said to Claude Rostand, 'The worst possible thing is to wish to follow the fashion when that fashion does not suit you.'

There can be no doubt that in his vocal works Poulenc gave the best of himself, and it is in these that he is most likely to confront successfully the test of time. Poulenc had a true vocation for vocal writing. In the first place it was because he loved the human voice, and song in itself had great appeal for him—a beautiful voice, a finely sung phrase, gave him intense joy. Secondly, his inspiration never flowed with greater spontaneity than when he felt the urge to set a literary text. It is astonishing to realize to how great a degree the words, their colours, their accents, the rhythm of a phrase or of a line as well as its sense, the general movement, the pulsation, the form of the poem or literary text in addition to its meaning, all combined to awaken in Poulenc the musical inspiration. And this was from a threefold point of view—rhythmic, harmonic and melodic.

During an epoch in which young composers seem to scorn problems of prosody (since they go so far, so they say, as to pulverize the poem), Poulenc attached the greatest importance to such problems and resolved them with an exceptional sense of French declamation. This is one of the main ways in which he serves his poets so well. From the harmonic point of view, his incredible ease in modulating from one key to another, allowed him to retain the different fragments of a poem always in the key in which he had first conceived them, thus creating their atmosphere with extraordinary subtlety and sensuousness.

Finally, his gift for melody—perhaps the most precious gift a composer can possess—which was the very essence of his music, inspired in him the appropriate musical curve to amplify the expression of the literary text.

Therefore it is not surprising that the vocal works of Poulenc are not only his most remarkable but also the most numerous in the catalogue of his music. They embrace secular and religious choral works *a cappella* or with orchestra, operas and works for the stage, and lastly the 137 *mélodies*.

Since his childhood he had adored poetry, especially that of contemporary poets whose works he 'sniffed greedily' and attempted to set to music from the time he first began to compose. Of his complete list of songs only twenty are not on texts by contemporary poets. These modern poems are often rather obscure, but his musical setting always clarifies them. Through his music they are given their correct punctuation (for most of the poems are without punctuation, which can involve the reader in serious misconceptions). He finds their speed, breathing places, inflections—grasps their feeling and emotion—reveals their profound meaning and gives them life. 'It is Poulenc,' wrote Claude Rostand, 'who should be consulted by those who do not entirely understand the meaning of the poetry of Max Jacob, of Jean Cocteau, of Louise de Vilmorin, and above all of Guillaume Apollinaire and Paul Eluard; in his songs he uncovers all the mysteries.'

Here is what Poulenc himself said: 'When I have chosen a poem of which the musical setting at times may not come to my mind until months later, I examine it in all its aspects. When it is a question of Apollinaire or Eluard, I attach the greatest importance to the way in which the poem is placed on the page, to the spaces, to the margins. I recite the poem to myself many times. I listen, I search for the traps, at times I underline the text in red at the difficult spots. I note the breathing places, I try to discover the inner rhythm from a line which is not necessarily the first. Next I try to set it to music, bearing in mind the different densities of the piano accompaniment. When I am held up over a detail of prosody, I do not persist. Sometimes I wait for days, I try to forget the word until I see it as a new word. . . . I rarely begin a song at the beginning. One or two lines, chosen at random, take hold of me and very often give me the tone, the hidden rhythm, the key to the work. . . . I never transpose the tonality in which I have conceived a phrase, in order to save myself trouble.'

In these lines Poulenc can be seen at work. In a few other phrases which have occasionally found their way into print, he has also defined extremely well his attitude towards the poems he chose to set to music: 'I have never claimed to resolve poetic problems by means of the intellect; the voices of the heart and of intuition are more reliable.' . . . 'It is not only the lines of the poem that must be set to music, but all that lies between the lines and in the margins.' . . . And lastly: 'The setting to music of a poem must be an act of love, never a marriage of convenience.'

To end this short chapter, I would like to quote the following extract from an article by Jean-Joel Barbier, in which he speaks with great perception and sensibility of Poulenc, composer of *mélodies*:

In effect there are two kinds of composers. Those like Fauré, for whom a song is first of all a new piece of music, and those like Debussy, for whom a song is primarily a poetic event. Now, a song or a cycle by Poulenc is always a poetic event before being a new musical piece. It is this that gives the value and the unique quality to his music. His poetic understanding equals his musical gifts—understanding that is shown as much in his choice of texts as in the way he uses them. For it is not enough to choose a good poet or a good poem. It is a question of finding a text, beautiful in itself, which is adaptable to musical treatment, a text which will combine with the music one ventures to write and be enhanced by it. This implies a double comprehension: first of the poetry and then of oneself. This double comprehension Francis Poulenc possesses to a high degree. In the case of Apollinaire, for instance, he will not choose the most celebrated poems, but those that are best in view of the final result. This does not in the least mean that he will decide on the minor poems, but on texts that are either very short, or which contain contrasts or juxtapositions: those that leave a margin round the words, those which not being too rigidly designed, not being too closely welded at the outset, will warrant a welding of music, leaving room for a span of sound which without amplifying the words, will, on the contrary, give them a new dimension by placing them in a favourable light. He chooses poems which have within them sufficient room to tolerate the presence of music, seeing that from then onwards they will be fixed in time and place with a definite emotional aspect.

The miracle of Poulenc, the song writer, is precisely that he is never guilty of misconception. Not only is there no misconception of the inner meaning, of the quality of the emotion received from the words, but moreover, Poulenc's music at once gives them a luminosity, a new and immediate transparency which simultaneously causes all possible hidden meanings in a text to be apprehended. And this is due to a prosody that is cultured to a remarkable degree, the first concern of a composer who relives his texts like a poet before becoming alive to them as a musician. Furthermore, with him the one and the other make a single whole.

After 60 years spent in study of the art of song—first as a singer, then as a teacher—the years of my adolescence came clearly to my mind as I re-read the above lines. Why was I so irresistibly drawn towards singing? It was not because I had a superb and powerful voice, for this, alas, was not so. Neither was it because I was an exceptional musician, for I was not. When I was seventeen or eighteen I was strongly attracted by the problem of putting a literary text to music—its prosody, its accentuation, the blend of the poetic expression and the musical expression. Doubtless I asked myself, without realizing it, the question that Saint-Saëns propounded: 'Can song not emerge from poetry as a kind of blossoming? The rhythms, the sonorities of the lines do they not demand song to intensify them, song being only a superior kind of declamation?' Saint-Saëns himself has, at times, been quite successful in attaining this ideal, but unfortunately the quality of his musical inspiration too often rendered the attempt ineffectual.

At all events, I had a preconception of the part that the interpreter might play in the marriage of poetry and music. The magnificent role that could be his in serving the poets as well as the musicians, and this exciting prospect was enough to decide my life. It is understandable that my meeting with Poulenc often seemed to me to be predestined.

CHAPTER III

Performance and Interpretation

WHAT PROFIT, WHAT instruction can performers draw from the commentaries and quotations of the preceding chapter? First of all, they can but be confirmed in their fundamental attitude, which must be one of complete respect for the musical text. 'A sin against the spirit of a work,' said Stravinsky, 'always begins with a sin against the letter.' My experience both as a performer and as a teacher has led me to believe that the musical score is never read with sufficient attention. There are so many things that must be scrupulously observed: the rhythmic values, including the value of the rests, the indications of tempo, of phrasing, the liaisons or absence of liaisons, the nuances etc. . . .

Stravinsky also put it very well when he wrote, 'The first condition that must be fulfilled by anyone who aspires to the imposing title of interpreter, is that he be first of all a flawless executant.' Naturally there is no question of my speaking in this book of flawless vocal technique, which I take for granted; but Stravinsky's aphorism also implies, for vocal music, that the performance of the literary text must be as perfect as that of the music. The poet must be served as well as the musician.

The singer pays great attention to the quality of his voice and his phrasing—he must give the same care to his articulation and his pronunciation (which are two different things, for one can articulate well and pronounce badly). In vocal music, the music of the words is an integral part of the music itself. Marcel Beaufils wrote 'the word has one attribute, *meaning*, and another attribute, *sound*. The sonority, the accentuation, the rhythm of the words inspire the music as much and sometimes more than the sentiments that they express. The music *of* the poem is as important as the music written *on* the poem.'

But take care! The *legato* and the phrasing, are these not the most beautiful qualities of song? There certainly could be no question of sacrificing them in favour of the words. It is essential that the vocal line should always take first place in the singer's attention. This is of prime importance in the songs of Poulenc, who virtually never employs *parlando*, or only very rarely for a brief effect of contrast. Contrary to the experiments made by Ravel in the *Histoires Naturelles*, Poulenc's vocal line is always essentially melodic.

Vocal music does not only involve the realization of this mysterious alloy of word and melody, above all it involves the synthesis of the poetic idea and the musical idea. Again it is obvious that the musical idea must take precedence, since it is the musician who gives his personal interpretation of the poetic text, and it is essentially this that the performer must bring to life. He must strive to accord his own idea of the poem with that of the composer, without, of course, losing anything of his own personality. In this connection and in contrast to that which is only too often found in contemporary compositions, Poulenc's songs do not pose difficult problems for the singer. There is no disunity between the two conceptions which the interpreter has to express: that of the poet and that of the musician. On the material plane the setting of a poem by Poulenc is as exactly accurate as it could be, and on the spiritual plane his accordance with the poets of his choice is altogether exceptional.

*   *   *

Before beginning to give more practical advice to the two interpreters, advice which will, let it be admitted, chiefly concern the singer, I would like to say a few words about the piano part of Poulenc's songs. I say 'the piano part' advisedly because, of course, there is no question of what is sometimes wrongly called an 'accompaniment'. The art of the Lied and the mélodie is that of an ensemble—a singer and a pianist. Is there anything more difficult, for example, than to play really well the at times deceptively simple piano parts of Schubert's Lieder? Or of Debussy's mélodies with all their subtleties of sound colour?

Poulenc said that the best piano music he had written was in the piano part of his songs. He had no doubt exaggerated, but I would like to quote some lines which show clearly the importance he attached to this aspect of his songs and the great care he took:

I cannot express to what extent the exhibition of drawings by Matisse, for Mallarmé's poems, impressed me some years ago. One saw there the same subject, in particular a swan, in three or four stages of development, progressing through greater complexity, greater density (drawn in charcoal or crayon), to the most ideally simple and pure stroke of a pen. I have often sought, especially in the piano part of my songs, to take account of this lesson. If you knew how complex originally the first rough draft was of such songs as 'Le Pont', 'Fagnes de Wallonie', and above all 'La Fraîcheur et le Feu'.

In Poulenc's mind, the importance of the piano part of his songs was quite equal to that of the vocal line. Sometimes there is considerable technical difficulty in quickly moving songs, but also in comparatively easy songs great care is always required, as the following remark will stress: 'Lady accompanists, will you be kind enough not to forget that there is a *song* in the piano part, with its own accompaniment.'

Poulenc himself was an admirable accompanist in his own songs: he had a marvellous 'touch' with a fullness and a superb quality of tone which, when appropriate, could be suddenly percussive. But I cannot do better than to quote his own words concerning the performance of his works for piano solo, for all he says is equally applicable to the piano part of his songs: 'The great technical errors which disfigure my piano music to the point of rendering it unrecognisable are: rubato, avarice in the use of the pedal, and too clear articulation of certain patterns of chords and arpeggios which need, on the contrary, to be played with veiled sustained tone.' One often finds, in fact, in the piano part of these songs, chords, syncopated or not, which are only intended to prolong the harmony and give a certain pulsation; these must be veiled with pedal. The same applies to the arpeggios which should always be very little articulated and bound together as much as possible.

Again he writes: 'The use of the pedals is the great secret of my piano music (and the lack of it often its downfall). They will never use enough pedal! Never enough!' Poulenc certainly played like a composer, not like an 'accompanist'. His harmonic instinct, his feeling for breaths, and not only in his own music, was irreplaceable. But, as with all artists, he was more at home with some composers than with others. His own music may perhaps suggest that he would have been more in sympathy with Schumann than with Schubert, and more with Debussy than with Fauré.

*   *   *

The following remarks written by Poulenc concerning his piano music are of *extreme importance*: 'I hate rubato (it is understood that I am referring to my own music). Once a tempo has been adopted, it must not be altered at any price until I so indicate. Never prolong or shorten a beat—that drives me crazy. I would prefer all the wrong notes in the world.' While admitting that in his vocal music, because of his love for the voice, he was a little less strict at times (which was in fact true) in order to allow the singer to 'sing', to prepare certain effects, and to breathe, yet all the same he has here formulated the correct conception and performance of his music.

The chosen tempo must be immutably maintained, for few of the songs allow of changes of tempo, and when they do, the changes are clearly indicated. But in general, be it slow or fast, the tempo must be implacable.

(One sees at the end of numerous songs the indication, 'Surtout sans ralentir'—above all no *rallentando*.) The singer must achieve the ability to give suppleness to the vocal line and correct accentuation to the text, while still remaining within the unchanging framework of a piano part which will not yield obligingly, but on the contrary, will firmly maintain the tempo of the musical discourse. The responsibility of the pianist is considerable.

One could mention many songs which have a perpetual change of rhythm, of light and shade, and of expression, which, nevertheless, are of a constant and equal tempo. ('Dans le jardin d'Anna', for example.) This equality of tempo gives them their unity despite their continual modulations of tonality and expression.

This accepted, Poulenc knew better than anyone how to take a breath to prepare an unexpected modulation, or to hesitate for a sudden change of dynamics, but this without ever altering the basic tempo.

This tempo is always carefully indicated by a metronomic sign. It is advisable to hold strictly to this tempo and to depart from it as little as possible. I must add, that in the following pages I shall, nevertheless, occasionally call into question certain of these tempi. The feeling for a tempo varies slightly in the course of a long career as an interpreter: my experience in performance and also in hearing the recordings of the same works made at different times during my life, give me proof of this. Poulenc himself, in the course of our long association, varied his tempi slightly. He played more quickly (too quickly, in my opinion) in his youth than in his maturity.

*   *   *

The *mélodies* of Poulenc never contain rhythmic difficulties, but the rhythms, in their simplicity, must not be subjected to any distortion. For instance, consecutive quavers must be perfectly equal despite weak or strong syllables. It is also very important to maintain the value of rests precisely as they are written, something to which Poulenc attached great importance. For example, the exact value of the final note of a musical phrase must always be strictly observed.

*   *   *

It must be stressed once more, although it has already been said in the foregoing pages, that the mélodies of Poulenc must be very much *sung*. In his love for the human voice, he was more drawn to the Italian vocal style than to the German—his own music reveals this and explains why he was not against the use of certain Italianate vocal effects, of certain 'portamenti', used, of course, with discernment and taste. These effects will always be preferable to too much dryness or lack of legato and phrasing. Singers will find in many of his songs an opportunity—all too rarely offered in contemporary music—of surrendering to true lyricism; they must not allow this chance to elude them.

*   *   *

If Poulenc's songs are in general very vocal, this does not mean that they are always easy vocally. Their tessitura is often extensive, and one can observe his tendency to demand a low register of some volume, *f* or *mf*, and on the other hand a lightness on the top of the voice *p* or *pp*. (For example, 'C'est ainsi que tu es', 'Voyage', 'Aux Officiers de la Garde Blanche'. It is therefore essential for a singer who wishes to sing these songs, to have good resonance in the lower part of the voice, together with the ability to sing a true *piano* in the high register.

*   *   *

Singers often have a tendency to make what I call 'involuntary nuances', largely owing to technical difficulties but also to lack of care. That is to say, they vary the intensity of sound in their vocal line without any expressive or musical reason, which would certainly not be done by instrumentalists playing the same phrase. Why, for instance, make a *crescendo* every time the voice rises and a *diminuendo* when it descends? Nothing could be more tedious in effect. Why, on certain notes, through a lack of vocal control, make a *crescendo* or a *diminuendo* which is totally out of place? The effect of a whole phrase or a whole page of music without any involuntary change of dynamics can be so beautiful, and will be an excellent preparation for the contrast that will follow. I draw attention to this because in Poulenc's songs such vocal mastery is indispensable. He marks the phrasing fully and with the greatest care. It can be noticed that the level of dynamics often changes in successive and contrasting planes, covering the whole of a phrase, rather than a *crescendo* and *diminuendo* within a phrase. All these markings must be strictly observed. In short, the phrasing, whether contrasted or gradual, must always have a reason behind it, not only musical but also expressive.

*   *   *

I have said above that the setting of a poem to music by Poulenc, both on the material plane and on the spiritual plane, very rarely poses problems for the interpreter. Nevertheless, I find in my experience as a listener, and above all as a teacher, that singers do not attach as much importance as they should to the interpretation of the poems.

Poulenc wrote that if he were a professor of singing, he would insist on his pupils reading the poem attentively before working at a song. This is certainly a minimum requirement. I strongly advise singers to read the poem as it is printed in the literary edition, or, if this is not possible, to write out the poem, trying to find the versification. (This is not always easy with free verse that is unrhymed.) The poem should then be read aloud, spoken with all the interpretation that an actor would give to it. Is a singer not also an actor in the best sense of the word? Otherwise how would he be able to express the meaning of a literary text? How can he hope to sing a poem well if he is incapable of speaking it well? Through speaking the poem aloud one very often discovers the deeper meaning, the atmosphere, the vocal colour, the inflexions and expressive accents, thereby giving life to the interpretation which must then, of course, accord with the composer's conception.

*   *   *

There is one quality that is indispensable for the recitalist: to have a great variety of colours on his palette of sound. He needs, in a sense, to have a different voice for each of the songs he interprets, without that, a whole recital of songs can be terribly monotonous. Each new poem, each new piece of music, must suggest to him a new timbre, at times light, clear, transparent, suspended, or very dark, warm, rich, weighty etc. . . . at times poetic, tender and sweet, or very intense, dramatic and even tragic, emotional or cold, with more or with less vibrato in the voice, etc. . . . there is an infinity of shades of expression. Similarly, the declamation of a poem permits of a great variety of tone quality. Would one declaim, for instance, a charming poem by Verlaine and a great poem by Baudelaire in one and the same manner, with the same colour and vocal intensity?

Colouring the voice in this way certainly presupposes absolute mastery of vocal technique throughout its whole range, but finally depends essentially on the imagination of the singer, on his intelligence and sensibility, which mysteriously govern his nervous impulse and the control of his muscles.

This mechanism, both psychological and physical, must respond with extraordinary rapidity for the recitalist. A song is a musical form of generally short duration and of great musical concentration; there is no question of entering into its character little by little, and the singer of songs must be, in the course of an evening, not one but twenty different people. The interpreters, singer and pianist, must from the first notes create an atmosphere, and find the vocal colour and the pianistic sonority suitable to the work which they are going to interpret. Just as a painter chooses for each picture a harmony of different colours, so the singer and the pianist must make their choice for each song, not only of a certain scale of colour and sonority, but also of a certain scale of dynamics and intensity. Some songs will demand a range from pp to mp, or mf . . . others from mf to ff. Dynamics indicated by the composer must never be taken in an absolute sense, but in proportion to the general context. One could take as one example among many others, the last two songs of 'Calligrammes'. It is obvious that the ff marked in 'Aussi bien que les cigales', of which the dynamics range from mf to ff, will be infinitely more intense than the f marked in 'Voyage', ranging from pp to mf. The same applies to the breadth of the declamation, and as I have repeated with some insistence, of the choice of vocal colour. There are also many songs of Poulenc which demand numerous changes of colour in the course of one song. A typical example is 'Tu vois le feu du soir', of which the enumerative poem absolutely demands these contrasts.

*   *   *

I have already urged interpreters to have at their command an extensive palette of sound colour, for there is perhaps no repertoire which demands a greater variety of interpretation than the *mélodies* of Poulenc. If the majority of the songs are essentially poetic, they can also be of very differing character, ranging from the most touching gravity to manifest sensuality, from sincere lyricism to waggish Parisian humour and even to crazy buffoonery. This is due to the extraordinary diversity of the poems that have inspired them, and also to the invention and personal fantasy of the composer. It is therefore imperative that the interpreter should succeed in conveying to the listener the nature of these widely varied songs. But I would like to give a warning, and later I shall return several times to this particular point.

It must be acknowledged that some songs by Poulenc can lend themselves to exaggeration in the interpretation. I have in mind, for instance, certain poems of Apollinaire, of Max Jacob, of Louise de Vilmorin, of others also, in which the interpreters can be tempted to go <u>too far</u> in exaggerating their effects in order to capture their audience. I have had, alas, the experience of hearing certain concerts and certain recordings which I am sure Poulenc would have detested. His art is an art of <u>suggestion</u>. I <u>beg</u> the interpreters never, figuratively speaking, to hold out their hand to their audience. They must always stay within the limits of a classical style, as far from coldness as from exaggeration. If, at times, one must suggest a type of popular song, the *mélodies* of Poulenc are <u>never</u> popular songs. If one needs to suggest a certain vulgarity, it must never be vulgar. Even the irony and the drollery must never go beyond suggestion. There must always be a dignity, a

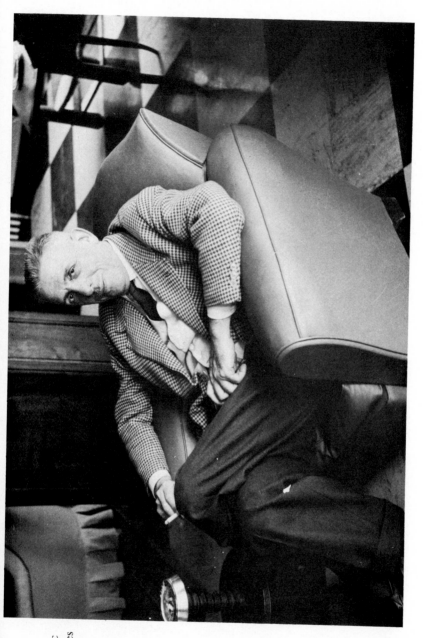

Francis Poulenc
during the fifties

Guillaume Apollinaire   Louise de Vilmorin

Nusch and Paul Eluard

Paul Eluard by Picasso

Pierre Bernac during the sixties

distinction, which must never be abandoned. There is great subtlety in all this, to which I shall return, while doing all I can to incite the interpreters to remain within the limits of good taste, to keep the restraint which Poulenc never lost.

*　　　*　　　*

The whole of this chapter underlines the tremendous responsibility of the interpreter, who can in a moment cause a bad or a good opinion to be formed of the work with which he has been entrusted. Paul Valéry wittily wrote: 'A musical work which is still only a piece of writing, is a cheque drawn on the fund of talent of an eventual artist.' I have stressed at length the importance of fidelity to the written work, but if this fidelity is a necessity for the performer, it is not enough for the interpreter, for whom there is very much more than the producing of sounds traced on paper, which in themselves are only 'potential' music. Moreover the composer may well have in his head the ideal interpretation of his work, but he is unable to indicate this interpretation by symbols. Liszt, who exemplifies the typical composer-performer, said that it would be an illusion to believe that the beauty of a performance can be set down on paper.

This inability to describe an interpretation is felt even more strongly by the present writer. How is he to indicate in written words the phrasing, the vocal colour, an inflexion, an expressive accent, a shade of meaning, etc. . . .

Referring to his song cycle, *La Fraîcheur et le Feu*, Poulenc wrote, 'The technical side must be perfected with cold precision, then, sure of oneself, one should forget everything and give an impression of improvising, listening only to one's instinct.' The choice of the word 'instinct' could be called into question, but one understands perfectly what he means by this phrase which can be applied to any musical work. It defines extremely well the procedure of the interpreter, for the music must seem to escape spontaneously from his lips or from his fingers.

In the following pages I can only try to awaken the intelligence and the sensibility of the interpreters, but in the end it is their <u>own</u> feeling, their sincerity, and not exterior effects, which will give to their interpretations expression, intensity and genuineness.

CHAPTER IV

Guillaume Apollinaire

'If on my tomb were inscribed: here lies Francis Poulenc, the musician of Apollinaire and Eluard, I would consider this to be my finest title to fame.'

Wilhelm Apollinaire de Kostrowitsky, known as Guillaume Apollinaire, was born in Rome in 1880, the natural son of Angelina de Kostrowsky and Francesco Flugi d'Aspremont. He was educated in various colleges in Monaco, Cannes and Nice. In 1898 he came to Paris; then for a time worked as a tutor in Germany. Returning to Paris he took up journalism. He formed many friendships among men of letters, and also painters, such as Alfred Jarry, Max Jacob, Picasso and Braque. At the end of 1914, although a foreigner, he joined the French Army, and in March 1916 he was wounded in the head by a shell splinter. After that he remained in Paris where he died on November 9th 1918, of Spanish influenza.

His principal prose works were, *L'enchanteur pourrissant* (1909), *L'Hérésiarque et Cie* (1910) and *Le Poète assassiné* (1916); his collections of poetry, *Le Bestiaire* (1911), *Alcools* (1913), *Calligrammes* (1918), *Les Mamelles de Tirésias*, a surrealist drama (1918), *Il y a* (1925).

Apollinaire led symbolist poetry along new paths which heralded surrealism. As an art critic he had great influence on the beginnings of the cubist movement.

*   *   *

BETWEEN THE YEARS 1918 and 1956 Francis Poulenc composed 35 songs on poems by Guillaume Apollinaire. 'Since my first songs,' he said, 'since *Le Bestiaire*, I have felt a definite and mysterious affinity with the poetry of Apollinaire.' As the poet had died in 1918, Poulenc barely had time to know him, having met him only a few times, generally at the home of Valentine Hugo.

With the exception of *Le Bestiare* and *Calligrammes*, almost all the poems which Poulenc chose to set to music from Apollinaire's works were drawn from the volume *Il y a*, published by Messein in 1925, which contained 41 poems (1895–1917) and articles on literature and painting.

*   *   *

First I must caution interpreters that there is a risk of committing grave faults of style in the songs composed by Poulenc on the poems of Apollinaire. I will, of course, try to indicate these hazards in my commentaries on the individual songs, but in the meantime here are two typical examples:

Apollinaire and Poulenc were often inspired by Paris. In this vein, their poetry and their music can, in a fashion, reflect a certain plebeianism. But take care! When Toulouse-Lautrec or Degas created paintings that represented certain circles (I am thinking of such works as *L'Absinthe*), did they become vulgar? Certainly not. In poetry and in music as in painting, the beauty is not born of the subject but of the treatment. This was well expressed by André Malraux when he said, 'Works of art do not derive their poetry from the subjects they represent, they use the subjects to discover their intrinsic poetry.' The works of Poulenc and Apollinaire are a striking example of this precept. It would therefore be unworthy of interpreters to vulgarize them for the sake of making an effect.

Then again in many of the songs there will be found a particular nuance of expression that has been extremely well described by Henri Hell as 'an irony always veiled by tenderness, a mischievous mockery always close to tears, a drollery always ready to change to lyricism.' I myself feel that the poetic melancholy in such songs is often tinged with humour to hide the depths of feeling behind it, as though the poet and the musician were smiling at their own sensibility. However this may be, the drollery and the irony must never be heightened and stressed, but <u>always</u> the tenderness, the lyricism, the poetry.

*

| LE BESTIARE | THE BOOK OF BEASTS |
| ou cortège d'Orphée | or Procession of Orpheus |

Poulenc was barely twenty years old when he wrote his first songs. He set twelve quatrains of *Le Bestiare* to music, but on the advice of his friend Georges Auric he finally kept only six.

Twenty years later Poulenc was himself astonished that these songs should be already so 'typically Poulenc'. 'The definite and mysterious affinity with the poetry of Apollinaire' was borne out by a letter written to him by Marie Laurencin, the celebrated painter who for ten years was the close friend of the poet: 'You cannot realize how well you have been able to express the nostalgia and the lyricism of these admirable quatrains. And what touches me so deeply is that I could believe it is Guillaume's voice speaking these verses.' The nostalgia and the lyricism—this definitely confirms Poulenc's assertion: 'To sing *Le Bestiare* with irony is a complete misconception. It would show no understanding whatever of Apollinaire's poetry or my music.'

Le dromadaire	*The Dromedary*
Avec ses quatre dromadaires	With his four dromedaries
Don Pedro d'Alfaroubeira	Don Pedro d'Alfaroubeira
Courut le monde et l'admira	roamed the world over and admired it
Il fit ce que je voudrais faire	he did what I would like to do
Si j'avais quatre dromadaires.	if I had four dromedaries.

   Does this poem not express in its own way the words which Jean de la Ville de Mirmont and Gabriel Fauré have used in the song cycle *L'Horizon Chimérique*: 'I feel within me an unappeased longing for great departures'? The indication 'very rhythmical and weighty' is excellent and ♩ = 76 also good. But together with the rhythm, the two interpreters must maintain a perfect *legato*.

   For the opening lines of the voice part, *f* is preferable to *mf* as it is in a low tessitura and needs a broad rich timbre. For the last two lines I suggest changing the indication *mf* to *p* for both singer and pianist—Poulenc and I always did this. Does it not intensify the nostalgic expression that I have suggested? Poulenc always made a slight *ritenuto* on the last bar of the final *allegro*, and despite his indication, he always used some pedal.

La chèvre du Thibet	*The Tibetan Goat*
Les poils de cette chèvre | et même	The hair of this goat and even
Ceux d'or pour qui prit	that hair of gold for which so much
tant de peine	trouble was taken
Jason ne valent rien au prix	by Jason are worth nothing to the value
Des cheveux dont je suis épris.	of the hair of her I love.

   This is a tender little poem of *happy* love. The tempo ♩ = 72 must be very supple but regular. Accent the word 'ceux'. The fifth and sixth bars of the piano part should be very flowing. The song ends with a *rallentando* on the last bar which must be illuminated by a smile, both in the voice and in the eyes.

La sauterelle	*The Grasshopper*
Voici la fine sauterelle	Here is the delicate grasshopper
La nourriture de Saint Jean	the nourishment of St. John
Puissent mes vers être comme elle	may my verses be likewise
Le régal des meilleures gens.	the feast of superior people.

Four lines, four bars. These are enough for the poet and the musician to express the wish that their work should be a feast for people of taste. Tempo ♩ =66 and imperturbable. An expressive breath between the second and the third bar. The vocal effect on the last two bars is difficult to achieve well. I suggest that the singer attacks *p* to allow for a further *diminuendo* to *pp*. The *rallentando* of the last bar can end with a short pause.

Le dauphin	*The Dolphin*
Dauphins vous jouez dans la mer	Dolphins you sport in the sea
Mais le flot est toujours amer	yet the waters are always briny
Parfois ma joie éclate-t-elle	at times my joy bursts forth
La vie est encore cruelle.	but life is still cruel.

The poem suggests extremely well the contrasts that must be made in this song: the first and the third lines are *mf* and rhythmic, the second and the fourth *p* and legato—thus the right expression in the declamation is found quite naturally. The indication of the tempo is without any doubt too fast. ♩ =120 is preferable. Make a *rallentando* on the last bar only.

L'écrevisse	*The Crayfish*
Incertitude | o! mes délices	Uncertainty O! my delights
Vous et moi nous nous en allons	you and I we progress
Comme s'en vont les écrevisses	just like the crayfish
A reculons à reculons.	backwards backwards.

A gentle philosophy pervades and explains itself in this poem and this music. The indication of tempo is not good, ♩ =88 is much better. The piano part must be very legato. The first 'à reculons' is *f* and the second is *p*, an echo and a *rallentando* (more than 'a little'), with a long pause on the final note.

La carpe	*The Carp*
Dans vos viviers dans vos étangs	In your fish-ponds in your pools
Carpes que vous vivez longtemps	carp how long you live
Est-ce que la mort vous oublie	is it that death has forgotten you
Poissons de la mélancolie?	fish of melancholy?

The pianist and the singer must rival one another in their quality of sonority and legato to express the poetic melancholy of this beautiful song. The indicated tempo is rather too fast, ♩ =54 is preferable. I insist that the singer should sustain every note well and stretch each vowel. A little

crescendo on the low C ♭ 'de la mélan' makes it possible to sing the upper C
much more *p* with a very slight *ritenuto*.

Curiously enough Poulenc set to music another quatrain from *Le Bestiaire*
but not until 38 years later.

La souris	*The Mouse*
Belles journées, souris du temps,	Lovely days, mouse of time,
Vous rongez peu à peu ma vie.	little by little you nibble away my life.
Dieu! Je vais avoir vingt-huit ans,	Heavens! I shall soon be twenty-eight years old,
Et mal vécus, | à mon envie.	and wasted years, I fear.

This song was composed in honour of Maria Freund* on the occasion of
her eightieth birthday, which explains the choice of the little poem.
Poulenc says: 'Since time nibbles away our years like a mouse, I am putting
this poem of Apollinaire to music. Immediately the melancholy I felt when I
was twenty comes back to me.'

The indication *doucement mélancolique* (with tender melancholy) is
therefore excellent. The tempo ♩ = 56 is good. The beginning should be
well sustained to emphasize the sudden *quasi parlando* of the bar 'Dieu! je vais
avoir vingt huit ans!', before returning to legato for 'et <u>mal</u> vécus, à mon
envie', with an expressive accent on '<u>mal</u>'. The regret for lost youth has
always inspired poets and musicians.

*

TROIS POÈMES DE LOUISE LALANNE

It may be surprising to find these songs among those written on poems by
Guillaume Apollinaire. Part of a letter written to Poulenc by Marie
Laurencin, one of the poet's great loves, will explain the reason:

I saw that you had set three poems by Louise Lalanne to music. Two of
these three poems are by me, 'Hier' and 'Le présent'. Eugène Montfort, at
that time director of *Marges*, had conceived the idea of inventing an
imaginary poetess. Naturally Guillaume, delighted with this idea,
accepted. At the moment of going into print Guillaume, who was laziness
itself, had done nothing, and I remember that we hunted through the
notebooks of my young days, full of nonsense, and ended by finding these
little verses, 'Hier' and 'Le Présent', which I think are nothing at all out of
the ordinary.

* Well known as a Lieder singer at the turn of the century.

In the first chapter I spoke of her collaboration with Poulenc over his ballet
Les Biches.

<table>
<tr><td>

LE PRÉSENT

Si tu veux je te donnerai
Mon matin, mon matin gai
Avec tous mes clairs cheveux
    Que tu aimes;
    Mes yeux verts
    Et dorés
    Si tu veux.
Je te donnerai tout le bruit
    Qui se fait
    Quand le matin s'éveille
    Au soleil
    Et l'eau qui coule
    Dans la fontaine
    Tout auprès;
Et puis encor le soir qui viendra vite

    Le soir de mon âme triste
    A pleurer
    Et mes mains toutes petites |
Avec mon cœur qu'il faudra près du
    tien
    Garder.

</td><td>

THE PRESENT

If you wish I will give you
my morning, my gay morning
with all my bright hair
    that you love;
    my eyes green
    and gold
    if you wish.
I will give you all the sound
    which is heard
    when morning awakens
    to the sun
    and the water that flows
    in the fountain
    nearby;
and then again the evening that will
    come quickly
the evening of my soul sad enough
    to weep
and my hands so small
with my heart that will need to be close
    to your own
    to keep.

</td></tr>
</table>

This poem, deliciously feminine, first enumerates the freshest and most
charming presents, which in the second part become suddenly coloured by
sadness and sentiment, until the final 'présent' which justifies the singular
noun of the title: 'mon coeur qu'il faudra près du tien garder'. The
interpreters must mark this contrast well. It will help if they carefully
observe the markings: *ff* and *f* for the first part, and *p* for the second part.

The indicated tempo ♩ =152 is good, but Poulenc gives this
commentary:

Generally a rhythmic fault is made in not allowing the strict equality of
the semiquavers at the beginning. I could have written it all in 2/4
adjusting the rests of the first bars. It seemed more acute to write in 3/8
followed by a breath. It is for the singer to give an impression of intensity
by slight breathlessness. The song must flow without a shadow of rubato.
Influenced by the writing of the end of the Chopin Sonata.

CHANSON	SONG
Les myrtilles sont pour la dame	Myrtle is for the lady
Qui n'est pas là	who is absent
La marjolaine est pour mon âme	marjoram is for my soul
Tralala!	tra-la-la!
Le chèvrefeuille est pour la belle	Honeysuckle is for the fair
Irrésolue.	Irresolute.
Quand cueillerons-nous les airelles	When do we gather the bilberries
Lanturlu.	Lan-tur-lu.
Mais laissons pousser sur la tombe	But let us plant on the tomb
O folle! | O fou!	O crazed! O mazed!
Le romarin | en touffes sombres	Rosemary in dark tufts
Laïtou!	La-i-tou!

Completely meaningless. Do not seek for a meaning in this poem, for none exists. Poulenc says: 'The rhythm of this song must be imperturbable. I think of it as a counting song: "Am-stram-gram-pic-et-pic et colegram".'

Care must be taken in this 'imperturbable rhythm' to observe the rests and the legato passages as they are written. The tempo $\quarternote = 132$ is very difficult, it should be as near to it as possible.

HIER	YESTERDAY
Hier, c'est ce chapeau fané	Yesterday is this faded hat
Que j'ai longtemps trainé	that I have trailed about so long
Hier, c'est une pauvre robe	yesterday is a shabby dress
Qui n'est plus à la mode.	no longer in fashion.
Hier, c'était le beau couvent	Yesterday was the beautiful convent
Si vide maintenant	so empty now
Et la rose mélancolie	and the rose-tinged melancholy
Des cours de jeunes filles	of the young girls' classes
Hier, c'est mon cœur mal donné	yesterday, is my heart ill-bestowed
Une autre, une autre année!	in a past, a past year!
Hier n'est plus, ce soir, qu'une ombre	Yesterday is no more, this evening,
	than a shadow
Près de moi dans ma chambre.	close to me in my room.

This poem by Marie Laurencin, so tenderly nostalgic, is quite authentically and typically feminine, and it inspired Poulenc to compose a song which foreshadows the tender, lyrical vein in which he was to write his most beautiful songs. Poulenc says: 'While writing it I imagined an interior painted by Vuillard. If you think of the words you are saying, the colour will come of itself.'

The indicated tempo ♩=66 is excellent for it must not drag, and from the third bar this tempo becomes more animated, and *mf*, instead of the initial *p*. 'Et la rose mélancolie des cours de jeunes filles' will be *pp*, but 'Hier c'est mon cœur mal donné une autre année' will be *mf*, very intense and expressive. 'Hier n'est plus ce soir qu'une ombre' is *pp*. At this period Poulenc did not yet indicate dynamics as carefully as he did later.

*

QUATRE POÈMES

While he was writing the *Trois Poèmes de Louise Lalanne*, Poulenc also composed four other songs for which he always had a great liking. They belong in fact to the best and most authentic Poulenc/Apollinaire settings.

L'ANGUILLE	THE EEL
Jeanne Houhou la très gentille	Jeanne Houhou the nice creature
Est morte entre des draps très blancs	is dead between very white sheets
Pas seule Bébert dit l'Anguille	not only Bebert known as the Eel
Narcisse et Hubert le merlan	Narcisse and Hubert the whiting
Près d'elle faisaient leur manille	close to her played their card game
Et la crâneuse de Clichy	and the swanker of Clichy
Aux rouges yeux de dégueulade	with the red eyes of the spewer
Répète Mon eau de Vichy	repeats My Vichy water
Va dans le panier à salade	go in the prison van
Haha sans faire de chichi	without making a fuss
Les yeux dansants comme des anges	eyes dancing like angels
Elle riait | elle riait	she laughed she laughed
Les yeux très bleus les dents très blanches	her eyes very blue her teeth very white
Si vous saviez si vous saviez	if you knew if you knew
Tout ce que nous ferons dimanche	all that we shall do on Sunday

Here for the first time we find Poulenc with the accent of Parisian slang (*parigot*). Other examples will be found. Concerning a song of which I shall speak later, Poulenc writes: 'When the subject is Paris I am often moved to tears and to music.' And also: 'I have so often wandered round Paris at night that I believe I know better than any other musician the rhythm of a slipper gliding along the asphalt on an evening in May.'

And here is his commentary on this song: 'L'Anguille, which evokes the atmosphere of a shady hotel, has the rhythm of little steps of shoes made of felt, and must be <u>touching</u>. Sing this song without irony, believing in it.'

Perhaps one needs to be Parisian and to know the Parisian slang in order to interpret this song. But the warning that I gave in my introduction to the songs of Apollinaire, and to which I ask the reader to refer, is here applicable. I must ask interpreters to take care! In this particular type of song, where Poulenc purposely adopts a plebeian accent, it is <u>essential</u>, while giving the song its character, to avoid any hint of <u>vulgarity</u>. None understood better than Poulenc the dark poetry of a certain sordid Parisian atmosphere. It is this poetry that one must try to recreate.

When Poulenc wishes to evoke Paris, as in this song, he often uses the rhythm of the 'valse-musette' suggesting the accordion of the popular dance halls: 'Voyage à Paris', for example, in a mood of gaiety; 'Le Disparu', in tragic mood.

As in many of his early songs, Poulenc has indicated here a metronomic tempo which is rather too fast. $\cdot = 100$ is about right, but it must be implacable. It is of the first importance to observe carefully the value of the rests. Nevertheless (and this should have been corrected in the printed edition), between the two phrases, 'si vous saviez', the bar's rest should not be observed, but instead the top G should be held for two bars. The 'slang' is written into the music; all the same it is possible to mark certain accents on some first syllables: '<u>gentille</u>', '<u>Bébert</u>', '<u>manille</u>', '<u>dégueulade</u>', '<u>chichi</u>', '<u>Dimanche</u>', on this last word, a little *portamento* should be made between the F sharp and the C.

CARTE POSTALE

L'ombre de la très douce est évoquée ici,
Indolente et jouant un air dolent aussi:
Nocturne ou lied mineur qui fait pâmer son âme
Dans l'ombre où ses longs doigts font mourir une gamme
Au piano qui geint comme une pauvre femme.

POSTCARD

The ghost of one who is very sweet is evoked here
indolent and playing an air that is doleful too
nocturne or Lied in a minor key that makes her soul swoon
in the shadow where under her long fingers a scale is dying
on the piano that laments like a poor woman

Taken from a series of nine poems: 'Les dicts d'Amour à Linda' (The discourse of love to Linda). This little poem has no title but it is preceded by this indication: (Postcard of the 19th of May 1901 for the charming young lady Linda M. de S.). It concerns Linda Molina de Silva, sister of a comrade of Apollinaire, whom he tried without success to seduce. The initials of these five lines form an acrostic, LINDA. Poulenc's commentary is 'Imperturbable rhythm. Thought of Missia Sert at the piano painted by Bonnard. Emphasize the intimate character of this song.'

Poulenc's marking is *sans trainer* (without dragging). ♩=96 and this is the maximum of speed. He also says *sans nuances* (without change of dynamics), but all the same with perfect *legato*, it needs very beautiful phrasing. (*Subito p* on the higher C of 'âme' is excellent.)

AVANT LE CINÉMA	BEFORE THE CINEMA
Et puis ce soir on s'en ira Au cinéma	And then this evening we will go to the cinema

Les Artistes que sont-ce donc
Ce ne sont plus ceux qui cultivent les
   Beaux-Arts
Ce ne sont plus ceux qui s'occupent de
   l'Art
Art poétique ou bien musique
Les Artistes ce sont les acteurs et les
   actrices
	What kind of artists are they
	they are no longer those who cultivate
	   the Fine Arts
	not those who go in for Art
	
	poetic art or even music
	the Artists are the actors and actresses

Si nous étions des Artistes Nous ne dirions pas le cinéma Nous dirions le ciné	If we were the Artists we would not say the cinema we would say the ciné

Mais si nous étions de vieux
   professeurs de province
Nous ne dirions ni ciné ni cinéma
Mais cinématographe
	but if we were old professors from the
	   provinces
	we would say neither ciné nor cinema
	but cinematograph

Aussi mon Dieu faut-il avoir du goût	Dear me we must have good taste

The irony of this poem must not be underlined. It will explain itself if it is sung with almost exaggerated seriousness. Nevertheless a certain emphasis can be given to the word 'cinématographe'. Poulenc himself said, 'Sing this quite straight.' The tempo, ♩=126, is very good. The articulation, difficult at times, must be incisive. The piano part must be played in strict time until the last chords.

1904   1904

A Strasbourg en 1904 [diznœfsãkatr]	In Strasbourg in nineteen hundred and four
J'arrivai pour le lundi gras	I arrived on the Monday before Lent
A l'hôtel m'assis devant l'âtre	at the hotel I sat by the fireside
Près d'un chanteur de l'opéra	close to a singer from the opera
Qui ne parlait que de théâtre	who spoke of nothing but the theatre
La Kellnerine rousse avait	The red haired waitress had
Mis sur sa tête un chapeau rose	put a pink hat on her head
Comme Hébé qui les dieux servait	such as Hebe who served the gods
N'en eut jamais | ô belles choses	never possessed O lovely things
Carnaval chapeau rose | Ave!	Carnival pink hat all hail!
A Rome | à Nice et à Cologne	To Rome to Nice and to Cologne
Dans les fleurs | et les confetti	in the flowers and the confetti
Carnaval j'ai revu ta trogne √	Carnival I have seen your bloated mug again
O roi plus riche et plus gentil	O king richer and kinder
Que Crésus Rothschild et Torlogne	than Croesus Rothschild and Torlogne
[Krezys] [Rɔtʃild] [Tɔrlɔɲ]	
Je soupai d'un peu de foie gras	I supped on a little foie gras
De chevreuil tendre à la compote	on tender venison with compote
De tartes flancs etc [etcetera]	on tartlets and so on
Un peu de kirsch me ravigotte	a little kirsch bucked me up
Que ne t'avais-je entre mes bras	If only you had been in my arms

'How much I like this kaleidoscope of words,' said Poulenc. The poet, after having seen the carnival at Rome, at Nice, and at Cologne, tells what happened at Strasbourg in 1904 (Kellnerin is the German word for a waitress in a restaurant). Poulenc advises, 'do not underline with exaggeration the satiated and erotic side of the final cadence. There is already sufficient in the musical writing.'

The indicated tempo, ♩ = 104, is almost impossible and too hurried. About ♩ = 96 is good. The accents and the rests must be carefully observed and the tempo strictly maintained until the *très lent* (very slow) of the final bars. (In some editions there is a flat omitted in the voice part on the word 'compote'.)

*

DEUX MÉLODIES
DANS LE JARDIN D'ANNA ALLONS PLUS VITE

Of all Poulenc's songs, these two undoubtedly present the greatest interpretative difficulties. They illustrate two very different aspects of Apollinaire's poetry set to music by Poulenc with such marvellous understanding.

DANS LE JARDIN D'ANNA

Certes si nous avions vécu en l'an dix-
  sept cent soixante
Est-ce bien la date que vous déchiffrez,
  | Anna, sur ce banc de pierre

Et que par malheur j'eusse été allemand,
Mais que par bonheur j'eusse été près
  de vous
Nous aurions parlé d'amour de façon
  imprécise
Presque toujours en français
Et pendue éperdûment à mon bras
Vous m'auriez écouté vous parler de
  Pythagoras
En pensant aussi au café qu'on
  prendrait
Dans une demi-heure.

Et l'automne eût été pareil à cet
  automne
Que l'épine-vinette et les pampres
  couronnent

Et brusquement parfois j'eusse salué très
  bas
De nobles dames grasses et
  langoureuses

J'aurais dégusté lentement | et tout seul

Pendant de longues soirées
Le tokay épais | ou la malvoisie
J'aurais mis mon habit espagnol
Pour aller sur la route par | laquelle
Arrive dans son vieux carrosse

IN ANNA'S GARDEN

To be sure had we lived in the year
  seventeen hundred and sixty
is it not the date which you decipher,
  Anna, on this stone bench

and if by mischance I had been German,
but if by good fortune I had been close
  to you
we would have spoken of love in a
  vague way
almost always in French
and hanging passionately on my arm
you would have listened to me speaking
  to you of Pythagoras
while also thinking of the coffee we
  would take
in half-an-hour.

And the autumn would have been
  like this autumn
crowned with berberis and vine
  branches

and I would at times have abruptly
  made a deep bow
to stout languorous ladies of the
  nobility

I would have sipped slowly all by
  myself
during long evenings
heavy tokay or malmsey wine
I would have donned my Spanish coat
to go out on the road along which
will arrive in her old fashioned carriage

Ma grand'mère qui se refuse à
   comprendre l'allemand

my grandmother who refuses to
   understand German

J'aurais écrit des vers pleins de
   mythologie

I would have written lines full of
   mythology

Sur vos seins la vie champêtre et sur les
   dames

on your breasts on the pastoral life
   and on the ladies

Des alentours

of the neighbourhood

J'aurais souvent cassé ma canne

I should have often broken my
   walking stick

Sur le dos d'un paysan

on a peasant's back

J'aurais aimé entendre de la musique |
   en mangeant

I should have liked to hear music while
   eating

Du jambon

ham

J'aurais juré en allemand je vous
   le jure

I should have sworn in German I
   assure you

Lorsque vous m'auriez surpris |
   embrassant à pleine bouche

when you caught me kissing full on
   the mouth

Cette servante rousse

this red haired serving-wench

Vous m'auriez pardonné dans le bois |
   aux myrtilles

you would have forgiven me in the
   myrtle wood

J'aurais fredonné un moment

I should have hummed for a moment

Puis nous aurions écouté longtemps
   les bruits du crépuscule

then we would have listened long to
   the sounds of twilight

This poem has an extravagant degree of verve and fantasy. It displays by turns irony, tenderness, parody, it is bombastic, farcical, erotic, down to earth, poetic, . . . all this without transitions, in phrases which follow one another in a whirl of images. It would seem impossible to follow such a diversity of contrasting nuances more closely and with greater accuracy than Poulenc has done. This means that the interpreters on their part must prove to have the virtuosity of an acrobat in the rapidity and the abruptness of all these contrasts of expression and these contrarieties of vocal colour, which must never cause a change in the implacable tempo, in which Poulenc never accords the singer the saving grace of a bar's rest!

In order to facilitate the study of the song we can divide it arbitrarily into fourteen clearly contrasted sections of two or three lines, that is to say two to seven bars.

Section 1 Alsace is obviously evoked in this poem, but, said Poulenc, 'in spite of my one eighth part of Alsatian blood, I never had that in mind at all.' An old stone bench where he is sitting with his Anna sets the scene for this fantasy of the poet, who imagines what their life would have been had they lived in the eighteenth century. The first four bars, all in very precise rhythm, should have a tempo slightly less than ♩ = 100, and must give the impression of a recitative which is entirely objective.

A *crescendo* leads to

Section 2, of two bars strictly in tempo which are non legato and *f*; here the indicated accents should be observed but without changing the dynamics, because, Section 3, of three bars, is subito *mp* legato, and as Poulenc indicates, 'monotone', with a kind of feigned indifference. A *crescendo* is needed in the voice part at the end of the third bar to correspond with the *crescendo* in the piano part.

Section 4, of four bars. Here is a complete change of vocal colour to great warmth, great lyricism, a certain grandiloquence, *f* and *crescendo*. Bring out the word 'éperdûment' by accenting the syllable '<u>per</u>'.

Section 5, of three bars. *Subito p legato, avec charme*, says Poulenc, to emphasize the love of good food and the comfortable middle class background. On the last bar a slight *rallentando* is needed and a good breath before attacking

Section 6, of seven bars which, *mf*, must suddenly bring in a poetic element by means of perfect legato and very lyrical phrasing. Again a total change of colour for the first five bars of

Section 7, *f* and broadly ceremonious. A good breath must be taken before the *p subito* of the seven bars of

Section 8. The *très expressif* indicated by Poulenc must suggest the poet drinking 'lentement' and 'longuement', '<u>et tout seul</u>'. Underline these three words with their touch of self-satisfaction and egotism. At the end of the seventh bar, observe carefully in the piano part the *subito f et très sec* (very crisp) to introduce the five bars of

Section 9. The Spanish music demanded by the text in the last two bars is *staccato* for the piano. The voice sings *f non legato*, strongly articulated, very gay and ironical. Again a good breath before attacking the six bars of

Section 10, and once more a total change of colour and of atmosphere, *p*, *avec charme*, legato, lyrical and a little bombastic. The two bars of

Section 11 are *f* and exaggeratedly *marcato*. And suddenly, for the six bars of Section 12, the warm sensuality of the poem must be defined, *f* and *ff*. Poulenc has indicated perfectly how to perform the phrase 'cette servante rousse': *bref, précis et parlé* (short, precise and spoken), and I would add: very simply, *mf*, and *a tempo* after a short pause. In the piano part take care not to hurry the bar of 6/4 that precedes

Section 13 with, according to Poulenc, its 'erotic irony' underlined by his music, which neatly suggests an implication for the forgiveness in the

myrtle wood . . . and which motivates the off-handedness of 'J'aurais fredonné un moment'. A slight slowing down leads to the
Last Section which, with a little slackening of tempo, expresses the calm sensuousness of this marvellously poetic ending with its beautiful piano part.

The over long but necessary dissection of this song shows to what extent the interpreters must use variety and fantasy and above all their imagination. But, I insist on this point, all the effects must be made without any *rubato*. This song could be disparate, but not if an inexorable tempo gives it its unity.

ALLONS PLUS VITE

Et le soir vient | et les lys meurent
   Regarde ma douleur beau ciel qui me
      l'envoie
     Une nuit de mélancolie

     Enfant souris | ô sœur écoute
Pauvres marchez sur la grand'route
   O menteuse forêt qui surgis à ma
      voix
     Les flammes qui brûlent les
      âmes

   Sur le boulevard de Grenelle
Les ouvriers | et les patrons
   Arbres de mai cette dentelle
   Ne fais donc pas le fanfaron
Allons plus vite nom de Dieu

   Allons plus vite

Tous les poteaux télégraphiques
Viennent là-bas le long du quai
Sur son sein notre République |
A mis ce bouquet de muguet

Qui poussait dru le long du quai
   Allons plus vite nom de Dieu

   Allons plus vite

COME ALONG MAKE HASTE

And the evening comes and the lilies die
  beautiful sky see my suffering which
    you send to me
   a night of melancholy

   Smile child O sister listen
poor folk walk on the high road
  O deceptive forest risen at my
    voice
   the flames which burn souls

  On the Boulevard de Grenelle
the workers and the employers
  trees of maytime this lace
  do not flaunt it so much
come along make haste for God's
  sake
  come along make haste

All the telegraph poles
reach yonder along the quay
on the breast of our Republic
they have put this bouquet of
  lilies of the valley
which grew densely along the quay
  come along make haste for God's
  sake
  come along make haste

La bouche en cœur Pauline honteuse	Simpering bashful Pauline
Les ouvriers | et les patrons	the workers and the employers
Oui-dà oui-dà belle endormeuse	O yes O yes beautiful humbug
Ton frère	your brother
Allons plus vite nom de Dieu	come along make haste for God's sake
Allons plus vite	come along make haste

If Apollinaire had used punctuation, there would obviously be a comma between 'Allons' and 'plus vite' in this title.

Here again is an example, and perhaps the most striking example, of Parisian inspiration in the work of Apollinaire and Poulenc. All that I have already said on this subject in the introduction to the Apollinaire songs concerning 'L'Anguille' is, of course, valid for this song, and I ask readers to turn to it. In my experience it is the most difficult of Poulenc's songs from the aspect of interpretation, for the poem is somewhat obscure, and in spite of the illumination thrown on it by the music, it is very difficult to 'put over' to the public. Here are Poulenc's own words:

The poem by Apollinaire opens like Baudelaire; then, abruptly, after taking flight with a few lofty lines, comes to earth on a Parisian pavement. After an opening in A minor I have jealously reserved the major key to convey this effect of surprise.

These 'few lofty lines' which incline towards surrealism (the poem is dated 1917) are not to be explained rationally, but they create an astonishing poetic climate, perfectly high-lighted by the music. They should be sung very legato, observing carefully the indicated dynamics (the first four bars rather *mp* to make the most of the following *pp*). During the five bars which precede the modulation of which Poulenc speaks, the level must be at least *mf*. (There is a very bad fault of orthography in the musical edition: 'qui surgit à ma voix' should of course read 'surgis', and the s should be carried in liaison.)

Here now is the 'coming to earth' on the Parisian pavement. . . . Poulenc says:

If the sexual melancholy of the poem is not understood, it is useless to sing this song. For Apollinaire and for me the Boulvevard de Grenelle is as rare and poetic as the banks of the Ganges are for others. To tell the truth I was not specifically thinking of the Boulevard de Grenelle while I was writing the music, but of its twin brother the Boulevard de la Chapelle that I passed through on so many evenings, when I lived in Montmartre. I imagined Pauline at the door of the Hotel Molière. Czechoslovakian prostitutes are seen there in shiny rubber boots, for a hundred sous. . . .

Could the setting be better staged or the atmosphere better created according to Poulenc's wishes? He again gives the indication, *ému et doucement poétique* (moved and tenderly poetic) on the phrase 'sur le boulevard de Grenelle . . .' Before beginning this modulation, take a good breath and sing *p* and *legato*; then observe carefully the indicated dynamics but without changing the expression. In this mood you will reach the phrase which, like a refrain, recurs three times: 'Allons plus vite. . . .' One can picture the man addressing the women (Pauline?) as they stroll along the Boulevard. This refrain should be said with authority, certainly, but the first time without impatience, with a kind of compliance. Afterwards the poetic atmosphere returns (with a *crescendo* on: 'Viennent là-bas le long du quai'). What may be the meaning of these lines? The Boulevard de Grenelle leads to the bank of the Seine. The bouquet of lilies of the valley—could this perhaps be formed by the white insulators of the telegraph poles?

Now comes the second refrain which this time is harsher and more impatient. The vocal effect on 'Pauline honteuse' should be very sustained to contrast with *sec et un peu narquois* (crisp and a little quizzical) indicated in the following line. The two 'Oui-dà's should be definitely *f* with *portamenti*. 'Ton frère' incredulously, and with a shrug of the shoulders. The last refrain is peremptory, pitiless, strictly in time. It is a tiny and pitiful little drama which must be encircled by a poetic halo.

*

LA GRENOUILLÈRE (THE FROGGERY)

This was the name of a small island in the Seine on the outskirts of Paris, with a restaurant, where on Sundays at the end of the nineteenth century writers and painters came boating. The famous picture by Renoir *The Boatmen's Luncheon*, which is on show at the Moscow Museum, has immortalized the scene brilliantly.

LA GRENOUILLÈRE

Au bord de l'île on voit
Les canots vides | qui s'entre-cognent

Et maintenant
Ni le dimanche √ ni les jours | de la
semaine √

THE FROGGERY

By the shore of the isle one sees
the empty boats that bump against
each other

and now
neither on Sunday nor on weekdays

Ni les peintres ni Maupassant ne se
  promène

Bras nus sur leurs canots avec des
  femmes à grosse poitrines
    Et bêtes comme chou

Petits bateaux vous me faites bien de
  la peine

Au bord de l'île

neither the painters nor Maupassant
  set out

with bare arms in their boats with
  their women friends full-bosomed
    and stupid as a cabbage*

little boats you make me very sad

by the shore of the isle

* sweetly silly.

We are fortunate in having a commentary by Poulenc on this song:

I have tried to make it touching throughout and above all to cause no amusement with 'les femmes à grosses poitrines et bêtes comme chou'. 'La Grenouillère' evokes happy days of a past that is lost, Sundays of ease and contentment. I certainly had in mind these boatmen's lunches, as painted by Renoir, where the bodices of the women and the rowing vests of the men harmonize not only in colour. It is the bumping together of their boats that motivates the rhythm of this tenderly affecting song. Do not sing it if you do not believe in it, if you are going to introduce sidelong looks and a false knowing air. You must be the dupe of your heart. Two bars recall Moussorgsky. It would be childish to hide this influence, such a subterfuge would be repugnant to me. I despise sons who blush at their likeness to their father.

So it can be realized that the 'bumping' of the boats in the piano part must be absolutely regular, 'very veiled by the pedals' and *pp*, while the vocal line is *mf* sung legato and well phrased, with the nostalgic character emphasized by Poulenc's commentary and indicated in his score, *très las et mélancolique* (very relaxed and melancholy). The tempo ♩ = 56 is perfect. A breath should be taken between 'Ni le dimanche' and 'ni les jours', and do not observe the rest before 'de la semaine'. The bar of *crescendo*, 'ni Maupassant ne se promènent', must be clearly articulated, because it is difficult to make it understood. *mp* suffices for 'avec des femmes à grosses poitrines et bêtes comme chou', with perfect equality of the triplets, and very legato. Of course no hint of humour, as Poulenc advises. Thus *p* is used for the two Moussorgsky bars, 'Petits bateaux vous me faites bien de la peine'; and the last line is again *mf*, as at the beginning of the song.

*

BLEUET	YOUNG SOLDIER
Jeune homme de vingt ans	Young man of twenty years
Qui a vu des choses si affreuses	you who have seen such terrible things
Que penses-tu des hommes de ton enfance	what do you think of the men of your childhood
Tu connais la bravoure et la ruse	You have seen bravery and cunning
Tu as vu la mort en face plus de cent fois	you have seen death face to face over a hundred times
Tu ne sais pas ce que c'est que la vie	you do not know what life is
Transmets ton intrépidité	Hand on your fearlessness
A ceux qui viendront |	to those who will come
Après toi	after you
Jeune homme	Young man
Tu es joyeux ta mémoire est ensanglantée	you are full of joy your memory is steeped in blood
Ton âme est rouge aussi	your soul too is red
De joie	with joy
Tu as absorbé la vie de ceux qui sont morts près de toi	you have absorbed the life of those who fell beside you
Tu as de la décision	you have resolution
Il est dix sept heures | et tu saurais	it is five o'clock and you would know how
Mourir	to die
Sinon mieux que tes aînés	if not better than your elders
Du moins plus pieusement	at least with more piety
Car tu connais mieux la mort que la vie	for you know death better than life
O douceur d'autrefois	O sweetness of former days
Lenteur | immémoriale	slow moving beyond all memory

This is a wartime poem; we shall find others in Apollinaire's work. It was written in 1917 when the poet had returned to Paris after having been wounded in the head by a shell splinter. The title plays on the word 'bleu' which is a colloquialism for a young soldier. The name of the flower 'bleuet' (cornflower) is thus a pleasing diminutive.

Poulenc wrote this song in October 1939, at the beginning of the Second World War, and it is easy to understand his having been inspired by this poem. Here are his words, after which all other commentary would seem superfluous:

I felt no heroic attitude of mind in writing this song. That would moreover not have suited me, because there is nothing of the bard about me. I was quite simply moved to the depths of my being by the intensely human overtones of Apollinaire's poem. Humility, whether it concerns prayer or the sacrifice of a life, is what touches me most.

> Il est dix sept heures et tu saurais
> mourir
> Sinon mieux que tes aînés
> Du moins plus pieusement

That is for me the key to the poem, the perfect clarification of the drama. We are far away from 'Ceux qui pieusement sont morts' (those who have died piously), with grand playing of the organ, with marble, with draped candelabra, with flags. It is more befitting, I believe, for that mysterious moment when leaving the mortal remains in the vestiary the soul flies away after a long, last look at 'La douceur d'autrefois'. All this proves what a misconception it would be to sing 'Bleuet' grandiloquently. Intimately should perhaps have been my marking for the initial expression.

'Intimately' and also 'very *legato* and with simplicity'. The quiet pace ♩ = 53 seems just right. Care should be taken over certain markings: *p très doux*. Do not be too sweet in the expression, which must always remain virile and serious, for example, 'Tu connais le bravoure et la ruse' and 'Tu ne sais pas ce que c'est que la vie'. (Of course there is no breath, but only a suspension of sound between 'pas' and 'ce'.) I suggest that the marking *p* should be changed to *mf* on 'Transmets ton intrépidité. The *animato* and *crescendo* are well indicated. But above all take well into consideration what I have just said on the *très calme et très doux* (very calmly and very softly) on 'Il est dix sept heures . . .'. Observe carefully the *mf*, 'car tu connais mieux la mort que la vie', and take a long breath before attacking *pp*, and in a totally different colour, a vocal colour which will not have been used before in this song: 'O douceur d'autrefois lenteur immémoriale'. The piano part, which most of the time comprises a counter-melody, must be played with extremely sensitive lyricism.

*

BANALITES (BANALITIES)

This collection of five poems is not in any sense a cycle (as *Tel jour telle nuit* for example). In fact the poems have no connection with each other, neither has the music. If Poulenc united these songs under a single title, it is because they form a well constructed group to be performed in this order, but it is obvious that each song can be performed separately.

Here, according to Poulenc, is the origin of *Banalités*:

I have already spoken of my inveterate habit of putting certain poems on one side in advance. I had chosen 'Sanglots' a long time before, and the curious 'Fagnes de Wallonies'. Going through my library in October 1940, I turned the pages once again—and with how much emotion—of those literary reviews which in 1914 to 1923 had enchanted my adolescence. This time, the series of issues of *Littérature* particularly held my attention. Could it be that so many beautiful poems had appeared there in such modest guise? But that is the unassuming privilege of this type of review. All at once one came upon a poem by Valéry, now a pride of all the anthologies. In the present instance, as far as Apollinaire was concerned, I chose only the delicious lines of doggerel, 'Voyage à Paris' and 'Hôtel', grouped under the title *Banalités*. To anyone who knows me it will seem quite natural that I should open my mouth like a carp to snap up the deliciously stupid lines of 'Voyage à Paris'. Anything that concerns Paris I approach with tears in my eyes and my head full of music. 'Hôtel' is again Paris; a room in Montparnasse. Nothing more was needed for my decision to undertake a cycle in which 'Sanglots' and 'Fagnes' would appear. It remained to find an opening rhythmical song since 'Sanglots' would conclude the cycle with gravity. Then I remembered a song, a little Maeterlinck in style, that Apollinaire had inserted in a strange and beautiful prose piece entitled *Onirocritique*.

This collection of songs shows the varied aspects that Poulenc's music can adopt to express with remarkable fidelity the diversity of Apollinaire's poems.

CHANSON D'ORKENISE

Par les portes d'Orkenise
Veut entrer | un charretier.
Par les portes d'Orkenise
Veut sortir un va-nu-pieds.

Et les gardes de la ville
Courant sus au va-nu-pieds:
'Qu'emportes-tu de la ville?'
'J'y laisse mon cœur entier.'

SONG OF ORKENISE

Through the gates of Orkenise
a carter wants to enter.
Through the gates of Orkenise
a tramp wants to leave.

And the town guards
hasten up to the tramp:
'What are you taking away from the town'
'I leave my whole heart there.'

Et les gardes de la ville	And the town guards
Courant sus_au charretier:	hasten up to the carter:
'Qu'apportes-tu dans la ville?'	'What are you bringing into the town?'
'Mon cœur pour me marier!'	'My heart to be married!'
Que de cœurs, dans_Orkenise!	What a lot of hearts in Orkenise!
Les gardes riaient, riaient.	The guards laughed, laughed.
Va-nu-pieds la route est grise,	Tramp, the road is hazy,
L'amour grise, | ô charretier.	love makes the head hazy, O carter.
Les beaux gardes de la ville	The fine-looking town guards
Tricotaient superbement;	knitted superbly;
Puis les portes de la ville	then the gates of the town
Se fermèrent lentement.	slowly closed.

The preliminary indication is excellent: *Rondement, dans le style d'une chanson populaire* (briskly, in the style of a folk song), ♩ = 126, clearly suggests that the tempo must not vary throughout all the changes of dynamics, of colour and expression. The pianist must always use plenty of pedal on the semi-quaver sextuplets each time they come, and they are always *mf* in contrast to the preceding *f*. The vocal line is very rhythmical. Take care to make the quavers equal. (For example 'Or-ke'.)

The first quatrain is *f*, without change in dynamics and without purport. But with the second quatrain rapid and difficult contrasts begin. A certain brusqueness can suggest the town guards dashing up to the tramp, then to the carter, and putting their questions. Bring out well: 'emporte', 'de', and 'apportes', 'dans'. The reply of the tramp *p subito* must be deeply nostalgic, but above all without any simpering. The reply of the carter very lively with a touch of coarseness. Neither of them are people of refinement. Poulenc has clearly indicated the expression that he wishes for 'Que de cœurs dans Orkénise': *p, très tendre* (very tenderly). But make no mistake, it must also be ironic, for the guards were 'laughing, laughing'! And suddenly here is the poetry: *pp très doux* (very softly) on the two lines: 'Va-nu-pieds la route est grise, L'amour grise, ô charretier'. (The word 'grise' in French can mean 'grey' and also 'tipsy'.) The last two lines. 'Les beaux gardes de la ville Tricotaient superbement', *f subito*, broadly declaimed and very emphatic. (They certainly have large moustaches!)

Then the picture of the heavy doors of the gates of Orkenise closing *slowly*, must nevertheless be expressed without *rallentando*, for the long value of the notes suffices to suggest it. It is preferable to ignore the quaver rest between 'Les beaux gardes' and 'de la ville'.

HÔTEL	HOTEL
Ma chambre a la forme d'une cage	My room is shaped like a cage
Le soleil passe son bras par la fenêtre	the sun puts its arm through the window
Mais moi qui veut fumer	but I who would like to smoke
Pour faire des mirages	to make smoke pictures
J'allume au feu du jour ma cigarette	I light at the fire of day my cigarette
Je ne veux pas travailler	I do not want to work
Je veux fumer.	I want to smoke.

Without doubt the 'laziest' song ever written! But make no mistake, there must be no hint of sadness. On the contrary it is a happy laziness! The poet is in his small hotel room, among the roof tops in Montparnasse, he stretches and yawns. A ray of sunlight shines through the window, and in his blissful mood the only thing he wants to do is to light a cigarette 'au feu du jour' (at the sun's fire)! We might say that the interpreters, singer and pianist, must themselves give the impression of stretching in a perfect *legato*, for which the indicated tempo, ♩ = 50, is excellent. (The semiquaver rest between 'soleil' and 'passe' should be disregarded.) There is no reason to sing *p* on the first line: the dynamics should preferably be *mf* and *f*. This will increase the marvellous vocal effect '*pp subito*' on 'J'allume au feu du jour ma cigarette'. Make a slight elongation of the quaver 'j'al' (take care not to pronounce the double ll). The semiquaver rest between 'jour' and 'ma' should be deleted and the whole phrase sung in one breath and kept in tempo. The effect of a slight suggestion of vulgarity in the *portamento* 'ga-rette' must be achieved with the most perfect taste. The secret is to anticipate slightly the 'g' of 'cigarette'. All the end of the song should be on the whole *mf* for the voice. There should be an accent on 'travailler and a slight dwelling on each of the notes 'Je veux fu' with an accent on 'fu'; and delay slightly the first beat of ' . . . mer', *pp*, and above all with a single 'm', I would say half an 'm'.

The two last bars of the piano are *subito mf*, like a happy conclusion to this marvellous song.

FAGNES DE WALLONIE	WALLOON UPLANDS
Tant de tristesses plénières	Overwhelming sorrow
Prirent mon cœur aux fagnes désolées	seized my heart in the desolate uplands
Quand las j'ai reposé dans les sapinières	when tired I rested in the fir plantation
Le poids des kilomètres pendant que râlait	the weight of the kilometres while blustered

le vent d'ouest
J'avais quitté le joli bois
Les écureuils | y sont restés
Ma pipe essayait de faire des nuages
  Au ciel
Qui restait pur obstinément

Je n'ai confié aucun secret √ sinon
  une chanson | énigmatique
Aux tourbières humides

Les bruyères fleurant le miel
Attiraient les abeilles
Et mes pieds endoloris
Foulaient les myrtilles et les
  airelles

Tendrement mariée
  Nord
  Nord
La vie s'y tord
En arbres forts
  Et tors
La vie y mord
  La mort
A belles dents
Quand bruit le vent

the west wind
I had left the pretty wood
the squirrels stayed there
my pipe tried to make clouds
  in the sky
which remained obstinately clear

I did not confide any secret except
  an enigmatic song
to the damp peat bog

the heather fragrant with honey
attracted the bees
and my aching feet
crushed the bilberries and the
  blaeberries

tenderly united
  north
  north
life twists itself there
in strong trees
  and twisted
life bites there
  death
ravenously
when the wind howls

The Fagnes de Wallonie are a high plateau in the Belgian Ardennes, where, at Stavelot, Apollinaire passed his holidays in 1899. It is a country of heath and peat-bogs, of gnarled trees twisted by the wind. Therefore the poem and the music that describes it must be interpreted from beginning to end like a great gust of wind, even though the tempo ♩=88 seems preferable to ♩=92.

All the first part of the song is *f* and very *legato*. It is only when reaching 'J'avais quitté le joli bois', *p*, that the colour must suddenly change. (Note that in the ninth bar there is a sharp omitted on the D in the left hand.) Give an accent on the 'râ' of the word 'râlait.' In the two first lines of Page 8, there are two quaver rests which must assuredly be disregarded and replaced by dotting the crotchets and singing in one breath, 'Je n'ai confié aucun secret', and also, 'sinon une chanson énigmatique'. In the bar after these words, the piano has a true *f* and a big *diminuendo* for the complete change of colour, *p clair* (*p* clear), fresh as the scent of the heather. For both voice and piano on 'Et mes pieds endoloris . . .', *mp* is preferable to *f*, in order to be able, after a big *crescendo* for the piano, to attack *f* and very rhythmically, 'Tendrement mariée'. *Always f* throughout to the end, despite the dynamics indicated by Poulenc! And with very biting articulation. A *crescendo-diminuendo* on the word 'vent' gives the impression of a last gust of wind.

The piano coda, *above all no rallentando*, should sooner be *accelerando*, particularly on the final chords.

VOYAGE A PARIS	TRIP TO PARIS
Ah! la charmante chose	Ah! how charming
Quitter un pays morose	to leave a dreary place
Pour Paris	for Paris
Paris joli	delightful Paris
Qu'un jour dut créer	that once upon a time love must have
l'Amour	created

To set to music these 'deliciously stupid doggerel verses', Poulenc has used, as in 'L'Anguille' (q.v.), the rhythm of the '*valse musette*', for this is again a song with a Parisian accent. In fact, for those who have had the joy of hearing Maurice Chevalier, it is his style that comes irresistibly to mind. This great music hall singer was, for half a century, the incarnation of a certain type of sentimentality and of Parisian badinage which never descends into vulgarity, but always remains instinct with graciousness and poetry. It suffices to say that this must be the style of interpretation for 'Voyage à Paris'.

The indicated tempo is excellent: ♩. =96, certainly no slower, and with gaiety and good humour, jovial and *f*. The touch of Parisian slang can be brought out by always giving a strong accent (with a strongly articulated 'P') on the first syllable of 'Paris'. It is essential to delete the quaver rest in the second bar of the voice part, and the phrase, 'Ah! la charmante chose' *must not* be broken. When these words return for the second time, the effect of charm, *p*, must be done wittily, then *f subito* on 'Pour Paris'. The tempo should be well maintained and there must be a portamento on 'joli' to reach the falsetto high G which must be very clean and crisp. It must be full of gaiety to the end and Poulenc's indication: *très aimable* (very amiably) is exactly right. The pianist must make much of the big final *crescendo*, with, of course, no *rallentando*.

*

SANGLOTS (SOBS)

This is one of the most beautiful and most inspired among the lyrical songs of Poulenc. It is as difficult in execution as it is in interpretation. 'The poem,' says Henri Hell, Poulenc's biographer, 'one of the most poignant, the most unpretentiously heart-rending of Apollinaire's poems, evokes the whole human race that each one of us has borne within himself since the beginning of time.'

It must be conceded that the poem is not always easy to understand. But Poulenc had such feeling for this poetry that, as always, his music clarifies the text, giving it its form, its rhythm, its intensity, and interpreters should have no difficulty in adopting his conception. Nevertheless I believe it necessary to reproduce here the arrangement of the poem on the page as in the literary edition. I have added, for sake of greater clarification, some parentheses for certain recessed lines, because there are, in a way, two poems in one. Without the lines in parenthesis the poem is much easier to understand, and it will be realized that the lines in parenthesis are connected with each other. Despite Poulenc's great ability, it is without doubt difficult to bring out all the points.

SANGLOTS	SOBS
Notre amour est réglé par les calmes étoiles	Our love is ordered by the calm stars
Or nous savons qu'en nous beaucoup d'hommes respirent	now we know that in us many men have their being
Qui vinrent de très loin | et sont un sous nos fronts	who came from very far away and are one under our brows
C'est la chanson des rêveurs	it is the song of the dreamers
Qui s'étaient arraché le cœur	who tore out their heart
Et le portaient dans la main droite	and carried it in the right hand
Souviens-t'en cher orgueil de tous ces souvenirs	(remember dear pride all these memories
Des marins qui chantaient comme des conquérants	of the sailors who sang like conquerors
Des gouffres de Thulé des tendres cieux d'Ophir	of the chasms of Thule of the gentle skies of Ophir
Des malades maudits de ceux qui fuient leur ombre	of the cursed sick people of those who fled from their shadow
Et du retour joyeux des heureux émigrants	and of the joyous return of happy emigrants)
De ce cœur il coulait du sang	this heart ran with blood
Et le rêveur allait pensant	and the dreamer went on thinking

A sa blessure délicate	of his wound delicate
Tu ne briseras pas la chaîne de	(You will not break the chain of
ces causes	these causes)
Et douloureuse | et nous disait	and painful and said to us
Qui sont les effets d'autres	(which are the effects of other
causes	causes)
Mon pauvre cœur mon cœur brisé	my poor heart my broken heart
Pareil au cœur de tous les hommes	resembling the heart of all men
Voici voici nos mains que la vie	(here here are our hands that
fit esclaves	life enslaved)
Est mort d'amour ou c'est tout	has died of love or so it seems
comme	
Est mort d'amour et le voici	has died of love and here it is
Ainsi vont toutes choses	such is the way of all things
Arrachez donc le vôtre aussi	tear out yours also
Et rien ne sera libre jusqu'à la	(and nothing will be free until
fin des temps	the end of time)
Laissons tout aux morts	let us leave all to the dead
Et cachons nos sanglots	and hide our sobs

The indicated tempo, ♩=66, is the maximum of speed, but clearly intimates that there must be no dragging in creating the extraordinary serenity of the opening. The pianist must find a quality of sound that is soft and transparent, and the singer a suspended *mezza voce* with perfect *legato*. Poulenc and I never made the *mf* on the fourth line of the voice part, because the same colour and the same atmosphere should remain until the modulation into E flat minor. (In the bar of 6/4 on the fifth beat in the piano part, there is obviously a misprint for D♮.) From the modulation, 'C'est la chanson . . .', there is a total change of colour: both singer and pianist must now achieve a rich and round sonority, and begin an *animato* which continues for seventeen bars. After the seven first bars of the *crescendo*, reserve the possibility of a *f subito* on, 'Souviens-t'en cher orgueil', for it is the start of the second poem.

In continuing the *animato* a big *crescendo* is again made which leads to 'Des malades maudits'. These triplets must be very *marcato* and dramatic. Then (and this is not indicated in the score, although Poulenc intended to mark it in later editions), it is imperative to make a *ritenuto* and a *diminuendo* on the two bars, 'de ceux qui fuient leur ombre', and thus to highlight the marvellous musical and expressive modulation: 'Et du retour joyeux des heureux émigrants' (with an accent on the B♮ of '*joy*'). After the *ritenuto* that I have just indicated you will find yourself in a slower tempo, but it must not be too slow to allow for a further slowing down to return to the *tempo primo* of the E♮ section (first poem). This tempo should not again vary, despite the difficulties posed by the poem.

Continue *p* for eight bars until the terribly difficult parenthesis (second poem), 'Tu ne brisera pas la chaîne de ces causes', which should be a true *f*, disregarding the semiquaver rest between 'pas' and 'la'. Return again to the *p* of 'délicate' to continue the first poem with the same intensity: 'Et douloureuse, et (le rêveur) nous disait' (And the dreamer told us sadly). On this line Poulenc's indication is still incorrect because singer and pianist must be *p* and very intense. Thus the second parenthesis (second poem) will be *f* *subito* like the first. Return to *p* with tenderness for the continuation of the first poem; and the following parenthesis is *mf*, and above all without hurrying, which is everyone's tendency.

A *ritenuto* of one bar introduces the great lyricism, *f*, of: 'Est mort d'amour ou c'est tout comme'. And a superb effect is made by the repeat of the phrase, *pp*, like an echo with a very slight *rubato* on the second: 'Est mort d'amour'. The modulation into major should be *mf*, and completely *a tempo*. (Cut out the quaver rest between 'Arrachez donc' and 'le votre aussi'.)

The second poem returns, 'Et rien ne sera libre', for which a *mf* is preferable to the *f* which is indicated. Make a little *decrescendo* up to the end of the song which must nevertheless retain all the richness of the voice in the low register, and great intensity of expression. There is a *rallentando* only on the last two bars of the piano part.

*

MONTPARNASSE · HYDE PARK

MONTPARNASSE

MONTPARNASSE	MONTPARNASSE
O porte de l'hôtel | avec deux plantes vertes	O door of the hotel with two green plants
Vertes qui jamais	green which never
Ne porteront de fleurs	will bear any flowers
Où sont mes fruits? Où me planté-je?	where are my fruits? where do I plant myself?
O porte de l'hôtel | un‿ange est devant toi	O door of the hotel an angel stands in front of you
Distribuant des prospectus	distributing prospectuses
On n'a jamais si bien défendu la vertu	virtue has never been so well defended
Donnez-moi pour toujours | une chambre à la semaine	give me for ever a room by the week
Ange barbu vous‿êtes‿en réalité	bearded angel you are really
Un poète lyrique d'Allemagne	a lyric poet from Germany
Qui voulez connaître | Paris	who wants to know Paris

Vous connaissez de son pavé   you know on its pavement
Ces raies sur lesquelles | il ne faut pas   these lines on which one must not
    que l'on marche   step
        Et vous rêvez   and you dream
D'aller passer votre Dimanche à   of going to pass your Sunday at
    Garches   Garches

Il fait un peu lourd | et vos cheveux   it is rather sultry and your hair is long
    sont longs
O bon petit poète | un peu bête et   O good little poet a bit stupid and
    trop blond   too blond
Vos yeux ressemblent tant | à ces deux   your eyes so much resemble these
    grands ballons   two big balloons
Qui s'en vont dans l'air pur   that float away in the pure air
A l'aventure   at random.

It seems probable that the poet included himself in the scene of this poem,
and that it evokes his arrival in Paris from the Rhineland ten years earlier.
(The poem is dated 1912.)

'Let us imagine,' said Poulenc, 'this Montparnasse suddenly discovered
by Picasso, Braque, Modigliani, Apollinaire. The more I re-read
Apollinaire, the more I am struck by the poetic rôle that Paris plays in his
work.'

In this song Poulenc is once more inspired by Paris, but in a style which is
quite different from certain Parisian songs of which we have just spoken.
Here one finds no more Parisian slang, the atmosphere is nearer to that of
'Hôtel'. I would say a happy nonchalance.

'It took me four years,' said Poulenc, 'to write "Montparnasse". I do not
regret the time I spent on it for it is probably one of my best songs. As I _never_
transpose the key of music which I have just conceived for a certain line or
even for several words, just to make things easier for myself, it follows that
the linking up is often difficult, and I need to take time to find the exact
place where at times I am obliged to modulate.'

The tempo, ♩ = 58, is the maximum of speed, _p_, but also very well sung
with beautiful _legato_. The dynamics are well indicated, nevertheless I advise
that the phrase, 'distribuant des prospectus', should not be sung too _p_ to
allow for the _pp_ on 'on n'a jamais si bien défendu la vertu' which by contrast
should be almost spoken, without any irony. All the following section is
extremely lyrical: a little _rubato_ on 'poète' to give comfortable time for the
pianist's arpeggio, but the movement must not slow down and the voice
must not _decrescendo_ in the descent to the lower notes. The word 'Paris' can
be brought out by accenting the first syllable, and an expression of

admiration. The following section should be very *dolce pp*, with a *mf* on 'et vous rêver d'aller passer', to give the effect of *pp subito* on 'votre Dimanche à Garches' (with an exaggerated G), this residential suburb of Paris which seems to the poet the ideal countryside. The pianist should take a good breath before attacking his counter-melody in octaves (a little accent on 'bête'). The whole end of the song should be very lyrical and very poetic, but above all not sad.

HYDE PARK	HYDE PARK
Les faiseurs de religion	The promoters of religions
Prêchaient dans le brouillard	were preaching in the fog
Les ombres près de qui nous passions	the shadowy figures near us as we passed
Jouaient à collin-maillard	played blind man's buff
A soixante-dix ans	at seventy years old
Joues fraîches de petits enfants	fresh cheeks of small children
Venez venez | Eléonore	come along come along Eleonore
Et que sais-je encore	and what more besides
Regardez venir les cyclopes	look at the Cyclops coming
Les pipes s'envolaient	the pipes were flying past
Mais | envolez-vous-en	but be off
Regards impénitents	obdurate staring
Et l'Europe l'Europe	and Europe Europe
Regards sacrés	worshipping looks
Mains énamourées	hands in love
Et les amants s'aimèrent	and the lovers made love
Tant que prêcheurs prêchèrent	as long as the preachers preached

Apollinaire created this little picture of London the same year, in 1912, when he was in London with the painter Picabia. It is an etching of Hyde Park in a London fog, with the preachers standing on their packing-cases haranguing the passers-by near Marble Arch; the old lady with a skin like a baby; the pipe smokers—one-eyed monsters in the fog; and the loving couples embracing on the grass whatever the weather. . . .

For Poulenc it was nothing but a sketch, nothing more than a bridging song intended to show to advantage the lyrical song which should follow in the programme.

There are no great subtleties of interpretation. It should be descriptive and brilliant, the tempo pitiless, and the indicated dynamics followed with precision. There must be contrasts of vocal colour and of *legato*: 'Les ombres près de qui nous passions etc. . . .', and of *non legato*: 'A soixante-dix ans etc. . . .'. Do not miss the *p subito* 'very tender' on 'Regards sacrés mains énamourées Et les amants s'aimèrent', in order to highlight the final *f* of the inexhaustible preachers.

*

LE PONT · UN POÈME

LE PONT

Deux dames le long du fleuve
Elles se parlent par-dessus l'eau
Et sur le pont de leurs paroles
La foule passe et repasse en dansant

un dieu   c'est
                                             pour
    tu reviendras   toi
                                             seule
       Hi! oh! là-bas √   que
                                             le
       Là-bas √   sang
                                             coule

Tous les   enfants savent pourquoi

      Passe mais passe donc
      Ne te retourne pas

   Hi! oh! là-bas là-bas

Les jeunes filles qui passent sur le pont léger
      portent dans leurs mains
      le bouquet de demain
Et leurs regards s'écoulent
    Dans ce fleuve à tous étranger
Qui vient de loin qui va si loin
Et passe sous le pont léger de vos paroles
    Ô bavardes le long du fleuve
      Ô bavardes │ ô folles le long du fleuve

THE BRIDGE

Two women along the river
they speak to each other across the water
and upon the bridge of their words
the crowd passes to and fro dancing

a god
                                             it is
                                             for
    you will come back   you
                                             alone
        Hi! Oh! over there   that
                                             the
            over there   blood
                                             flows

all the children know why

        go on but go on then
        do not turn back

    Hi! Oh! over there over there

The young girls who cross over the airy bridge
        carry in their hands
        the bouquet of tomorrow
and their gaze pours
        into this river stranger to all
that comes from far away that goes so far away
and passes under the airy bridge of your words
    O chatterers along the river
    O chatterers O foolish ones along the river

Here again is a song which, like 'Montparnasse', Poulenc took several
years to write. In studying the song let us see what he has to say about his
method of working. For 'Le Pont' he remarks:

> I hope that, in spite of the long polishing, this song gives the impression of
> an effortless flow. Above all it needs to suggest the rippling effect of water
> and of the conversation over the water, conversation that becomes 'the
> bridge of their words'. . . . 'Le Pont' is certainly one of the most exacting
> of Apollinaire's poems to set to music.

In truth this poem is made up of so many incidents (and it is also
curiously placed on the page in the literary edition), that the guiding

thread of Poulenc's music is certainly needed, for it gives the poem its form. 'Play "Le Pont" with great evenness in one single movement and without *rubato*,' he says.

The preliminary indication, 'very fast, in a single impulse, $\jmath \cdot = 60$', is misleading because the metronomic speed is <u>*right*</u> but it is <u>*not very fast*</u>. The important point is to feel the rhythm definitely one beat in the bar. The dynamics are well indicated and should be scrupulously observed.

Two accents on '*passe*' and '*repasse*', a slight breathing space before 'Tous les enfants', *p. f subito* and *marcato* on '<u>Passe</u> mais passe donc' cutting out the semiquaver rest. Breathe before 'Les jeunes filles. . . .' *p.* The *crescendo-diminuendo* must be observed on 'Qui vient de loin qui va si loin', but without *any rubato*. The indication of a liaison in the poem between 'Ô bavardes' and 'Ô folles' is absurd and impossible. The piano slows down only in the last three bars.

UN POÈME	A POEM
Il est entré	He came in
Il s'est assis	he sat down
Il ne regarde pas le pyrogène aux cheveux rouges	he did not look at the pyrogene with its red hair
L'allumette flambe	the match flamed
Il est parti	he went

'I have always liked,' said Poulenc, 'the postage stamp size of "Un Poéme", which suggests with so few words a great silence and a great emptiness.'

The silent scene is evidently set in a café, for, at the beginning of the century, on all the tables in the cafés were little stoneware pots called 'pyrogènes', in which the matches stood upright, their phosphorescent heads looking like red hair. The matches were struck on the roughness of the pot.

Up to the deliberate nudity of the simple chord of C major which ends it, this short song is probably Poulenc's most dissonant. This may be explained by the dedication to Dallapiccola: at this time we had just given the first performance of one of his works. It is certainly true that the song can give a strange impression of silence and emptiness surrounding solitude provided it is sung with perfect *legato* and very clear diction, but with a total absence of phrasing, with gravity and without expression. Poulenc has obviously tried to indicate this: 'The whole song *quasi parlando* but very tied', which seems a contradiction.

As always the dynamics are well indicated. I recommend the *pp* 'L'allumette flambe'. There is an obvious omission of a bass clef in the left hand under the words: 'Il est parti'.

*

CALLIGRAMMES (CALLIGRAMS)

As I have already said, all the poems by Apollinaire that Poulenc had set to music up to this point, except *Le Bestiare*, were taken from the volume *Il y a*, but Poulenc wrote the following words in 1952:

The more I turn the pages of this volume, the more I feel that I shall no longer find what I need. Not that I like the poetry of Apollinaire any less (I have never liked it so much), but I feel that I have exhausted all that is suitable for me. In 1948 I began on *Calligrammes*. I write these lines four years after having composed this collection, which allows me to pass a cool judgement. Dare I write my own opinion. It represents for me the culmination of a whole range of exploration concerning the setting to music of Apollinaire.

The exact title of this volume is *Calligrammes, Poems of Peace and of War (1913–1916)*. It was published in 1918, and it is the last book of which Apollinaire was able to correct the proofs.

In this volume there are several poems in the form of ideograms. The cover of the musical edition, where a fragment of the poem, 'Cœur, couronne et miroir', is reproduced, shows an example, the form of which suggests a mirror. Several of the poems Poulenc chose were printed in this way in the literary edition, where 'Voyage', 'Il pleut' and 'Aussi bien que les cigales', appear in the form of ideograms. It must be confessed that this is a puerility that adds nothing to the value of the poems but merely makes them more difficult to read.

Among the poems set by Poulenc, only 'Voyage' and 'Il pleut' are about peace, the others are war poems. Apollinaire enlisted in the French army (although a foreigner) at the end of 1914, and his poems reflect, in one way or another, his life as a soldier and the mentality peculiar to war-time.

L'ESPIONNE

Pâle espionne de l'Amour
Ma mémoire à peine fidèle
N'eut pour observer cette belle
Forteresse √ qu'une heure un jour

THE SPY

Pale spy of love
my memory scarcely to be trusted
having watched this beautiful
fortress for but one hour one day

Tu te déguises ǀ	disguise yourself
A ta guise	as you will
Mémoire espionne du cœur	memory spy of the heart
Tu ne retrouves plus l'exquise	you find no longer the exquisite
Ruse √ et le cœur seul est vainqueur	trickery and the heart alone is victorious
Mais la vois-tu cette mémoire	but do you see this memory
Les yeux bandés √ prête à mourir	eyes blindfolded at the point of death
Elle affirme qu'on peut l'en croire	it affirms that it can be believed
Mon cœur vaincra sans coup férir	my heart will conquer without a shot

While he was at the front, the poet took refuge in his memory of happy days, and of his loves. His fiancée at that time, Madeleine Pagés, whom he compares here to a 'lovely fortress', he had not been able to hold in his arms for longer than one hour of one day. Musically a rhythm is found here that Poulenc often used in his songs on the poems of Eluard, but, said Poulenc: 'The tone is different, more sensual here than lyrical.' The indicated tempo seems excellent. Perfect legato is obviously of prime importance, with beautiful phrasing. As always the indications of dynamics, which are numerous and precise, should be strictly observed. Take care, for instance, not to make any *crescendo* in the first bar. (In the sixth bar of the first page, in the vocal line, the D should be D ♮ .) The interpretation of this song should be very poetic but very virile.

MUTATION   MUTATION

Une femme qui pleurait	A woman who wept
Eh! Oh! Ah!	Eh! Oh! Ah!
Des soldats qui passaient	Soldiers who passed
Eh! Oh! Ah!	Eh! Oh! Ah!
Un éclusier qui pêchait	A lock-gate keeper who was fishing
Eh! Oh! Ah!	Eh! Oh! Ah!
Les tranchées qui blanchissaient	The trenches that grew white
Eh! Oh! Ah!	Eh! Oh! Ah!
Des obus qui pétaient	Shells that burst
Eh! Oh! Ah!	Eh! Oh! Ah!
Des allumettes qui ne prenaient pas	Matches that did not strike
Et tout	And all
A tant changé	Has so much changed
En moi	In me
Tout	All
Sauf mon amour	But my love
Eh! Oh! Ah!	Eh! Oh! Ah!

The total change, the mutation, supervening in the life of the poet, is here evoked by descriptive pictures of his life as a soldier. These pictures can initially be well diversified by the interpreters by strict observation of the indicated dynamics. 'Presto, très rythmé' (very rhythmical), ♩=192, is very good. No slower.

The first 'Eh! Oh! Ah!' must suggest the weeping women, *ff* and very legato. The second 'Eh! Oh! Ah!', *f*, should be *marcato* and *non legato*, to suggest the marching past of the soldiers. The third is *pp subito* to suggest a touch of peacefulness in the picture of this lock-gate keeper fishing with his rod not far from the front. The fourth is *mf*, with simplicity, evoking the trenches dug in the white chalk of Champagne. The fifth is very intense, for the shells that 'pétaient' (burst), with a strong accent on the 'pé'. The suggestion of boredom, 'des allumettes qui ne prenaient pas', because of the humidity of the trenches, can be achieved by an almost exaggerated legato. And the whole end of the song, *ff* with brilliance, to proclaim his unchanging love, the last 'Eh! Oh! Ah!' being very legato.

VERS LE SUD

Zénith
　　Tous ces regrets
　　　　Ces jardins sans limite
Où le crapaud module un tendre cri
　　d'azur
La biche du silence éperdu passe vite

Un rossignol meurtri par l'amour
　　chante sur
Le rosier de ton corps dont j'ai cueilli les
　　roses
Nos cœurs pendent ensemble au même
　　grenadier
Et les fleurs de grenade | en nos
　　regards écloses
En tombant tour à tour ont jonché le
　　sentier

TOWARDS THE SOUTH

Zenith
　　all these regrets
　　　　these limitless gardens
where the toad modulates a tender
　　cry of blue
the doe in bewildered silence passes
　　quickly
a nightingale anguished by love sings
　　on
the rose bush of your body from which
　　I have gathered the roses
our hearts hang together on the
　　same pomegranate tree
and the pomegranate flowers opened
　　in our sight
falling one by one have strewn our path

A poem of regret for happy days; days passed in the south of France with his mistress ('Le rosier de ton corps dont j'ai cueilli les roses'), Louise de Coligny Chatillon. 'These limitless gardens', and 'the blue cry of the toad', 'the song of the nightingale', the 'roses', 'the pomegranate flowers', inspired Poulenc to write an enchanting lyrical song, with wonderful vocal effects which must on no account be missed. Therefore above all a perfect legato and the strict observance of the changes of tempo, exceptionally numerous, and of dynamics, and expression very carefully indicated. Thus a poetic and lyrical climate will be achieved.

IL PLEUT	IT RAINS
Il pleut des voix de femmes comme si elles étaient mortes mêmes dans le souvenir	It is raining women's voices as though they were dead even in memory
C'est vous aussi qu'il pleut merveilleuses rencontres de ma vie ô gouttelettes	it is you also that it is raining marvellous encounters of my life O droplets
Et ces nuages cabrés se prennent à hennir tout un univers de villes auriculaires	and these rearing clouds begin to neigh a whole universe of auricular cities
Ecoute s'il pleut tandis que le regret | et le dédain pleurent | une ancienne musique	listen if it is raining while regret and disdain are weeping an ancient music
Ecoute tomber les liens qui te retiennent | en haut et | en bas	hear the bonds falling that hold you high and low

This poem calligram-ideogram was printed in five lines almost vertical and almost parallel. Thus suggesting the rain. Poulenc says: 'From the technical point of view, it is in the field of subtlety of pianistic writing that I was experimenting here, attempting in "Il pleut" to achieve a kind of musical calligram.'

The piano part of the song is, in fact, more difficult than the vocal part, which is without subtlety of execution or of interpretation. In contrast to the piano it must be very flowing and very *legato*. All the first page should be *p* in order to effect a *f subito* from the second page onwards. After the bars marked *cédez* (slower) and *cédez encore* (still slower), the coda for the piano must be *a tempo*.

LA GRÂCE EXILÉE	EXILED GRACE
Va-t'en va-t'en mon arc-en-ciel	Away, go away my rainbow
Allez-vous-en couleurs charmantes	away charming colours
Cet exil t'est | essentiel	this exile is essential for you
Infante aux écharpes changeantes	Infanta of the changing scarves
Et l'arc-en-ciel est exilé	and the rainbow is exiled
Puisqu'on exile qui l'irise	since she is exiled who gives it iridescence
Mais un drapeau s'est envolé	but a flag is flying
Prendre ta place au vent de bise	to take your place in the North wind

This concerns yet another love of Guillaume Apollinaire—his love of long duration: Marie Laurencin. During the war she was 'exiled' in Spain. Her works are extremely well evoked by the lines, 'couleurs charmantes', 'infante aux écharpes changeantes'. But other colours, those of the flag of France in war-time, have taken their place.

As indicated, the tempo *très allant* (quickly moving), ♩= 88, must be taken up gradually on the three first quavers. I suggest a *mf* for the voice and the piano on the bars, 'Puisqu'on exile qui l'irise', in order to contrive a *f subito*, with a marked change of colour and expression on 'Mais un drapeau s'est envolé prendre ta place', and a *diminuendo* only on 'au vent de bise'.

This short song must be given great charm, with a certain nostalgic melancholy.

AUSSI BIEN QUE LES CIGALES

Gens du midi gens du midi
vous n'avez donc pas regardé les cigales
que vous ne savez pas creuser
que vous ne savez pas vous éclairer ni
   voir
Que vous manque-t'il donc pour voir
   aussi bien que les cigales
Mais vous savez encore boire comme
   les cigales
ô gens du midi gens du soleil
gens qui devriez savoir creuser
et voir aussi bien
pour le moins | aussi bien que les
   cigales
Eh quoi! vous savez boire et ne savez
   plus pisser utilement comme les
   cigales
le jour de gloire sera celui où vous
   saurez creuser pour bien sortir au
   soleil
creusez buvez pissez comme les cigales
gens du midi il faut creuser voir boire
   pisser | aussi bien que les cigales pour
   chanter comme elles

LA JOIE ADORABLE DE LA
   PAIX SOLAIRE

AS WELL AS THE CICADAS

Folk of the south folk of the south
so you have not watched the cicadas
since you cannot dig
since you cannot make light or see

What are you lacking that you cannot
   see as well as the cicadas
But yet you can drink like the cicadas

O folk of the south folk of the sun
folk who should know how to dig
and see as well
as least as well as the cicadas
What! you can drink and no longer
   know how to pee to some purpose
   like the cicadas

the day of glory will come when you
   know how to dig your way out
   into the sun
dig see drink pee like the cicadas
folk of the south you must dig see
   drink pee as well as the cicadas to
   sing like they do

THE ADORABLE JOY OF THE
   SUN-FILLED PEACE

This poem, again, is printed as a calligram, the significance of which is not very easy to understand. The folk of the south are evidently his war-time comrades, since Apollinaire had enlisted in an artillery regiment at Montpellier. Poulenc suggests clearly the style of the song in these words:

> I like 'Aussi bien que les cigales' because of its style which is half-way between a chanson (ribald or folk) and a true mélodie. As often with Apollinaire, the poem quickly goes on its way to abut on a coda of another rhythm. I think I have succeeded rather well in expressing 'La joie adorable de la paix solaire' in a rhythm which recalls the sunshine of *Animaux modèles.**

The preliminary indications are excellent, and it is essential to have precise and percussive diction. The dynamics range from *mf* to *ff*. The indication of *p* on the last bar of the first page is impossible, all the more so since the voice is in a low register. Suddenly there is a short *legato* phrase on the words 'gens qui devriez savoir creuser'. The *accelerando* from 'Le jour de gloire' should begin very gradually, but very markedly, as also the *rallentando* on the bar, 'pour chanter comme elles'. The 'coda' mentioned by Poulenc which is printed in large letters in the literary text, should be sung *largo* and *maestoso* with full voice, and an expression of joy and of deliverance. The piano part brilliant, with the demi-semiquavers (32^{nds}) as short as possible.

VOYAGE

Adieu amour nuage qui fuit et n'a pas
  chu pluie féconde
refais le voyage de Dante

Télégraphe
oiseau qui laisse tomber ses ailes partout

Où va donc ce train qui meurt au loin

Dans les vals et les beaux bois frais du
  tendre été si pâle?

La douce nuit lunaire et pleine d'étoiles

C'est ton visage que je ne vois plus

JOURNEY

Farewell love cloud that flies and has
  not shed fertile rain
take again the journey of Dante

telegraph
bird who lets its wings fall everywhere

Where is this train going that dies
  away in the distance

in the vales and the lovely fresh woods
  of the tender summer so pale?

The gentle night moonlit and full
  of stars

it is your face that I no longer see

---

* Poulenc's ballet, 1940/41.

There must be a long silence before commencing this song. It is essentially a poem of peace. Again it is printed as a calligram in a way that is very complicated and seemingly rather arbitrary: differences of direction of the lines straight or curved, differences also in the size and type of the letters. Before the word 'Télégraphe' there is even a vignette representing the insulators and the electric wires, which could stand for the words, 'oiseau qui laisse tomber ses ailes partout', evoking the movement of the cables between the poles along the railway track when the train speeds up. Here is an important commentary by Poulenc:

'Voyage' is *certainly* one of the two or three songs which I value the most. Greatly superior to 'Sanglots' of which certain points will always trouble me. By the interjection of unexpected and sensitive modulations, 'Voyage' goes from emotion to silence, passing through melancholy and love. It must be accompanied by a great deal of pedal, to veil, as I ceaselessly repeat, the harmonies and to make the piano sing as intensely and as smoothly as the voice. 'La douce nuit' and the phrase which follows must be *pp*. 'C'est ton visage' tenderly and suddenly *f* as though the clouds had all at once unveiled a ray of moonlight. The end is, for me, the silence of a night in July when, on the terrace of my childhood home at Nogent, I heard in the distance the trains 'that were leaving on holiday' (as I used to think then).

The indicated tempo is excellent and the two executants must try to achieve the greatest possible *legato*.

I suggest for the singer a breath between 'nuage qui fuit' and 'et n'a pas chu', and only a suspension of sound before 'pluie féconde'. The following phrases remain *pp*. Observe carefully the 'à peine plus vite' (scarcely any faster), and the indications, *très poétique et mystérieux* (very poetic and mysterious), and *infiniment doux* (infinitely tender). A little *crescendo* should be made on 'Dans les vals et les beaux bois frais' then a big *diminuendo* on 'du tendre été si pâle'. This last word must be *pp*. Poulenc's commentary is extremely precise and suggestive for the following lines, but it is of prime importance that the moon is suddenly veiled again on the syllable 'sa' of the word 'visage', *pp*, with infinite tenderness and nostalgia prolonged until the end by the beautiful coda for the piano.

*

ROSEMONDE   ROSEMONDE

Longtemps | au pied du perron de   Long I stood at the foot of the steps
La maison où entra la dame   of the house where the lady entered
Que j'avais suivi pendant deux   whom I had followed for two
Bonnes heures | à Amsterdam   good hours in Amsterdam
Mes doigts jetèrent des baisers   my fingers threw kisses

Mais le canal était désert   But the canal was deserted
Le quai aussi et nul ne vit   the quay also and no one saw
Comment mes baisers retrouvèrent   how my kisses found her again
Celle à qui j'ai donné ma vie   to whom I had given my life
Un jour pendant plus de deux heures   one day for more than two hours

Je la surnommai Rosemonde   I named her Rosemonde
Voulant pouvoir me rappeler   wishing to be able to recall
Sa bouche fleurie en Hollande   her flowery mouth in Holland
Puis lentement je m'allai   then slowly I went away
Pour quêter la Rose du Monde   to seek the Rose of the World

In 1954 Poulenc was again inspired by a poem of Apollinaire. It is the only one taken from the celebrated collection, *Alcools*, which resembles almost all the poems written between 1898 and 1913. This one, a poem of three stanzas of five lines of eight feet, is obviously a poem of his youth. Its meaning is clear—it evokes a charming memory for the poet, who all his life had been in search of love.

This delicious song is without difficulties in the interpretation, provided it is well 'sung', *molto legato*, while observing the markings. (In some editions there is an obvious misprint in the piano part: in the line, 'Comment mes baisers retrouvèrent', under the syllable 're' in the right hand, the G should be changed to a B♭♭.

I suggest a good breath for both executants before the second stanza, 'Je la surnommai Rosemonde . . .'. The pianist must take care over the charming final *ritournelle*. In this song the atmosphere is one of happy nostalgia. Poulenc's fondness for the beautiful quays of Amsterdam, the city to which our concerts had brought us each season for over twenty years, was undoubtedly the reason for his choice of this little poem.

CHAPTER V

Paul Eluard

Eugene Emile Paul Grindel, known as Paul Eluard, the name of his maternal grandmother, was born at St Denis, a northern suburb close to Paris, on December 14th 1895.

His father was first a chartered accountant, later becoming a well-to-do estate agent, a profession which assured to his family more than comfortable material prosperity, from which Paul, an only son, was to benefit all his life. His mother, at the time of his birth, was a dress-maker.

He was educated first at a public elementary school, and later at a higher primary school. Interrupted by illness, he spent some time at the Sanatorium of Davos, where he met the girl who was to become his first wife: Gala, who later married Salvador Dali.

Having witnessed the horrors of war, he was attracted by liber-tarian and pacifist ideas.

In 1918 he published his first small volume of verse: *Le devoir et l'inquiétude*. He participated in the scandalous and subversive 'Dada' movement, which proved ephemeral but led to Surrealism. In 1924 Eluard was, with Breton, Soupault and Aragon, one of the founders of this important movement. In 1926 he joined the Communist Party.

Also in 1926 he met Nusch who was to be his new companion and inspired many of his love poems.

Eluard's work did not cease to grow in stature. Among other titles may be cited: *Mourir de ne pas mourir* (1926), *Capitale de la douleur* (1926), *Les yeux fertiles* (1936), *Donner à voir* (1939). But events were destined to carry this poetry to a vaster field. The Spanish war and Guernica, the defeat of France in 1940 and the German occupation, revealed to him the extent of human misery. He became known as a 'poet of the Resistance', on account of 'Liberté' from *Poésie et Vérité* (1942), and a later collection, *Au rendez-vous allemand* (1944).

In 1946 Nusch, who by then had been his wife for twelve years, died suddenly. Eluard himself died in 1952 of a heart attack, shortly after having published *Le Phénix*, a poem of love, symbol of the renascence of love's union, and dedicated to his last wife, Dominique, whom he married in 1951.

*　　　*　　　*

PAUL ELUARD WAS the outstanding lyric poet of his time; no other has sung more eloquently of love—both human love and love of humanity. He was the most important poet of the Surrealist Movement. A *Manifeste du Surréalisme* was published in 1924. In it the Movement was defined as 'Purely psychic automatism by which it is proposed to explain, be it verbally, be it in writing or by quite other means, the true functioning of thought. Dictated by thought in the absence of all control by reason, outside all aesthetic or moral preoccupations, Surrealism rests on the belief in the superior reality of certain forms of associations, formerly neglected, and in the transcendent power of dreams released from any interference by thought. It tends definitely to destroy all other psychic mechanisms and to take their place in the resolution of the principal problems of life.'

It must therefore be realized how useless it would be to attempt to give a precise meaning to these poems, or to understand them in an exact sense. Rather they should be felt intuitively and left to the 'transcendent power of dreams'. Interpreters of the songs of Francis Poulenc will find themselves greatly aided by the composer, who had an extraordinary understanding of this poetry. Eluard himself acknowledged the debt by sending him a poem 'To Francis Poulenc'. This is a translation of the second part:

>Francis I did not listen to myself
>Francis I owe it to you that I hear myself
>on a white pathway
>in an immense countryside
>where light strengthens itself

>At night there are no longer any roots
>the shadow is behind the mirrors
>Francis we dream of expanse
>as a child of endless games
>in a starry countryside

>which only reflects youth.

It may appear surprising that Poulenc did not set to music poems by Eluard until 1935. He had in fact met the poet for the first time in 1917, together with Breton and Aragon, at the celebrated bookshop of Adrienne Monnier, 'Aux Amis des Livres', rue de L'Odéon, which was a meeting place for young writers of many countries. From their very first meeting, Poulenc had felt an immediate bond of sympathy with this poet 'of the voice warm, gentle and violent by turns'.

At once I took a liking to Eluard. Firstly because he was the only surrealist poet who could tolerate music. And next because the whole of his work is musical vibration.

Subsequently Georges Auric often urged Poulenc to set the poems of Eluard, but it was not until 1935 that the composer truly came to know the work of the poet—this was, as he said himself, 'one of the most important encounters of my life'.

Ultimately Poulenc wrote 34 songs on these poems, and many very important choral works: *Seven Songs* for mixed choir *a cappella* (except two of these which are on poems by Apollinaire), *Un soir de neige* for six mixed voices *a cappella*. And *Figure Humaine*, a cantata for double mixed choir *a cappella*, published clandestinely during the German occupation. This work contains the celebrated poem, 'Liberté'.

*

CINQ POÈMES DE PAUL ELUARD

'It will never be sufficiently realized,' said Poulenc (forgive me for this quotation), 'how much I owe to Eluard, how much I owe to Bernac. It is due to them that lyricism entered into my vocal work. In 1935, a small booklet printed on pink paper came into my hands when I was hoping to write some new songs for the first recital of our ensemble Bernac-Poulenc. These five poems opened up for me all the poetry of Eluard. At last I had found a lyric poet, a poet of love, be it human love, or love of liberty.' Concerning these songs he again wrote: 'Feeling my way in this work. Key turned in the lock. Trying to give the piano the maximum with the minimum of means. In composing these songs I often thought of an exhibition of drawings by Matisse for a book by Mallarmé [see p. 43], where the same pencil drawing could be seen, full of hatching, of repetitions finally retaining nothing but the essential, in a single outline. I regret having burned the draft of "Peut-il se reposer". A Swiss critic who never failed me could see where my "simplistic writing" came from. It is piano reduced to the essential, that's all.'

It must be said that these songs are of unequal merit and difficult for the interpreters, perhaps precisely because Poulenc had not yet found his own Eluardian lyricism.

The five songs of the collection were chosen from among the 29 that comprised the slender volume, *A toute épreuve* (printed, it is true, on pink paper), published in 1930. They are of greatly differing character and atmosphere, passing from tenderness to violence.

I

Peut-il se reposer celui qui dort
Il ne voit pas la nuit ne voit pas
    l'invisible
Il a de grandes couvertures
Et des coussins de sang sur des coussins
    de boue

Sa tête est sous les toits et ses mains sont
    fermées
Sur les outils de la fatigue
Il dort pour éprouver sa force
La honte d'être aveugle dans un si
    grand silence.

Aux rivages que la mer rejette
Il ne voit pas les poses silencieuses
Du vent qui fait entrer l'homme dans
    ses statues
Quand il s'apaise.

Bonne volonté du sommeil
D'un bout à l'autre de la mort.

I

Can he rest this man who sleeps
he does not see the night does not see
    the invisible
he has thick coverings
and pillows of blood on pillows of mud

His head is under the roofs and his
    hands are closed
upon the tools of weariness
he sleeps to test his strength
the shame of being blind in so great
    a silence.

On the shores rejected by the sea
he does not see the silent postures
of the wind which causes a man to
    enter into his images
when he is appeased

A willing acceptance of sleep
from one end to the other of death.

1. *Peut-il se reposer*. The two contrasted metronomic movements are excellent, ♪=72 and ♩=138. The first and the last stanzas with their surprising unison, should be sung and played with perfect immobility and *legato* without any *rubato*, *p* rather than *pp*, without any involuntary changes of dynamics. They must create a strangely tragic atmosphere without any *vibrato*. Thus the violent outbreak of the central part will tell. It is important to sing very *legato* on the phrase, 'La honte d'être aveugle dans un si grand silence', and not too *p*, as the *tessitura* is very low. The same applies to the bars, 'Aux rivages que la mer rejette', the piano part being rather *pp* with a rapid *crescendo* to lead to the *ff*. All the end of this section without *diminuendo* and without *rallentando*. Some beautiful effects of *pp* on the high notes must be made in the final stanza, but above all without affectation.

2

Il la prend dans ses bras	He takes her in his arms
Lueurs brillantes | un instant | entrevues	brilliant rays glimpsed for a moment
Aux omoplates | aux épaules | aux seins	on the shoulder blades on the shoulders on the breasts
Puis cachées par un nuage.	then hidden by a cloud
Elle porte la main à son cœur	She raises her hand to her heart
Elle pâlit | elle frissonne	she grows pale she trembles
Qui donc a crié?	Who has cried out?
Mais l'autre s'il est encore vivant	But the other if he is still living
On le retrouvera	will be found
Dans une ville inconnue.	in an unknown town.

2. *Il la prend dans ses bras*. This poem suggests a melodramatic nocturnal scene of a street in Paris. Poulenc says: 'This second song is horribly difficult. It is necessary to know Eluard well, because the tempo, that no metronome can mark with precision, must be divined.'

It is true that the composer, in seeking the desired effect, has not completely attained his goal, and that the changing tempo creates difficulties for the interpreters. Poulenc has been led into multiplying the interpretative indications. It is therefore advisable to observe them <u>all</u> with precision, and to pay attention to the notes of short value which often terminate the phrases. The value of the rests in this song are of prime importance and the interpreters must make them alive, expressive and varied, with great dramatic feeling.

3

Plume d'eau claire pluie fragile	Jet of clear water fragile rain
Fraîcheur voilée de caresses	freshness veiled with caresses
De regards | et de paroles	with looks and with words
Amour qui voile ce que j'aime.	love that veils that which I love.

4

Rôdeuse au front de verre	Prowler with brow of glass
Son cœur s'inscrit dans une étoile noire	her heart inscribes itself on a black star
Ses yeux montrent sa tête	her eyes show her head
Ses yeux ont la fraîcheur de l'été	her eyes have the freshness of summer
La chaleur de l'hiver	the heat of winter
Ses yeux s'ajourent rient très fort	her eyes light up full of laughter
Ses yeux joueurs gagnent leur part de clarté.	her playful eyes win their share of clarity.

Of these two songs Poulenc says, 'They are, I think, the best of the collection'. In the nine bars of *Plume d'eau claire* he has succeeded in creating for this entrancing poem, a poetic climate of irresistible attraction which the interpreters must recreate with *legato* and phrasing. Without bad taste but with great charm. The dynamics are clearly indicated, as also the tempo, ♩=72, which must be without *rubato*. No *rallentando* on the last line but considerable *diminuendo*.

Rôdeuse au front de verre suggests a more troubled atmosphere; but the eyes of this loiterer reveal that she is, nevertheless, not without her share of brightness. This belongs to the extremely melodic type of song by Poulenc, which demands a sustained *legato* with sufficient strength in the lower register and a perfect *pp* for the high notes. I suggest that after the small *animer un peu* (a little faster) there should be a return on 'les yeux joueurs' to the *tempo primo* maintained to the end.

5

Amoureuses

Elles ont les épaules | hautes
Et l'air malin
Ou bien des mines qui déroutent
La confiance est dans la poitrine
A la hauteur où l'aube de leurs seins
    se lève
Pour dévêtir la nuit.

Des yeux | à casser des cailloux
Des sourires sans y penser
Pour chaque rêve
Des rafales de cris de neige
Et des ombres déracinées.

Il faut les croire sur baiser
Et sur parole et sur regard
Et ne baiser que leurs baisers

Je ne montre que ton visage
Les grands orages de ta gorge
Tout ce que je connais | et tout ce
    que j'ignore
Mon amour ton amour ton amour ton
    amour.

5

Lovers

They have haughty shoulders
and a cunning air
or else looks that lead astray
the confidence is in the chest
at the height where the dawn of
    their breasts rise
to strip the night.

Eyes to break stones
thoughtless smiles
for each dream
squalls of cries of snow
and uprooted shadows

They must be believed on kiss
and on word and on look
and to kiss only their kisses

I show only your face
the great storms of your throat
all that I know and all that I do not
    know
my love your love your love your
    love.

5. *Amoureuses*. Here again is a picture of a street in Paris; there is therefore no reason to fear a slight accent of Parisian slang, but without vulgarity, as I have stressed several times when speaking of certain songs on poems by Apollinaire. The indication, *très vite et haletant* (very fast and breathless) ♩ = 152, is excellent and applies also to the piano part, but with the singing melody of the left hand very *legato*, and, later, that of the right hand also. How could Poulenc have committed such a fault of prosody: 'La confiance est dans la poitrine'? There is evidently a crotchet (1/4) on 'an' with an elision of the 'e' mute: 'c'est'. All the opening is *mf*, but is already increasing to *f* on 'où l'aube de leurs seins se lève' and *sempre f*. 'Des yeux à casser des cailloux' is very *marcato*, then *p subito* on 'et des ombres déracinées'.

Begin again *mf*, 'Il faut les croire sur baiser', but 'Et ne baiser que leurs baisers' is already *f*, which must be maintained to the end, except for the three dynamic changes *molto diminuendo* on 'mon amour'. The last phrase is murmured but very intense. A strange and difficult song; but one which makes a big effect if an immutable tempo is maintained throughout.

TEL JOUR TELLE NUIT (SUCH A DAY SUCH A NIGHT)

The poems which constitute the cycle *Tel jour telle nuit* are taken from a collection by Paul Eluard entitled *Les yeux fertiles*. 'Such a title is good for a book,' wrote Poulenc, 'but is not necessarily good for a collection of songs.' Finding this 'too visual' he asked Eluard to send him another. (He also asked him in 1944 for a title for his ballet, *Les animaux modèles*.) 'Eluard's friendship lent itself to all my exigencies,' he said.

In a letter of January 2nd 1937, Eluard sent him several titles to choose from, including this one, *Tel jour telle nuit*. It was none too soon, since we were to give the first performance of the work on the following February 3rd.

In this cycle of nine songs Poulenc has definitely mastered his Eluardian style, and it is indisputably one of his greatest achievements in the domain of song. The musicologist and critic, Roland Manuel, thought fit to write that this cycle is worthy to be compared with the greatest cycles of German Lieder, such as *Die Winterreise* of Schubert, or *Dichterliebe* of Schumann.

Tel jour telle nuit constitutes a cycle in the true sense of the word. These songs should not be separated from one another. Poulenc says: 'In my opinion a song in a cycle must have a colour and a special architecture.' The value of each one depends on its place in the ensemble, on the song which precedes it and that which follows. In fact some of the songs are intended only to form a transition in order to heighten the effect of the following one. The first and the last are in the same key and in the same tempo, establishing the atmosphere of calm and serenity which imbues almost the whole of the cycle.

Poulenc has this to say about the starting point of the work: 'When I have been working for some weeks far away from Paris, it is truly with a heart full of love that I return to "my town". One Sunday in November '36, I was feeling completely happy strolling by the side of the Bastille. I began to recite the poem from *Les yeux fertiles*: "Bonne journée". That evening the music came of itself.'

May I be allowed to tell two anecdotes? At Christmas in 1936 I was at Noizay for a short stay in order to make the most of this free time to prepare the programmes for our forthcoming tours, and in particular the new songs that Poulenc had written and which we were going to perform at our annual recital in Paris. They were settings of poems by Jean Cocteau titled 'Plain-chants'. The evening I arrived Poulenc went to the piano and let me hear them. Frankly I did not feel enthusiastic, and he must have sensed this from my reaction. Suddenly, to my alarm, to my horror, Poulenc took his manuscript and threw it on the big fire that was burning in the grate. He began to laugh and said, 'Don't worry, you will have something much better for February 3rd!' It was to be *Tel jour telle nuit*.

All these songs in fact were composed at Noizay in December 1936, or in Paris or Lyons in January 1937, as can be seen in the musical edition. As always when we passed through Lyons on one of our tours, we stayed with our friends Professor and Mme Latarjet. I remember during dinner we tried to persuade Poulenc to leave the piano—'Francis, it will all be cold!' He was composing 'Nous avons fait la nuit', one of the most beautiful songs that he had ever written.

<table>
<tr><td align="center">I</td><td align="center">I</td></tr>
<tr><td>

Bonne journée j'ai revu qui je
   n'oublie pas
Qui je n'oublierai jamais
Et des femmes fugaces dont les yeux
Me faisaient une haie d'honneur
Elles s'enveloppèrent dans leurs
   sourires

Bonne journée j'ai vu mes amis sans
   soucis
Les hommes ne pesaient pas lourd
Un qui passait
Son ombre changée en souris
Fuyait dans le ruisseau

</td><td>

A good day I have again seen whom I
   do not forget
whom I shall never forget
and women fleeting by whose eyes
formed for me a hedge of honour
they wrapped themselves in their
   smiles

a good day I have seen my friends
   carefree
the men were light in weight
one who passed by
his shadow changed into a mouse
fled into the gutter

</td></tr>
</table>

J'ai vu le ciel très grand	I have seen the great wide sky
Le beau regard des gens privés de tout	the beautiful eyes of those deprived of everything
Plage distant | où personne n'aborde	distant shore where no one lands
Bonne journée qui commença mélancolique	a good day which began mournfully
Noire sous les‿arbres verts	dark under the green trees
Mais qui soudain trempée d'aurore	but which suddenly drenched with dawn
M'entra dans le cœur √ par surprise.	invaded my heart unawares.

1. *Bonne journée . . .* (In the collection *Les yeux fertiles* this poem is entitled 'à Pablo Picasso'. It must be connected with the journey that Eluard made to Spain for the first retrospective Picasso exhibition in Barcelona, Madrid and Bilbao, from January to May 1936.)

The poem is one of the easiest to understand; the song must suggest joy, a peaceful happiness marked with gravity. My advice is to sing all the first stanza (♩=63) *mp* with warm timbre and perfect *legato*, without any change of dynamics. Take care not to make a *crescendo* on 'Elles s'enveloppèrent dans leurs sourires'. The second stanza should be begun *mf* in the lower register, making a *diminuendo* on the ascending scale, 'j'ai vu mes amis sans soucis', which ends *p*. Then frankly *mf* on the following phrases. (Bind together with thought, in spite of the quaver ($\frac{1}{8}$) rest, 'Son ombre changée en souris fuyait dans le ruisseau'.) Observe the *crescendo* indicated on the ascending scale, 'Le beau regard des gens privés de tout'. An expressive breath, and begin *subito p*, 'Plage distante où personne n'aborde'.

On the following bar of the piano part, Poulenc slowed down a little in order to prepare the re-entry of the initial theme which should be only *mp*. The *crescendo* should already begin on the B♭ before 'Mais qui soudain', and the voice should end *mf*, leaving the *pp* for the coda of the piano part. The quality of the timbre of the voice must suggest this invasion of the heart by the dawn. It is certainly not easy, especially with the sudden change of vocal *tessitura*.

There must be no hurry in beginning the next song:

2	2
Une ruine coquille vide	A ruin an empty shell
Pleure dans son tablier	weeps into its apron
Les enfants qui jouent | autour d'elle	the children who play around it
Font moins de bruit que des mouches	make less sound than flies

La ruine s'en va | à tâtons   the ruin goes groping
Chercher ses vaches dans‿un pré   to seek its cows in the meadow
J'ai vu le jour vois cela   I have seen the day I see that
Sans‿en avoir | honte   without shame

Il est minuit comme‿une flèche   It is midnight like an arrow
Dans‿un cœur à la portée   in a heart within reach
Des folâtres lueurs nocturnes   of the sprightly nocturnal glimmerings
Qui contredisent le sommeil.   which gainsay sleep.

2. *Une ruine coquille vide*. (In the literary edition this poem is entitled 'Je croyais le repos possible'.) 'This song,' Poulenc says, 'must be sung with a sense of complete unreality', and his preliminary indications are *Très calme et irréel* (very calm and unreal) ♩ = 60. I would gladly add 'and mysterious', both for the surprising atmosphere that the music must evoke and for the meaning of the poem. At all events, as I have often been asked, the ruin is certainly not an old lady! I myself imagine that the apron into which the ruin weeps is suggested by the heavy masses of ivy hanging down the old walls; and would it not be the moving shadow which 'va à tâtons chercher ses vaches dans un pré'? The pianist must, from the beginning of the two bars of introduction, create, by the quality of his touch and the constant use of both pedals, this unreal and mysterious impression, and must not change it, always *pp*, until the end of the song, in no way being influenced by the few changes of dynamics in the voice part. This latter begins *pp* and very *legato* for the first four bars. The four following bars, however, will be definitely *mp* (the breath indicated by Poulenc after 'les enfants', seems to me not indispensable), and there is a return to *pp subito* for the four following bars.

This section of four bars continues on 'J'ai vu le jour . . .', this time boldly *mf* despite the piano part which remains *pp*. 'Il est minuit comme une flèche dans un cœur' is obviously *pp* with a strangely mysterious character; *mp* is sufficient (not *mf*) to begin 'à la portée des folâtres lueurs nocturnes', with a *crescendo* on these last words in order to begin the last phrase *p*. Above all no *crescendo* towards the high G which must be *p mezza voce*, with beautiful sonorous quality. The coda of the piano part remains always *pp* and must vanish into silence. Having allowed the expressive value of this silence to spend its effect, attack *subito f, Le front comme un drapeau perdu*.

3

3

Le front comme un drapeau perdu	The brow like a lost flag
Je te traîne quand je suis seul	I drag you when I am alone
Dans des rues froides	through the cold streets
Des chambres noires	the dark rooms
En criant misère	crying in misery

Je ne veux pas les lâcher	I do not want to let them go
Tes mains claires et compliquées	your clear and complex hands
Nées dans le miroir clos des miennes	born in the enclosed mirror of my own

Tout le reste est parfait	all the rest is perfect
Tout le reste est encore plus inutile	all the rest is even more useless
Que la vie	than life

Creuse la terre sous ton ombre	hollow the earth beneath your shadow

Une nappe d'eau près des seins	a sheet of water reaching the breasts
Où se noyer	wherein to drown oneself
Comme une pierre.	like a stone.

3. *Le front comme un chapeau perdu.* (In the literary edition the title of this poem is 'être'.)

As Poulenc stressed, this is a song of the cycle that must not be separated from its context. It begins in violence and concludes with a strange appeasement. The first four bars are *f* with very strong articulation. The indication ♩=132 is excellent, for it must be possible to accelerate on the four following bars and thus reach almost ♩=144. (There is a mistake in the text which should be, 'Dans des rues froides Des chambres noires'.) This latter tempo must be inexorably maintained until the end of the song. The beginning of the second page is *legato* and *p* (not too much so). All the dynamic indications should then be followed but, in my opinion, without ever reaching a true *p* or *pp*, and always with almost dramatic intensity. Poulenc made very little of the pause mark on the bar of 2/4.

4

4

Une roulotte couverte en tuiles	A gypsy wagon roofed with tiles
Le cheval mort un enfant maître	the horse dead a child master
Pensant √ le front bleu de haine	thinking his brow blue with hatred
A deux seins √ s'abattant sur lui	of two breasts beating down upon him
Comme deux poings	like two fists

Ce mélodrame √ nous arrache √	this melodrama tears away from us
La raison √ du cœur.	the sanity of the heart.

4. *Une roulotte couverte en tuiles.* 'I really believe,' says Poulenc, 'that I saw the child of the gypsy wagon somewhere on a late afternoon in November at Ménilmontant.'*

This striking and unusual poem evokes for me the sordid outlying quarters of Paris, like a picture by Picasso of the period when he was painting young acrobats. *Très lent et sinistre* (very slow and sinister), ♪=80, is Poulenc's indication. In my opinion ♪=72 is still better, *mf* and *parlando*. The indicated accents must be very marked. 'Pensant le front bleu de haine . . .' is suddenly legato and without any *crescendo*, in order to achieve a *subito f* on 'comme deux poings'. Observe carefully the rhythm on this last word so as to end exactly with the piano and have a distinct silence before beginning the last phrase *pp* and *parlando*. The vocal effect on 'La raison du cœur' is simply a matter of attacking the last B underneath and letting out some breath. (In the first two bars in the piano part, on the fourth beat, the A is obviously natural. Same thing in the third bar before the end.)

5

5

A toutes <u>bri</u>des toi dont le fantôme
<u>Pia</u>ffe la nuit sur un violon
Viens ré<u>gner</u> dans les <u>bois</u>

Riding full tilt you whose phantom
prances at night on a violin
come to reign in the woods

Les verges de l'ouragan
Cherchent leur chemin par chez toi
Tu n'es pas de celles
Dont ‿on ‿invente les désirs

the lashings of the tempest
seek their path by way of you
you are not of those
whose desires one imagines

Viens boi<u>re</u> ‿un baiser par ici
Cè<u>de</u> ‿au feu qui te désespère.

come drink a kiss here
surrender to the fire which drives
    you to despair.

5. *A toutes brides.* (This poem, and also 'Je n'ai envie que de t'aimer' and 'Figure de force' bear the numbers II, V and IV in a series of poems of which the title is *Intimes*.) This song again belongs entirely to the cycle. 'It has no other pretension,' says Poulenc, 'than to highlight the following song "Une herbe pauvre".'

The piano part suggests the tuning of a violin. *Prestissimo* ♩=112 is excellent. The voice should be resonant with strong articulation. (There is a very bad misprint in some editions at the sixth bar in 7/8: in the left hand part there should obviously be a bass clef.) The bars of piano solo (bars 7 to 10) should be even more animated, but it is good to return to ♩=112 from

* A popular district of Paris.

'Les verges de l'ouragan' and continue thus until the end of the song which is *f* or *ff*, with the exception of the lines. 'Tu n'es pas de celles Dont on invente les désirs', which is more *p avec douceur* (with gentleness), as also the two following bars in the piano part. All the end is brilliant, *éclatant* with an inclination towards *accelerando*. A long silence is then necessary before beginning:

6	6
Une herbe pauvre	Scanty grass
Sauvage	wild
Apparut dans la neige	appeared in the snow
C'était la santé	it was health
Ma bouche fut émerveillée	my mouth marvelled
Du goût d'air pur qu'elle avait	at the savour of pure air it had
Elle était fanée.	it was withered.

6. *Une herbe pauvre*. (The third poem in the series 'Balances'.) 'This poem of Eluard,' says Poulenc, 'has for me a divine savour. It recalls for me that invigorating bitterness of a flower I once plucked and tasted in the surroundings of the Grande Chartreuse.'

When spring comes in the mountains, the first blade of grass, the first flowers to appear through the melting snow, give such an impression of purity that one cannot resist picking one and tasting its 'invigorating bitterness'. But already 'elle était fanée'.

This translucent and limpid atmosphere is wonderfully expressed musically, and the interpreters must succeed in suggesting it by a soft and pure clarity of timbre, perfect *legato*, and an immutable tempo, ♩=60. The first lines are *p*, but bear in mind the necessity of a still softer *p* for the repeat of the theme.

'C'était la santé Ma bouche fut émerveillée' is *mf*, and there is an excellent effect not to be missed on 'Du goût d'air pur qu'elle avait', in making a *crescendo* in descending as far as the E and then a *diminuendo* in ascending.

'Elle était fanée' should not be too *p*, to prepare the effect of *subito pp* on the repeat of the first line, and above all without *crescendo* in ascending to the high G which must be *pp*, and always *pp* until the end without any *rallentando*.

7	7
Je n'ai envie que de t'aimer	I long only to love you
Un orage emplit la vallée	a storm fills the valley
Un poisson la rivière	a fish the river

Je t'ai faite à la taille de ma solitude	I have formed you to the pattern of my solitude
Le monde entier pour se cacher √	the whole world to hide in
Des jours des nuits pour se comprendre √	days and nights to understand one another
Pour ne plus rien voir dans tes yeux	to see nothing more in your eyes
Que ce que je pense de toi	but what I think of you
Et d'un monde à ton image	and of a world in your likeness
Et des jours et des nuits réglés par tes paupières.	and of days and nights ordered by your eyelids

7. *Je n'ai envie que de t'aimer*. 'This charming poem of happy love,' says Poulenc, 'must be sung in a single curve, a single impulse.'

The tempo, ♩.= 100, is in fact fast enough and the music flows from beginning to end, but must never give a feeling of agitation. Observe carefully the dynamic markings that are indicated. A good expressive breath must be taken before attacking, *p subito*, 'Pour ne plus rien voir dans tes yeux', but with a slight *crescendo* in descending to the lower register. To be certain of avoiding any slowing down towards the end of the song, it is advisable to make a slight *accelerando* on 'réglés par tes paupières'. It is not until the last two bars of the song that the piano may slow down slightly.

8

Figure de force brûlante et farouche	Image of fiery wild forcefulness
Cheveux noirs │ où l'or coule vers le sud	black hair wherein the gold flows towards the south
Aux nuits corrompues	on corrupt nights
Or englouti étoile impure	engulfed gold tainted star
Dans un lit jamais partagé	in a bed never shared
Aux veines des tempes	to the veins of the temples
Comme au bout des seins	as to the tips of the breasts
La vie se refuse	life denies itself
Les yeux nul ne peut les crever	no one can blind the eyes
Boire leur éclat ni leurs larmes	drink their brilliance or their tears
Le sang │ au dessus d'eux triomphe pour lui seul	the blood above them triumphs for itself alone
Intraitable démesurée	intractable unbounded
Inutile	useless
Cette santé bâtit une prison.	this health builds a prison.

8. *Figure de force brûlante et farouche*. With its contrasts of vehemence and calm, here again is a song of transition.

The violent *Presto*, ♩ = 138, with as incisive articulation as possible, becomes faster and faster from 'Aux nuits corrompues' until 'jamais partagé'. Then, after a long silence, the tempo *Lent* (slow), ♩ = 66, with a voice *morne* (dismal), with neither *vibrato* nor phrasing, but extremely *legato*, and *p*, but not *pp*. Keep the same tempo in attacking *ff* the final bars.

'This terrific climax is there,' says Poulenc, 'to increase the effect of the kind of silence which begins:'

9

Nous avons fait la nuit je tiens ta main je veille	We have made night* I hold your hand I watch over you
Je te soutiens de toutes mes forces	I sustain you with all my strength
Je grave sur un roc l'étoile de tes forces	I engrave on a rock the star of your strength
Sillons profonds | où la bonté de ton corps germera	deep furrows where the goodness of your body will germinate
Je me répète ta voix cachée ta voix publique	I repeat to myself your secret voice your public voice
Je ris encore de l'orgueilleuse	I laugh still at the haughty woman
Que tu traites comme une mendiante	whom you treat like a beggar
Des fous que tu respectes des simples où tu te baignes	at the fools whom you respect the simple folk in whom you immerse yourself
Et dans ma tête qui se met doucement d'accord | avec la tienne avec la nuit	and in my head which gently begins to harmonize with yours with the night
Je m'émerveille de l'inconnue que tu deviens	I marvel at the stranger that you become
Une inconnue semblable à toi semblable à tout ce que j'aime	a stranger resembling you resembling all that I love
Qui est toujours nouveau.	which is ever new.

* We have turned out the light.

9. *Nous avons fait la nuit*. (This poem is not, as are the others, from *Les yeux fertiles*, but from the collection *Facile*.) Poulenc says: 'At the time I wrote this song, I was most deeply moved. I hope that this will be apparent.'

This admirable poem of love did, in fact, inspire one of his most beautiful songs, the lyricism of which is scarcely equalled in the vocal literature of the twentieth century. Poulenc also said: 'It is very difficult to make interpreters understand that <u>calm</u> in a poem of love can <u>alone</u> give intensity.' To obtain this 'calm' and this 'kind of silence' that he demands, it is essential to wait several seconds before beginning the song with the most perfect *legato* possible.

The quiet tempo ♩=60 must keep its equality consistently until the end of the song, including the long *coda* for the piano, with a firmness that will exclude all sham sentimentality, and will confer a strong and virile profundity to the feelings described by the poet and the musician with such wonderful lyricism. The two lovers may be imagined side by side on the bed, having turned out the light, 'fait la nuit', the man holding the woman's hand and sustaining her with all his strength, while he calls to mind all her human qualities. Gradually she escapes into sleep, becoming someone unknown, someone resembling herself, an embodiment of all that he loves which is always new.

The *p* of the opening must not be *pp* because of the low *tessitura* and because the timbre of the voice must be warm and full. Thus the *tessitura*, higher from the fifth bar, should continue with the same intensity, to make the sudden contrast of a real *pp* on 'Sillons profonds . . .' as soft and as clear as possible without the least *crescendo* on 'germera'. A good breath for both interpreters before attacking 'Je me répète', which should be only *p*. Then *f subito* and a complete change of expression on 'Je ris encore de l'orgueilleuse'.

From this bar onwards the piano must continue to sing its melodic line, while remaining *p* and *dolce*, although the voice part is *mf*. The key changes to three flats at the start of the great lyrical section of the song. It is preferable to begin only *mf*, 'et dans ma tête', and to maintain this during the following bars to reserve the true *f* for 'Je m'émerveille'. There should then be a *diminuendo* in order to prepare another big *crescendo* on 'une inconnue semblable à toi', truly *f*; and I find that the *p* marked by Poulenc on the last lines is not advisable, at least a *mf* is needed, very intense with an accent on '<u>nou</u>veau'.

All this section must give an impression of complete wonderment prolonged throughout the long coda for the piano which becomes more and more serene in its peaceful happiness. 'This coda,' says Poulenc, 'is essential. Play it in strict tempo, without hurrying (to make sure of applause for the singer).'

The last bars look back to 'Bonne journée', thus forming a logical conclusion to this cycle of songs.

*

MIROIRS BRÛLANTS (BURNING MIRRORS)

Under this title two songs are combined which are composed on poems that appeared in the revue *Mesures* and later formed part, with several others, of the collection *Chanson complète*. 'Tu vois le feu du soir' bore the title 'Nous sommes'.

Poulenc once again asked Eluard to give him a title, and the poet replied in this wise in the month of October 1938:

My dear Francis, this is really absurd. I am not writing a book but a title, and for these two poems, one of which is health and the other suffering, I can think of nothing but titles which are anti-public.

But the following November 1st, he wrote again:

My dear Francis, do not reproach me for not having found this title. Your music, had I known it, would surely have guided me and this title would have been its own. *Miroirs brûlants* had occurred to me, the meaning fits both poems.

In the end it was this title that Poulenc chose, using it as a heading for the two poems. He wrote about the first song as follows:

No one will ever sing this song like Bernac, it is for this reason that I have dedicated it to him. I wonder if in the 'desert island game' this might not be the one I would choose from my songs to take with me. It was born of chance and happy encounters.

One morning in August 1938, just before leaving to take the train to Anost,* I bought, below my apartment in the rue de Médicis, at Corti, the issue of *Mesures* which included this poem by Eluard. What a marvellous coincidence! It was to this very countryside that I was going, it was the view from the room where I worked at Anost. Rarely have I worked so well anywhere, with so much lightness and oxygen in me. . . . If the conception of 'Tu vois le feu du soir' was spontaneous, the achievement of it none the less gave me a lot of trouble. As I have already written, à propos of 'Jardin d'Anna', an enumerative poem calls for an immutable rhythm. This long song (four minutes) where not a single semi-quaver disturbs the flow, must be saved from monotony by the refinement of the writing for the piano and the simplicity of the vocal line. I hope I have not failed in this programme. The arabesque leaps up

* A remote village in Burgundy where we were going to spend the summer months working.

and rebounds in two similar falls. A coda of a page gives to the whole a human significance.

Much hesitation over the prosody of 'l'été qui la couvre de fruits'. The syllable 'té', very closed, is in general rather difficult to pronounce on a high note. This was, however, my first version to which after many experiments I returned, in agreement with Bernac.

The pianist must scrupulously observe the strict value of the notes. Although it is conceived in a halo of pedals, the accompaniment must be played with no variation of tempo.

TU VOIS LE FEU DU SOIR . . .

YOU SEE THE FIRE OF EVENING

Tu vois le feu du soir qui sort de sa coquille
Et tu vois la forêt | enfouie dans sa fraîcheur

You see the fire of evening emerging from its shell
and you see the forest buried in its coolness

Tu vois la plaine nue aux flancs du ciel traînard
La neige haute comme la mer
Et la mer | haute dans l'azur

you see the bare plain at the edges of the straggling sky
the snow high as the sea
and the sea high in the azure

Pierres parfaites ‿ et bois doux secours voilés
Tu vois des villes teintes de mélancolie

perfect stones and sweet woods veiled succours
you see cities tinged with gilded melancholy

Dorée des trottoirs pleins d'excuses
Une place ‿ où la solitude a sa statue
Souriante √ et l'amour ⌐ une seule maison

pavements full of excuses
a square where solitude has its statue
smiling and love a single house

Tu vois les ‿ animaux
Sosies malins sacrifiés l'un ‿ à l'autre

you see animals
malign doubles sacrificed one to another

Frères ‿ immaculés | aux ombres confondues
Dans ‿ un désert de sang

immaculate brothers with inter-mingled shadows
in a wilderness of blood

Tu vois ‿ un bel enfant quand ‿ il joue quand ‿ il rit
Il est bien plus petit
Que le petit ‿ oiseau du bout des branches

you see a beautiful child when he plays when he laughs
he is smaller
than the little bird on the tip of the branches

Tu vois un paysage | aux saveurs
    d'huile et d'eau
D'où la roche est exclue où la
    terre abandonne
Sa verdure √ à l'été qui la couvre de
    fruits

Des femmes descendant de leur
    miroir ancien
T'apportent leur jeunesse √ et leur
    foi en la tienne
Et l'une √ sa clarté la voile √ qui
    t'entraîne
Te fait secrètement voir le monde
    sans toi.

you see a countryside with its savour
    of oil and of water
where the rock is excluded where the
    earth abandons
her greenness to the summer which
    covers her with fruit

women descending from their ancient
    mirror
bring you their youth and their faith
    in yours
and one of them veiled by her clarity
    who allures you
secretly makes you see the world
    without yourself.

The composer has chosen the tranquil tempo ♩ = 60, which must remain unchanged throughout the whole length of the song. The beauty of the poem and of its music, the manner in which the composer plays with the modulations must assuredly suggest to the singer ever-varied vocal colours.

The whole of the first page must be sung *pp* with a floating tone and no involuntary changes of dynamics. The three following bars are in *crescendo*. In the bar of 5/4 (the only bar in which the singer is silent!), the piano part reverts gradually to *pp*. Here there is a complete change of vocal colour. In the *pp* the timbre of the voice must be warm and mellow for 'Pierres parfaites et bois doux secours voilés'. Then *mf* is demanded because of the low *tessitura* and the meaning of the words.

The next, lyrical, section begins *mf* with a *crescendo* to *f*. 'Tu vois les animaux sosies malins sacrifiés l'un à l'autre' should be *mf* because the *tessitura* is low and it is the piano, in its upper part, that has the melodic line. Then a very intense *f* up to 'dans un désert de sang'. Then both performers should take a good breath and make a new change, *subito pp*, with a colour that is as clear and transparent as possible for five bars. In spite of the rest before 'du bout des branches', the whole phrase must hold together. The ten following bars are *mf* and *f*. The pianist, for once, should be a little accommodating to help the singer to prepare his top G ♯! (There is a possible alternative, but a C ♯ should be sung and not an E, which is indicated by mistake.) Note that there is a misprint in the literary text, which is, quite obviously, 'qui la couvre de fruits'.

In the two following bars the piano again has the melodic line, but the singer must avoid singing too *p* in the low *tessitura*. 'T'apportent leur jeunesse et leur foi en la tienne' is *mf crescendo*, very much declaimed and *marcato*, with the accents which I indicate. In the line 'Et l'une (sa clarté la voile) qui t'entraîne', the dynamics are very badly indicated and absent in the piano part. 'Et l'une' is frankly *f*, 'qui t'entraîne' is similar, and the parenthetical, 'sa clarté la voile', is *p*. The last line is *p* with a nicely sung G ♯ *pp*.

In this beautiful song the singer can and <u>must</u> show his vocal mastery in the perfect performance of the contrasting dynamics and changes of vocal colour. And not only show the perfection of his technique but above all the power of his imagination and his poetic sensibility.

JE NOMMERAI TON FRONT	I WILL NAME YOUR BROW
Je nommerai ton front	I will name your brow
J'en ferai un bûcher │ au sommet de tes sanglots	I will make of it a stake at the summit of your sobs
Je nommerai reflet la douleur qui te déchire	I will name reflection the sorrow which rends you
Comme une épée dans un rideau de soie	like a sword in silken curtain
Je t'abattrai jardin secret	I will destroy your secret garden
Plein de pavots │ et d'eau précieuse	full of poppies and precious water
Je te ligoterai de mon fouet	I will bind you with my whip
Tu n'avais dans ton cœur que lueurs souterraines	In your heart you had nothing but subterranean gleams
Tu n'auras plus dans tes prunelles que du sang	you will have nothing in the pupils of your eyes but blood
Je nommerai ta bouche et tes mains les dernières	I will name your mouth and your hands the last
Ta bouche écho détruit tes mains monnaie de plomb	your mouth destroyed echo your hands leaden coins
Je briserai les clés rouillées qu'elles commandent	I shall break the rusted keys that they command
Si je dois m'apaiser profondément un jour	If the day comes when I am completely calmed
Si je dois oublier que je n'ai pas su vaincre	if I must forget that I have not known victory
Qu'au moins tu aies connu la grandeur de ma haine.	at least let it be that you have known the extent of my hate.

(In the literary edition the poem is entitled 'Vertueux solitaire' ('Righteous recluse').) Poulenc's commentary on this song is short and severe: 'An unsuccessful song. I began it at Anost. After our departure, earlier than we anticipated (as Bernac's father was dying), I did not take it up again until much later at Noizay. I had lost the thread. It can't be helped.'

It is true that this song of violence and hate does not demand subtlety of expression. The *f* is maintained almost throughout with percussive diction. Do not fail to take advantage of several respites: the parenthesis *p subito* on the line, 'plein de pavots et d'eau précieuse'; and the beginning of the last page which is *p* and must prepare and allow for the big final *crescendo*.

Both Eluard and Poulenc were more successful in singing of love than of hate.

*

LA FRAÎCHEUR ET LE FEU (THE COOLNESS AND THE FIRE)

These seven songs were composed between April and July 1950, thirteen years after *Tel jour telle nuit*, and what years!—the war, the occupation and all that they stood for. The poems are taken from the collection, *Le livre ouvert I*, published in 1940. The poems concerned here are entitled *Vue donne vie* (Sight gives life) which once again Poulenc did not think suitable, and it was at his request that Eluard suggested *La Fraîcheur et le Feu*.

First let us give Poulenc's own words from his *Diary of my Songs*:

Indisputably the most concerted of my songs. I have written so many songs up to now that I have lost my inclination for them, and doubtless I shall write them less and less. If these are successful, and I believe they are, it is because a technical problem stimulated my appetite. In reality it is not so much a cycle as <u>one single poem</u> set to music, in separate sections exactly as the poem is printed. A rhythmic unity (two *tempi*, one rapid, one slow) lies at the base of the construction. The poem progresses admirably, it was easy for me to take as the culminating point the last song but one, *Homme au sourire tendre*. A certain litanist aspect of Eluard (*Liberté* is his most admirable example) blends with my religious feeling. There is, besides, a mystical purity in Eluard.

'These songs are terribly difficult to perform well. I fear that, after Bernac, I will never again hear them attain the golden mean. The piano here is economical to a degree. I have thought once again of Matisse. Each note, each breath is important. This is why the timing of the pauses between the songs is not left to chance. The metronomic speeds are implacable. The technical performance must be rehearsed again and again with cold precision, then, sure of oneself, forget it all and give the impression of improvising, while listening only to one's intuition. These songs are dedicated to Stravinsky because in a kind of way they stem from him. The third one in fact borrows the tempo and the harmonic feeling from the final cadence of his Serenade in A for piano.

This text by Poulenc contains invaluable indications. He particularly insists, as I myself have already repeatedly insisted right through this book, on the implacability of his metronomic speeds—an instruction again expressly written at the beginning of the musical score.

LA FRAÎCHEUR ET LE FEU

THE COOLNESS AND THE FIRE

I

Rayons des yeux et des soleils
Des ramures et des fontaines
Lumière du sol et du ciel
De l'homme et de l'oubli de l'homme
Un nuage couvre le sol
Un nuage couvre le ciel
Soudain la lumière m'oublie
La mort seule demeure entière
Je suis une ombre je ne vois plus
Le soleil jaune le soleil rouge
Le soleil blanc le ciel changeant
Je ne sais plus
La place du bonheur vivant
Au bord de l'ombre sans ciel
     ni terre.

I

Beams of eyes and of suns
of branches and of fountains
light of earth and of sky
of man and man's oblivion
a cloud covers the earth
a cloud covers the sky
suddenly the light is unmindful of me
death alone remains complete
I am a shadow I see no longer
the yellow sun the red sun
the white sun the changing sky
I know no longer
the place of living happiness
at the edge of the shadow with neither
     sky nor earth.

2

Le matin les branches attisent
Le bouillonnement des oiseaux
Le soir les arbres sont tranquilles
Le jour frémissant se repose.

2

In the morning the branches stir up
the effervescence of the birds
at evening the trees are peaceful
the rustling day is resting.

3

Tout disparut même les toits même le
     ciel
Même l'ombre tombée des branches

3

All disappeared even the roofs even
     the sky
even the shade fallen from the branches

Sur les cimes des mousses tendres
Même les mots et les regards bien
  accordés

Sœurs mirotières de mes larmes
Les étoiles brillaient | autour de ma
  fenêtre
Et mes yeux refermant leurs ailes
  pour la nuit
Vivaient d'un univers sans bornes.

4

Dans les ténèbres du jardin
Viennent des filles invisibles
Plus fines qu'à midi l'ondée

Mon sommeil les a pour amies
Elles m'enivrent en secret
De leurs complaisances aveugles.

5

Unis la fraîcheur et le feu
Unis tes lèvres et tes yeux
De ta folie attends sagesse
Fais image de femme et d'homme.

6

Homme au sourire tendre
Femme aux tendres paupières
Homme aux joues rafraîchies
Femme aux bras doux et frais
Homme aux prunelles calmes
Femme aux lèvres ardentes
Homme aux paroles pleines
Femme aux yeux partagés
Homme aux deux mains utiles
Femme aux mains de raison
Homme aux astres constants
Femme aux seins de durée

Il n'est rien qui vous retient
Mes maîtres √ de m'éprouver.

---

upon the tips of the soft mosses
even the words and the concordant
  looks

sisters mirroring my tears
the stars shone around my window

and my eyes closing their wings
  again for the night
lived in a boundless universe.

4

In the darkness of the garden
come some invisible girls
more delicate than the shower at
  midday

my sleep has them for friends
they elate me secretly
with their blind complaisance.

5

Unite the coolness and the fire
unite your lips and your eyes
await wisdom from your folly
make a likeness of woman and of man.

6

Man of the tender smile
woman of the tender eyelids
man of the freshened cheeks
woman of the sweet fresh arms
man of the calm eyes
woman of the ardent lips
man of the plenitude of speech
woman of the shared eyes
man of the useful hands
woman of the sensible hands
man of the steadfast stars
woman of the enduring breasts

there is nothing that prevents you
my masters from testing me.

<table>
<tr><td>7</td><td>7</td></tr>
</table>

La grande rivière qui va	The great river that flows
Grande au soleil et petite à la lune	big under the sun and small under the moon
Par tous chemins │ à l'aventure	in all directions at random
Ne m'aura pas pour la montrer du doigt	will not have me to point it out
Je sais le sort de la lumière	I know the spell of the light
J'en ai assez pour jouer son éclat	I have enough of it to play with its brilliance
Pour me parfaire au dos de mes paupières	so that I may perfect myself behind my eyelids
Pour que rien ne vive sans moi.	so that nothing lives without me.

1. *Rayons des yeux et des soleils. Allegro molto, emporté* (fiery), ♩ = 132, this vehement song allows but little subtlety of interpretation. Such contrasts of dynamics as are indicated should be carefully observed, particularly the *p subito* on 'Un nuage couvre le ciel'. In my opinion the *p* on 'Je ne sais plus la place du bonheur vivant' should preferably be *mp* owing to the lowness of the *tessitura*. The last five bars should be sung in one breath. (On the first beat of the seventh bar in the voice part, the A is of course A♭. On the third beat of the ninth bar it is obviously A♮.)

A short silence before beginning, *presto et très gai* ♩ = 132:

2. *Le matin les branches attisent*, which so well evokes the chirping and the fluttering of the birds in the freshness of the morning. Choose of course a light timbre. No *diminuendo* on the *rallentando* of the ascending scale, 'Le bouillonnement des oiseaux'. The two interpreters should take a good breath before beginning the evocation of the calm of evening, 'Le soir les arbres sont tranquilles . . .', for which I suggest *mp* rather than *p*, with a much warmer timbre and very legato—and gradually slower to the end. (In the piano part, fourth bar, the second beat G is ♮ not ♭.)

The silence should be rather short before beginning:

3. *Tout disparut. Très calme mais pas trop lent* (very calm but not too slow), ♩ = 69 is an excellent indication. The poet falls asleep thus this song is a tranquil nocturne, and should be sung with a very floating voice and peaceful legato, but certainly without any sadness.

Almost the whole of the first page is *pp*. Only the line, 'Même les mots et les regards bien accordés' is *mf*, returning immediately to *pp*, and only the line, 'Et mes yeux refermant leurs ailes pour la nuit' is again *mf*, with a *crescendo* that leads to a *f* (comparative of course) on the word 'nuit'. Again an immediate return to *pp* and a small *rallentando*. The coda for the piano is *a tempo*. (At the 16th bar of the piano part the D is D ♭ on the second beat. At the 24th bar, voice part, the D♯ is of course a minim (½ note), not a semibreve.)

4. *Dans les ténèbres du jardin*. The poet tells of a beautiful dream. *Molto vivace*, ♩ = 132, *mf* then *f* with a considerable *diminuendo* on 'Plus fine qu'à midi l'ondée' which must lead to *pp*. After a good breath for the two performers, the *mp* begins again, then *mf*, the summit of the *crescendo* being on the syllable 'aveugle'; above all no accent on the B♭, but mark well the two low Ds. The piano can make a slight *rallentando* with the *diminuendo* of the last bars.

A long silence before beginning:

5. *Unis la fraîcheur et le feu*. *Très calme* (very calmly), ♩=66, and imbued with gravity, this song must be performed with intensity. The piano introduction is *ff* and *marcato*. The voice very legato and on the whole *mp* because of the low *tessitura*. Take care over the equality of the quavers, 'De ta folie', and then the contrasted dotted note and semiquaver (1/16) on 'attends sagesse'. The last line is definitely *f* and *marcato*, and there is a rapid *diminuendo* for the piano.

A very long pause is needed (but without losing hold of the audience) to prepare the superb modulation and total change of vocal colour and expression for the opening, as *pp* as possible, of:

6. *Homme au sourire tendre*. *Très lent (very slow)*, ♩ = 50, and very tenderly. The poem in the form, familiar to Eluard, of a litany, has rightly inspired the musician to write a song based on groups of two bars. The two first groups remaining *pp*, the second *mf* then *f* with an immediate *diminuendo*. I suggest that this *diminuendo* should lead only to *p* instead of the indicated *pp*, in order to reserve the true *pp* for the beginning of the following group which mounts gradually to *mf*. From this point the tempo should be a little less slow and *f* for the following groups, with a *crescendo* reaching the *ff* on the beginning of 'Homme aux astres constants', soon followed by *molto diminuendo*.

The last lines must be a contrast in expression; it is the conclusion of all the preceding invocations to those who are the 'masters' of the poet, in his profound humanity. I prefer *p* rather than *pp*, and with broad declamation. Time must be taken for an expressive breath between 'Mes maîtres' and 'de m'éprouver'.

(In the piano part, second page, first bar, fourth beat, the top D is obviously D♮.)

The last song must be begun immediately:

7. *La grande rivière qui va*, which must flow *mf* (♩ = 120) like the river of the poem, and which in the second quatrain, *subito f*, recalls the vehemence of the first song, with its impulse and its incisive articulation. The pianistic introduction is also repeated to form the conclusion.

*

LE TRAVAIL DU PEINTRE (THE WORK OF THE PAINTER)

Poulenc composed this collection of songs in August, 1950, at Tremblay, the magnificent château in Normandy owned by his brother-in-law, André Manceaux. The following is an extract from his *Diary of my Songs*:

If I have not written any songs since *La fraîcheur et le feu* it is because other forms of music have specially taken up my time: religious music and opera. . . . However, I wrote this cycle, *Le travail du peintre*, about which I had spoken to Eluard some months before his death.

The seven poems which make up this collection are drawn from the volume *Voir*. I thought that it might revive my songs to *paint musically*, Picasso, Chagall, Braque, Gris, Klee, Mirò, Villon.

When I spoke to Eluard about my project I asked him for a poem on Matisse, whom I adore. Paul half promised me, I say half promised because he did not share my passion for this painter. To my mind, Matisse ought to have closed the cycle in joy and sunshine. As it is, Villon ends it lyrically and gravely. . . . All that I have said already about the interpretation of my songs holds good here. It is more than ever a duet in which the contents, vocal and instrumental, are closely woven. There is no question of an accompaniment.

1 PABLO PICASSO

Entoure ce citron de blanc d'œuf
    informe
Enrobe ce blanc d'œuf d'un azur
    souple et fin
La ligne droite et noire | a beau venir de
    toi
L'aube est derrière ton tableau

1 PABLO PICASSO

Surround this lemon with formless
    white of egg
coat this egg white with a malleable
    delicate blue
although the straight black line surely
    comes from you
the dawn lies behind your picture

Et des murs innombrables croulent	And innumerable walls crumble
Derrière ton tableau et toi l'œil fixe	behind your picture and you your eyes fixed
Comme un aveugle comme un fou	like a blind man like a madman
Tu dresses | une haute épée dans le vide	you put a tall sword in the empty space
Une main √ pourquoi pas une seconde main	A hand why not a second hand
Et pourquoi pas la bouche nue comme une plume	and why not a denuded mouth like a quill
Pourquoi pas un sourire | et pourquoi pas des larmes	why not a smile and why not tears
Tout au bord de la toile | où jouent les petits clous	on the very edge of the canvas where little nails are fixed
Voici le jour d'autrui laisse aux ombres leur chance	This is the day of others leave their food fortune to the shadows
Et d'un seul mouvement des paupières renonce.	and with a single movement of the eyelids renounce.

I continue to quote Poulenc's commentary:

> Picasso opens the collection: Honour to whom honour is due. His initial theme, likewise found a long time ago, served as *root-stock* for the theme of Mother Marie in *The Carmelites*. Here, as in my opera, it takes on a tone of pride, well suited to the subject. This song, in C major, recalls, from very far, the opening of *Tel jour telle nuit*, but many years have passed and, for the musician, C major no longer means peaceful happiness. It is the progress of the prosody, with its long run-on lines, that gives a proud tone to this song. Note, before the end, the vocal minim rest preceding the word 'renonce' which, to my mind, underlines the imperative side of Picasso's painting.

This 'proud tone' this 'imperative side' is first imposed by the dynamics which are almost always *f* and *ff* (even the *p* that occurs occasionally should be very relative), and also by incisive articulation and very broad declamation.

I saw, several years ago, a remarkable film on Picasso, in which he appeared painting. He began on a white canvas 'tout au bord de laquelle jouent les petits clous', with a powerful 'ligne droite et noire', 'comme une épée dans le vide', and, little by little, the work grew and became complicated and passed through various stages of beauty, until the moment when one longed to cry out to him: Enough, don't touch it any more, don't add anything more now! 'Voici le jour d'autrui laisse aux ombres leur chance Et d'un seul mouvement des paupières renonce.'

Great care must be taken over the balance with the piano, of which the *ff* can be for most of the time reduced to *f*, the voice being constantly in a low *tessitura*.

2 MARC CHAGALL

Ane ou vache coq ou cheval
Jusqu'à la peau d'un violon
Homme chanteur | un seul oiseau
Danseur agile avec sa femme

Couple trempé dans son printemps

L'or de l'herbe le plomb du ciel
Séparés par les flammes bleues
De la santé de la rosée
Le sang s'irise le cœur
      tinte
Un couple le premier reflet

Et dans un souterrain de neige
La vigne opulente dessine
Un visage aux lèvres de lune
Qui n'a jamais dormi la nuit.

2 MARC CHAGALL

Ass or cow cock or horse
even the skin of a violin
a singing man a single bird
agile dancer with his wife

Couple steeped in their springtime

The gold of the grass the lead of the sky
divided by the blue flames
of health and of dew
the blood grows iridescent the heart
      rings
A couple the first reflection

And in an underground cavern of snow
the opulent vine delineates
a face with moon-like lips
which has never slept at night.

'It is,' says Poulenc, 'a kind of rambling *scherzo*. Strange objects pass in the sky. A poetic fall brings us back to the human being.'

The tempo, *Molto prestissimo* ♩. =96, must be pitilessly maintained. At 'Ane ou vache', do not pronounce the final 'e', the consonant 'ch' articulated very strongly is sufficient. The first eight bars of the voice are *f*; the following four *mf*. There should be a *p* which is not indicated, but which we always made in performance, and which is imperative for both piano and voice, together with a lighter timbre, to evoke 'Danseur agile avec sa femme Couple trempé dans son printemps'. The piano resumes *f* for its four solo bars.

The following page is *mf*, but the *f* should be again resumed on the four bars, 'Un couple le premier reflet', because the following ten bars are only *mf* with a slight slackening of the tempo for the last two bars, in order to prepare the final *subito pp* which must be a little mysterious, very soft and poetic, and above all <u>without</u> *rallentando* (without any *crescendo* for the *ppp* of the F♯). To tell the truth we even made a slight *accelerando* on 'Qui n'a jamais dormi la nuit'.

3 GEORGES BRAQUE

Un oiseau s'envole,
Il rejette les nues comme un voile
inutile,
Il n'a jamais craint la lumière,
Enfermé dans son vol,
Il n'a jamais eu d'ombre.

Coquilles des moissons brisées par le
soleil.
Toutes les feuilles dans les bois disent |
oui,
Elles ne savent dire que oui,
Toute question, toute réponse
Et la rosée coule au fond de ce
oui.

Un homme aux yeux légers décrit le
ciel d'amour.
Il en rassemble les merveilles
Comme des feuilles dans un bois,
Comme des oiseaux dans leurs ailes
Et des hommes dans le sommeil.

3 GEORGES BRAQUE

A bird flies away
it throws off the clouds like a useless
veil,
it has never feared the light,
enclosed in its flight,
it has never had a shadow.

Husks of harvest grains split by
the sun.
All the leaves of the wood say
yes,
they can say nothing but yes,
every question, every answer
and the dew flows in the depth of this
yes.

A man with carefree eyes describes
the heaven of love.
He gathers its wonders
like leaves in a wood,
like birds in their wings
and men in sleep.

Poulenc's commentary: 'Braque is the most subtle of the songs, the most detailed of the collection. It is perhaps too mannered, but that is how I feel Braque. It must be accompanied with precision and, above all, from the beginning a tempo must be taken that is not too slow, suitable for the conclusion, "Un homme aux yeux légers", etc.'

For this 'tempo that is not too slow' the indication $\dot{\downarrow}=63$ is good in my opinion. The swaying of the 6/8 must be felt, very *legato*. (In the fifth bar, piano part, right hand, Poulenc has cut out the B♭ which is found in certain editions, giving three even quavers ($\frac{1}{8}$) on the first half of the bar.)

The song should begin no louder than *mf*, in order to reserve the *f* for the line, 'Il n'a jamais craint la lumière', after which the indication *p*, which is marked for the piano part, applies also to the voice, and should be given to the line, 'Enfermé dans son vol il n'a jamais eu d'ombre'. Again *f* for both piano and voice, *p subito* applying only to the line, 'Toutes les feuilles dans les bois disent oui'; and there is a return to *f* for the two following lines, which must be well united by their meaning. Take a good expressive breath before beginning the *pp très doux* (molto dolce), which must have a

complete change of colour and expression: the sudden tenderness for
Un homme aux yeux légers décrit le ciel d'amour'. Return immediately
to *mf* and even *f* for the two following lines, while nevertheless retaining the
same expression to the end of the song, making a very gradual *diminuendo* on
the last five bars, leading to a true *pp* on the word 'sommeil', and above all,
no *rallentando*. (The prosody of the line, 'Comme des oiseaux', is not very
good, the marking of the 'e' mute which falls on the second beat, must be
avoided by making an accent on 'Comme'.

   The important consideration in this song is to make sufficient contrast
between the first part inspired by Braque's numerous flights of birds, and
the second part full of human tenderness.

4 JUAN GRIS

De jour merci de nuit prends garde
De douceur la moitié du monde
L'autre montrait rigueur aveugle

Aux veines se lisait | un présent sans
   merci
Aux beautés des contours l'espace
   limité
Cimentait tous les joints des objets
   familiers

Table guitare et verre vide
Sur un arpent de terre pleine
De toile blanche d'air nocturne

Table devait se soutenir
Lampe rester pépin de l'ombre
Journal délaissait sa moitié

Deux fois le jour deux fois la nuit
De deux objets | un double objet
Un seul ensemble à tout jamais.

4 JUAN GRIS

By day give thanks by night beware
sweetness one half of the world
the other showed blind harshness

In the veins a merciless present was
   read
in the beauties of the contours limited
   space
cemented all the joinings of familiar
   objects

Table guitar and empty glass
on an acre of solid earth
of white canvas of nocturnal air

Table had to support itself
lamp to remain a pip of the shadow
newspaper abandoning half of itself

Twice the day twice the night
of two objects a double object
a single whole for ever and ever.

   Poulenc writes: 'Gris is the song that I first sketched several years ago. I
have always greatly admired this painter and very much liked him as a man,
the worthy and unfortunate Juan who only now begins to take the place he
deserves.

   'I have a liking for this song in which I have been able to underline the
rhythmic similarities that are found in the poem:

"De jour merci de nuit prends garde
Deux fois le jour deux fois la nuit"

and again:

"Table guitare et verre vide
Table devait se sountenir" '

The whole song is serious and sorrowfully melancholy. The pedal plays a key rôle here.

A long wait is needed, as Poulenc indicates, before beginning this song, in order to heighten the effect of the entrance of the voice without accompaniment. The song consists of contrasts in dynamics and expression. The clue to it is in the two lines, 'De deux objets un double objet Un seul ensemble à tout jamais'.

From the first line I think the dynamics should already be contrasted and modified thus: 'De jour merci' *p* and softly clear; then *mf* for the threatening, 'de nuit prends garde'; again *p* for 'de douceur la moitié du monde', and *mf* for 'l'autre montrait rigueur aveugle'. In the following three bars, which are *mp* for the voice, the piano should be *p* not *mf* which is indicated by mistake!

Subito f for six bars, then establish a *crescendo* through the three following lines: the first *pp*, the second *mf* and the third *f*. 'Table devait se soutenir' is *p*, and the two following lines are *f* with a *diminuendo* (not easy) on 'sa moitié'. The value of the quaver must be carefully respected in order to make a definite silence before beginning *pp*, and as though from afar, 'Deux fois le jour deux fois la nuit'. I suggest that the important following line, 'De deux objets un double objet', should be *p* instead of *pp*, with an accent on 'deux' and on 'double'. Begin the last line *mf* and enunciate very clearly 'Un seul ensemble', then *diminuendo*, but affirm with conviction 'à tout jamais'. This last note must remain as though suspended.

The piano coda is *pp* and *ppp*, with a slight *rallentando*.

5 PAUL KLEE

Sur la pente fatale le voyageur profite	On the fatal slope the traveller benefits
De la faveur du jour, verglas | et sans cailloux,	from the favour of the day, glazed with frost and without pebbles,
Et les yeux bleus d'amour, découvre sa saison	and his eyes blue with love, discovers his season
Qui porte à tous les doigts de grands astres en bague.	which bears on every finger great stars as rings.

Sur la plage la mer a laissé ses oreilles	On the shore the sea has left its ears
Et le sable creusé la place d'un beau crime.	and the hollowed sand site of a noble crime.
Le supplice est plus dur aux bourreaux qu'aux victimes	The agony is worse for the executioners than for the victims
Les couteaux sont des signes | et les balles des larmes.	knives are omens and bullets are tears.

This song is a song of transition between the preceding one and that which follows—genuinely part of a cycle. Poulenc admitted, 'I needed a *presto* here. A song that would go with a bang.'

This means that it does not need subtlety of interpretation. The tempo is *Implacablement vite* (implacably fast), ♩ = 144. The dynamics always *f* and *ff* with strong articulation. Try to achieve more *legato* on the only line that is *mf*.

It must be admitted that the poem and the music are not among the best.

6 JOAN MIRÓ

Soleil de proie prisonnier de ma tête,	Sun of prey prisoner of my head,
Enlève la colline, enlève la forêt.	remove the hill, remove the forest.
Le ciel est plus beau que jamais.	The sky is more beautiful than ever.
Les libellules des raisins	The dragonflies of the grapes
Lui donnent des formes précises	give precise forms to it
Que je dissipe d'un geste.	that I dispel with a gesture.
Nuages du premier jour,	Clouds of primeval day,
Nuages insensibles | et que rien n'autorise,	insensitive clouds sanctioned by nothing,
Leurs graines brûlent	their seeds burn
Dans les feux de paille de mes regards.	in the straw fires of my glances.
A la fin, pour se couvrir d'une aube	At the end, to cloak itself with dawn
Il faudra que le ciel soit aussi pur que la nuit.	the sky must needs be as pure as the night.

Poulenc says that this song is 'The most difficult to interpret with its sudden passing from a strident outburst to softness and lyricism on the words, "les libellules des raisins". The *cédez beaucoup* (*molto rallentando*) on "que je dissipe d'un geste", and the return to the tempo, cannot be explained. It must be felt.'

In fact, if his indications are rigorously observed, it is not so difficult, but it is seldom that one finds so many changes of tempo in a song by Poulenc. The preliminary indication is very exact: *Allegro giocoso*, ♩ = 144, *ff* for both performers. I would sooner say 'brilliant' than 'strident'. The bar of 5/4 for the piano fortunately allows the singer time to prepare for the *p subito* with the 'softness and lyricism' demanded by the composer, but at the same time keeping exactly the initial tempo. It is not until the time changes to 3/2 the *céder beaucoup* (*molto rallentando*) appears with a *diminuendo* to return from the preceding *mf* to *p* and another *rallentando*.

Then in the space of two bars there is a very gradual *accelerando* to return exactly to the original tempo on 'Nuages insensibles', conserving the dynamics *p*, so that the *f* should be sudden on 'Leurs graines brûlent'. (In the following bar in the piano part there is a mistake in some editions: the first G in the right hand is G♯ and the second G♮, and not the contrary.)

The vocal part remains *f* with a gradual slowing down on the words, 'de mes regards'. The 3/2 bar in the piano part should be supple and without strictness but must be immediately *a tempo* and *f* for the following bars. There can be only a slight slowing down on the words 'soit aussi pur que la nuit', because the note values become long, but there should be a big *diminuendo* to a true *pp* on the word 'nuit'.

The piano coda again picks up the initial tempo.

7 JACQUES VILLON

Irrémédiable vie
Vie à toujours chérir

En dépit des fléaux
Et des morales basses
En dépit des étoiles fausses
Et des cendres envahissantes

En dépit des fièvres grinçantes
Des crimes à hauteur du ventre
Des seins taris des fronts idiots
En dépit des soleils mortels

En dépit des dieux morts
En dépit des mensonges
L'aube l'horizon l'eau
L'oiseau l'homme l'amour

L'homme léger | et bon
Adoucissant la terre

7 JACQUES VILLON

Irremediable life
life ever to be cherished

Despite scourges
and base morals
despite false stars
and encroaching ashes

Despite grinding fevers
crimes belly-high
dried up breasts foolish faces
despite the mortal suns

Despite the dead gods
despite the lies
dawn horizon water
bird man love

man light-hearted and good
smoothing the earth

Eclaircissant les bois	clearing the woods
Illuminant la pierre	illuminating the stone
Et la rose nocturne	And the nocturnal rose
Et le sang de la foule.	and the blood of the crowd.

Here is Poulenc's commentary: 'Villon is with Gris the song I like best. It is known how much I like the litanist side of the poetry of Eluard. The prosody of "l'aube l'horizon l'eau l'oiseau l'homme l'amour" brings human relaxation to this severe and violent poem.'

In 25 years of collaboration this particular phrase was the only subject of argument I ever had with Poulenc concerning the interpretation of his songs. All the first part of the song is, of course, *ff* with diction as incisive as it can be, although I myself prefer 'Vie à toujours chérir' to be only *mf*. Then all the rest is *ff* with, if possible, a *crescendo* of intensity, in order to achieve, on the lines quoted by Poulenc and of which the prosody is so exactly right, an unexpected contrast, a complete relaxation, a sudden softness, a sudden wonder. In spite of everything love replaces hate. This is the reason that I felt, after an expressive breath, there should be a *p subito* instead of a *f* on 'L'aube l'horizon l'eau l'oiseau l'homme l'amour'. Poulenc never entirely accepted my point of view, but he came half way—*mf* with a very much lighter timbre and an immediate *decrescendo*, which must be an increase of intensity.

It is not desirable to sing *f* on 'L'homme léger et bon': *mf* is altogether preferable. The violence and intensity of the poem's opening, now gives way to pity and to hope in humanity.

*

It now remains to speak of four songs on poems by Eluard, which Poulenc composed at different times during his life.

First 'Ce doux petit visage', dated 1938. (I have not been able to discover from which collection of Eluard, Poulenc took the poem.)

CE DOUX PETIT VISAGE	THIS SWEET LITTLE FACE
Rien que ce doux petit visage	Nothing but this sweet little face
Rien que ce doux petit oiseau	nothing but this sweet little bird
Sur la jetée lointaine où les enfants faiblissent	on the distant jetty where the children wane
A la sortie de l'hiver	At the end of winter
Quand les nuages commencent à brûler	when the clouds begin to burn

Comme toujours	as always
Quand l'air frais se colore	when the fresh air is tinged with colour
Rien que cette jeunesse qui fuit devant la vie.	Nothing but this youth that flies in the face of life.

'I have a great liking,' Poulenc says, 'for this short song: the dedication bears witness. Raymonde Linossier was my best adviser for the music of my youth. How many times, during the years since her death, I would have liked to have had her opinion on this or the other of my works.

'I have tried here to transfuse musically all the tenderness of Eluard's poem. I think I have succeeded, particularly the prosody of the long phrase, "A la sortie de l'hiver", full of delicate difficulties.'

All the tenderness of Eluard's poem, of which the exact sense remains mysterious enough, is certainly to be found in the music, and the interpreters must succeed in emphasizing it. A clear timbre of voice (I prefer a soprano voice in this song), simplicity, purity, and a poetic sense of nostalgia and melancholy. (Memory and regret for lost youth?) Singers often have a tendency to take too slow a tempo. The initial indication, ♩=63, seems right to me, and as always without *rubato*. The first lines are *p* and very *legato*, without involuntary changes of dynamics, in order to prepare the *mf* on 'A la sortie de l'hiver . . .'. (Roll the 'r' well in the word 'brûler', with a slight accent on the first syllable.) The *mf* must be maintained to bring out the *subito p* or better still *pp* on 'Rien que cette jeunesse qui fuit devant la vie', the repetition of this line being *mf*.

Poulenc attached great importance to the *legato* of the piano part (observe the indicated fingering), and the use of the pedals.

In 1947 Poulenc composed two more songs on poems by Eluard.

. . . MAIS MOURIR	. . . BUT TO DIE
Mains agitées ǀ aux grimaces nouées	Restless hands with twisted expressions
Une grimace en fait une autre	one expression brings another
L'autre est nocturne le temps passe	the other is nocturnal time passes
Ouvrir des boîtes casser des verres creuser des trous	to open boxes break glasses dig holes
Et vérifier les formes invisibles du vide	and verify the useless forms of empty space
Mains lasses retournant leurs gants	tired hands turning down their gloves
Paupières des couleurs parfaites	eyelids of perfect colours
Coucher n'importe où	to lie no matter where
Et garder en lieu sûr	and to keep in a safe place

Le poison qui se compose alors	the poison which is engendered then
dans le calme mais mourir.	in the stillness but to die.

(This poem was chosen from the collection *La vie immédiate* where it bore the title, 'Peu de vertu' (Little courage), a title that Poulenc was wise to discard.) He writes: 'I like this song written in memory of Nush* Eluard. Nush's hands were so beautiful, and this poem seems to me quite specially intended to evoke them.'

Contrary to many of Poulenc's songs, where the piano part doubles the vocal line, in this song there is constantly a counter-melody in the right hand which must be *doucement en dehors* (gently brought out), the chords being, as always in his writing for piano, 'very veiled' and intended only to give pulsation and prolongation to the harmony.

A tempo not slow but without haste is needed, and the indication, ♩.=66, is excellent. As always it should be maintained from beginning to end, despite all the contrasts of dynamics that must be scrupulously observed. Nevertheless I advise an attack already *mf* on the words 'Ouvrir des boîtes', with an immediate *crescendo*, similarly on the word 'Paupières', *mf* and *crescendo*. All the other indications are perfect and will give scope for the changes of colour and expression suggested by the poem, which are not easy to bring into effect without changing the tempo.

MAIN DOMINÉE PAR LE CŒUR	HAND RULED BY THE HEART
Main dominée par le cœur	Hand ruled by the heart
Cœur dominé par le lion	heart ruled by the lion
Lion dominé par l'oiseau	lion ruled by the bird
L'oiseau qu'efface un nuage	The bird that a cloud effaces
Le lion que le désert grise	the lion intoxicated by the desert
Le cœur que la mort habite	the heart where death abides
La main refermée en vain	the hand closed in vain
Aucun secours tout m'échappe	No help all escapes me
Je vois ce qui disparait	I see that which disappears
Je comprends que je n'ai rien	I realize that I have nothing
Et je m'imagine à peine	and I barely imagine myself
Entre les murs │ une absence	An absence between the walls
Puis l'exil dans les ténèbres	then the exile into the darkness
Les yeux purs la tête inerte.	the eyes pure the head inert.

* Poulenc always misspelt Nusch.

(A poem taken from *Poésie et vérité 1942*, where it bore the title 'La main le cœur l'oiseau' (The hand the heart the bird).) Poulenc says: 'During the first seven lines the words return so delightfully to their source that Eluard proposed a title for me (too mysterious for the public), "La Gamme" (The Scale). I preferred "Main dominée par le cœur". I have already made a note of this essential point, that, in order to make my task easier, I never transpose the key in which I have chanced to conceive the music of a line of the poem. It follows that my modulations pass at times through a mouse-hole. Here, having begun this song at the first line and knowing what the music of the last line was to be, I have manipulated the modulations to benefit the words directly. Two arabesques of seven lines passing from C to C, with the key of D as the highest point (reached each time by different degrees) form, in my estimation, a logical whole.'

This song has, therefore, a very logical construction, but none the less retains its impetus and spontaneity. Does the first line not define to perfection Poulenc's art?

Here again the tempo and all the indications of dynamics are carefully marked and must be scrupulously observed, without ever interrupting the general impulse and spontaneity of the song. While remaining exactly *a tempo*, the last line, owing to the long note values of the voice part, will suddenly give an impression of immobility.

UNE CHANSON DE PORCELAINE

Une chanson de porcelaine bat des
   mains
Puis͜ en morceaux mendie et meurt
Tu te souviendras d'elle pauvre͜ et nue
Matin des loups | et leur morsure͜ est͜
   un tunnel
D'où tu sorͮ en robe de sang
A rougir de la nuit
Que de vivants͜ à retrouver
Que de lumières͜ à éteindre
Je t'appellerai V͟i͟s͟u͟e͟l͟l͟e͟
Et multiplierai ton͜ image.

A SONG OF PORCELAIN

A song of porcelain claps
   hands
then in pieces begs and dies
you will remember it poor and denuded
morn of the wolves and their bite is a
   tunnel
out of which you come robed in blood
to blush for the night
so many living beings to find again
so many lights to extinguish
I will call you Visual
and will replicate your face.

'Une chanson de porcelaine' was the last song composed by Poulenc on a poem by Eluard. It is dated 1958, and was written in homage to Jane Bathori, on the occasion of her eightieth birthday. She was a marvellous musician, who had, with untiring devotion, put her musicianship at the service of most early twentieth-century French composers, Ravel among others, by performing their works for the first time.

The poem was chosen by Poulenc from the collection *A toute épreuve* from which he took the poems by Eluard which he first set to music (see p. 93). Poulenc's commentary is brief. Evidently he did not attach great importance to this work: 'Song without surprise. The second part, not unlike *Travail du peintre* is well designed.'

He has omitted to indicate the metronomic speed, but *Andante semplice* suggests ♩=63. The first line is *p* and very *legato*. (There should be a slight accent on the anacrusis 'U' in order to avoid marking the first beat with the mute 'e' of 'ne'.) After the *f* of the fourth bar, I suggest a return to *p* and *legato* on the third line, 'Tu te souviendras d'elle pauvre et nue'. Again *f*, up to the *pp très doux et très lié* (*dolce* and *legato*) at 'A rougir de la nuit', which should be preceded by a good, expressive breath. (Take a breath before 'que de vivants' and before 'que de lumières'!) The line, 'Je t'appellerai Visuelle', with an accent on the syllable 'Vi', is a little less *p*, and the last line is *mf*, with a slight *diminuendo* to lead into the coda for the piano, on which there can be a slight *rallentando*.

CHAPTER VI

Louise de Vilmorin

Louise de Vilmorin was born in 1902, on the estate of Verrières-le-Buisson where her family, celebrated for the plant-seeds and flowers produced there, owned part of its gardens and its cultivation. She died in 1972. At that time she was living with André Malraux.

She wrote numerous small books, among which can be mentioned some collections of verse, *Fiançailles pour rire* (1938), *Le Sable du sablier* (1945);and the novels, *Sainte une fois* (1934), *La fin de Villavid* (1937), *Madame de. . . .* (1951).

*   *   *

MOST OF THE songs composed by Poulenc on poems by Apollinaire and Eluard were conceived for a man's voice, although there are many among them that can also be sung by a woman. But Poulenc wished to write some typically feminine songs, for, as he said:

> I need to believe in the words that I hear sung. I admit that when a lady (with the best intentions no doubt) begins: 'J'aime tes yeux, j'aime ta bouche, O ma rebelle, o ma farouche' (I love your eyes, I love your mouth, O my rebellious one, O my shy one), in spite of Fauré's music, I am not convinced, for fear of being too convinced. Thus what joy for me when, one day at the home of Marie-Blanche de Polignac, I read the poem, 'Aux Officiers de la Garde Blanche', which she had just received for Christmas.
>
> The poems of Louise de Vilmorin provide material for truly feminine songs. I am enchanted by that. Liking as a rule to group several songs together, I begged Louise for some more poems. During the summer of 1936 she wrote for me 'Le garçon de Liège' and 'Eau-de-vie! Au-delà!' during a visit to Kerbastic, the country house of Jean de Polignac and his wife, in Brittany.

I would like to say a few words here about Marie-Blanche de Polignac, to whom Poulenc has just referred, not only because these three songs are dedicated to her, for as can be seen he dedicated many others to her, but because her personality is often evoked in my commentary on this little triptych.

The Countess Jean de Polignac was the daughter of Jeanne Lanvin, the first couturier to become world famous. Marie-Blanche—it was by this Christian name that she was always known—was a great beauty, I have never seen a handsomer couple than Marie-Blanche and her husband (a nephew of the Princess Edmond de Polignac whom I have mentioned in Chapter I). She was a woman of remarkable intelligence, and an exceptional musician. At her house in the rue Barbet-de-Jouy she held the last remaining musical salon in Paris.

On Sunday evenings, well known French musicians and foreign virtuosi who were passing through Paris met and made music at her home without any formality, entirely for their own pleasure and for hers. Almost all Poulenc's new songs, which he and I were creating together, had their first hearing at her salon, before public performance. She was a very good pianist herself and often played duets for four hands with one or another of her visitors. She also had a delightful voice, to which the recordings of Monteverdi which she made under the direction of Nadia Boulanger will bear witness.

But above all her musical judgement was infallible. I have no better proof of this than the coda for piano of the last song of *La Fraîcheur et le Feu*, which in Poulenc's original version ended rather lamely. It was she who, when we performed the cycle for her, suggested to Poulenc that he should repeat the first bars of the cycle, thus giving a logical conclusion and a unity to the whole.

From Kerbastic, Louise de Vilmorin sent Poulenc a letter in which she agreed to his request. She wrote as follows:

It is you, Francis, it is you who first had the idea of 'commanding' some poems to put to music. Therefore it is you who decreed that I was a poet! Your confidence does me honour and pleases me all the more because I believe it to be stamped with the supreme charm of illusion. At Kerbastic I was only able to write 'Le garçon de Liège' and 'Eau-de-vie! Au-delà!' which I enclose. As for 'Aux Officers de la Garde Blanche' (which I also send you), I wrote this several months ago at Fourques, the home of Jean Hugo,* with him in mind. For me it is less a poem than a prayer and an avowal. If I become a poet it is your fault, and I wonder if I shall forgive you for having prevented me from stifling the sighs of my melancholy.

---

* Jean Hugo, the great-grandson of Victor Hugo, is a talented painter. Fourques is the name of his estate in the South of France.

These three poems were set to music by Poulenc and published under the title:

TROIS POÈMES DE LOUISE DE VILMORIN

Here is Poulenc's enchanting portrait of Louise de Vilmorin:

Few people move me as much as Louise de Vilmorin: because she is beautiful, because she is lame, because she writes innately immaculate French, because her name evokes flowers and vegetables, because she loves her brothers like a lover and her lovers like a sister. Her beautiful face recalls the seventeenth century, as does the sound of her name. I can imagine her as a friend of 'Madame', or painted by Ph. de Champaigne as an abbess, a rosary in her long hands. Louise always escapes childishness despite her country house where they play on the lawns.

Love, desire, illness, exile, and money difficulties, were at the root of her genuineness.

At a discussion concerning *Nouvelles Littéraires*, Poulenc commented in the following way:

I found in the poetry of Louise de Vilmorin a kind of sensitive audacity, of wantonness, of avidity which extended into song that which I had expressed, when very young, in *Les Biches* [ballet composed in 1923] with Marie Laurencin.

In this way he defined the elegance and the charm of these poems. 'Charm,' wrote Henri Hell in his book on Poulenc, 'where veiled eroticism plays a part. Transparent, easy, readily precious and capricious like embroidery: beneath the lightness of its style this audacious poetry is not without seriousness. Its elegance barely disguises a melancholy which is never renounced. And the shadow of death seems at times to caress her. This game of words that would be called nonchalant and facile knows the essential truths: desire, pleasure, melancholy and love. The whole adorned with romantic grace.' Louise de Vilmorin liked also, as many of her poems show, to play with words, with their sonority: 'Eau-de-vie! Au-delà!', and also on words, with their double meaning: 'Il vole' (in *Fiançailles pour rire*) and in the song that follows:

1 LE GARÇON DE LIÈGE	1 THE BOY OF LIÈGE

Un garçon de conte de fée
M'a fait un grand salut bourgeois,
En plein vent, au bord d'une allée,

Debout, sous l'arbre de la Loi.

Les oiseaux d'arrière saison
Faisaient des leurs, malgré la pluie,
Et, prise par ma déraison,
J'osai lui dire: je m'ennuie.

Sans dire un doux mot de menteur,
Le soir, dans ma chambre à tristesse,
Il vint consoler ma pâleur;
Son ombre me fit des promesses.

Mais c'était un garçon de Liège
Léger, léger comme le vent,
Qui ne se prend à aucun piège
Et court les plaines du beau temps.

Et dans ma chemise de nuit,
Depuis lors, quand je voudrais rire,
Ah! beau jeune homme, je m'ennuie,
Ah! dans ma chemise, à mourir.

A fairy-tale youth
boldly bowed low to me,
in the open air, on the verge of a
    pathway,
standing under the tree of the Law.

The birds of late autumn
were busy, in spite of the rain,
and, seized by a foolish whim,
I dared to say to him: I am bored.

Without one sweet deceiving word,
at evening, in my cheerless room,
he came to console my pallor;
his shadowy figure made me promises.

But he was a boy of Liège
light, light as the wind,
who would never be caught in a trap
and roams the plains in fine weather.

And in my nightdress,
ever since then, when I want to laugh,
Ah! handsome young man, I am bored,
Ah! in my nightdress, bored to death.

'Le garçon de Liège' (The boy of Liège—or of cork, light as the wind. In French, Liège means—cork). Poulenc says:

> This song must be sung at a dizzy speed. The *empirical* tempo of the metronomic indication ♩ = 176 is meant to safeguard the turbulent atmosphere of the song and to show to advantage the cadence of the poem. Besides, the writing for the voice requires a much less rapid delivery than that for the piano.

I suggest that the beginning of the song should be sung at least *mp*, because the piano part is very brilliant. The expression, 'l'arbre de la Loi', seems to be a favourite of Louise de Vilmorin, for she uses it again in the poem *Dans l'herbe*, the second song in the cycle *Fiançailles pour rire*. What did this phrase evoke for her? St Louis delivering justice under an oak, comes to mind. The whole line must be *mf* for the voice, being given a low *tessitura*, and *p* for the piano with a sudden *crescendo* at the end of the second bar, to prepare the *p subito* for the two performers on 'Les oiseaux d'arrière saison . . .'. I advise then a *mf* from 'Et prise par ma déraison'. Take an expressive breath before 'je m'ennuie' with the indicated dynamics which underline the meaning of the words. The following lines are *pp*, but I prefer *p* to *mf* on 'Son ombre me fit des promesses', then *p* again for 'Mais c'était un garçon de Liège'. The high G on the second 'léger' can have only the value of a quaver (1/8) with a quaver rest, and it should be reached with a light *portamento*. The following line is *mf* and truly *f* on the gusty 'Et court les plaines du beau temps'. The six following bars are in *crescendo* until the second 'Ah!' (F♯) on which there should be a *diminuendo*. Then take a good breath before *mf*, 'Dans ma chemise', and a slight break without breathing before 'à mourir', which must express all the boredom possible!

2 AU-DELÀ

Eau-de-vie! Au-delà!
A l'heure du plaisir,
Choisir n'est pas trahir,
Je choisis celui-là.

Je choisis celui-là
Qui sait me faire rire,
D'un doigt de-ci, de-là,
Comme on fait pour écrire.

Comme on fait pour écrire,
Il va par-ci, par-là,
Sans que j'ose lui dire:
J'aime bien ce jeu-là.

J'aime bien ce jeu-là,
Qu'un souffle fait finir,
Jusqu'au dernier soupir
Je choisis ce jeu-là.

Eau-de-vie! Au-delà!
A l'heure du plaisir,
Choisir n'est pas trahir,
Je choisis ce jeu-là.

2 AU-DELÀ

Eau-de-vie! Au-delà!
At the hour of pleasure
to choose is not to betray,
I choose that one.

I choose that one
who can make me laugh,
with a finger here, there,
as when one writes.

As when one writes,
he goes this way, that way,
without my daring to say to him:
I very much like this game.

I very much like this game,
that a breath can end,
until my last breath
I choose this game.

Eau-de-vie! Au-delà!
At the hour of pleasure,
to choose is not to betray,
I choose this game.

'Eau-de-vie! Au-delà!' Louise de Vilmorin wrote to Poulenc about this poem as follows:

You ask me why the text of this poem, in the volume which I have called *Fiançailles pour rire*, is not the same as the original text which you received from me long before the publication of the volume. Here is the reason: this poem which I had written without any particular intent, without the least thought of anything improper, brought me such teasing from Marie-Blanche that I am still feeling astounded. She assured me that the poem was indecency itself and contained some ideas and admissions that would cause the most broad-minded Father-confessor to blush for shame. And when I told her that it was just her dirty mind she replied that my unawareness was not, in her eyes, a proof of innocence. She was laughing, as you can imagine, but as for me I swear that I had a face like an omelette—an omelette 'aux fines herbes' to boot. In short, I dare not let it appear as it was, I modified it for everybody, and if I have not changed it for you it is because I wrote it for you and I knew that your music would have the power to render it innocent in its original form.

And here is what Poulenc himself wrote:

I regret that in her volume *Fiançailles pour rire* Louise has thought fit to tone down the veiled eroticism of *Eau-de-vie! Au-delà!* For nothing in the world would I make this alteration in my musical version, for that would create a positive misconception. The palpitation of the accompaniment would have no reason to exist. . . . This song should be sung very lightly, very simply, without any underlining, but at the same time without dissimulation. The *staccato* triplets of the piano must remain in the background while still being precise.

These indications given by Poulenc are invaluable. The metronome speed ♩.= 136 is very good. The first verse should be *mf* for the voice as also for the piano. There is a slight *crescendo* on 'me faire rire' to prepare the *p subito*, 'd'un doigt de-ci-de-là'; then again *mf*. The breath indicated before the second 'Comme on fait' should be scarcely perceptible. Above all the flow of the song must not be interrupted. Note that the *p* on 'Il va par-ci par-là' is important, as also the *sf* and *diminuendo* on 'sans que j'ose lui dire'.

The *subito pp* (*dans un souffle*), meaning that the phrase should seem to be whispered, implies the necessity for strong and precise articulation. Then once more a beautiful *legato* is needed. On the last word of 'Je choisis ce jeu-là' there should be a *crescendo* and at the same time a *portamento* to reach the *p subito* on 'Eau-de-vie! . . . .'. All the end of the song is *p absolument sans ralentir* (without any slowing down whatever). (In the fifth bar before the end in the piano part, it is much easier to play the C with the left hand in the same way as in the following bar an octave lower—this will preserve the equality of the right hand.)

I must repeat Poulenc's advice: 'sing this song very simply'. For a pretty, fresh voice that is able to sing *p* in the high register, it is a delightful piece to which the continuing triplets of the piano part transmit an irresistible impetus.

3 AUX OFFICIERS DE LA GARDE BLANCHE

Officiers de la Garde Blanche,
Gardez-moi de certaines pensées, la nuit,
Gardez-moi des corps à corps et de l'appui
D'une main sur ma hanche.

Gardez-moi surtout de lui
Qui par la manche m'entraîne
Vers le hasard des mains pleines
Et les ailleurs d'eau qui luit.

Epargnez-moi les tourments en tourmente
De l'aimer un jour plus qu'aujourd'hui,
Et la froide moiteur des attentes
Qui presseront aux vitres et aux portes
Mon profil de dame déjà morte.

Officiers de la Garde Blanche,
Je ne veux pas pleurer pour lui
Sur terre, je veux pleurer en pluie,
Sur sa terre, sur son astre orné de buis,

Lorsque plus tard je planerai transparente,
Au-dessus des cent pas d'ennui.

Officiers des consciences pures,
Vous qui faites les visages beaux,
Confiez dans l'espace, | au vol des oiseaux,

3 TO THE OFFICERS OF THE WHITE GUARD

Officers of the White Guard,
guard me from certain thoughts at night,
guard me from love's tussle and the pressure
of a hand upon my hip.

Guard me above all from him
who pulls me by the sleeve
towards the danger of full hands,
and elsewhere, of water that shines.

Spare me the tempestuous torment

of loving him one day more than today,

and the cold moisture of expectation
that will press on the windows and doors
my profile of a woman already dead.

Officers of the White Guard,
I do not want to weep for him
on earth, I would weep as rain
on his land, on his star of carved boxwood,

when later I float transparent,

above a hundred steps of weariness.

Officers of the pure consciences,
you who beautify faces,
confide in space, to the flight of the birds,

Un message pour les chercheurs de mesures,	a message for the seekers of moderation,
Et forgez pour nous des chaines sans anneaux.	and forge for us chains without rings.

Recalling the letter from Louise de Vilmorin which I have already quoted, 'For me it is less a poem than a prayer and an avowal', it is obvious that these Officers of the White Guard are angels. Here is Poulenc's commentary:

> It was after a great deal of reflection that I adopted the style of piano writing in this song. 'What poor stuff', the grouser* of Geneva will write on discovering the unchanging unison of the beginning. It has nevertheless given me a great deal of trouble. What a temptation to harmonize after the fourth bar, and yet I am convinced that it was necessary to resist this false richness. For my part I see more humility than misery in it. These repeated semiquavers (1/16) evoke the guitar that Louise used to take with her when she went to dine with her friends.

Poulenc also said: 'this song must be "very sung".' It is in fact typical of his lyrical songs, and demands a perfect *legato* and good phrasing.

The indicated tempo ♩ = 69 is excellent. All the opening is *p*, but I suggest *mp* on the line, 'Gardez-moi surtout de lui', but after the indicated *pp* on the following lines, attack *mf*, 'Epargnez-moi . . .'. (I have this indication in Poulenc's own hand.) Further on the *pp* is important on 'Qui presseront . . .' etc.

The invocation to the 'Officiers de la Garde Blanche' should be at least *mf* with very warm timbre on the low notes—the same for the following bars. Not too *p* on 'Je veux pleurer en pluie' in order to reserve the *pp*, after a good breath, for 'Lorsque plus tard . . .'. All the warmth of the voice is needed to sing very expressively the last invocation to the 'Officiers des consciences pures'. And then sing with a floating voice and without *vibrato* (very white, says Poulenc), on 'confiez dans l'espace . . .'. The last line should be *mf*; this indication is in the piano part but omitted for the voice. The coda for piano must be well phrased, taking account of the indicated dynamics and without *rallentando*.

This song, in its simplicity, is very difficult for the two interpreters. For the singer it implies the absolute necessity, on which I have insisted many times for the performance of songs by Poulenc: the ability to sing *p* on high notes, with an equal ability to sing low notes that are resonant and warm. For the pianist, the evenness and *legato* of the repeated notes is very subtle

---

* A critic who did not like Poulenc's music at all.

and delicate. 'They are only,' says Poulenc, 'an introduction, until the first invocation to the "Officiers de la Garde Blanche"' (page 5 of the musical score). In short, in this song, there must be intense lyricism with perfect taste.

The commentary of Louise de Vilmorin should be remembered: 'It is a prayer and an avowal . . .'. 'Gardez-moi de certaines pensées la nuit . . . Gardez-moi surtout de lui. . . .'

*

FIANÇAILLES POUR RIRE (WHIMSICAL BETROTHAL)

The three poems of which I have just written were later published in a collection entitled *Fiançailles pour rire*. Poulenc was to choose six other poems from this collection which he set to music at the end of 1939, that is at the beginning of the war when he was at his house in Noizay. Here is his commentary:

Had it not been for the war, I should doubtless never have written this cycle. I hasten to explain in order to excuse myself for an assertion which at first glance may seem paradoxical. I composed *Fiançailles pour rire* to be able to think more often of Louise de Vilmorin, imprisoned in her castle in Hungary for God knows how long. (She had married Count Palffy who had an estate in Slovakia.) This was the only connection between my work and this horrible tornado. It was obviously fortuitous.

In composing these songs Poulenc had in mind the writing of a work for a woman's voice that would be akin to *Tel jour telle nuit*. But first let it be said that this collection does not at all constitute a true cycle as does that written on the poems of Eluard. United under the title *Fiançailles pour rire*, which is that of the literary collection and has no bearing on the cycle as a whole, the songs form a well-constructed group for concert performance, nothing more; for there is no poetic or musical link of any kind between these effectively contrasted songs. They may, therefore, be performed separately. It must be added that these charming and elegant poems are not comparable in richness and substance to the admirable poems of Eluard—a comparison reflected in the music.

1 LA DAME D'ANDRÉ   1 ANDRÉ'S WOMAN FRIEND

André ne connaît pas la dame   André does not know the woman
Qu'il prend aujourd'hui par la main.   whom he took by the hand today.
A-t-elle un cœur à lendemains,   Has she a heart for the tomorrows,
Et pour le soir a-t-elle une âme?   and for the evening has she a soul?

Au retour d'un bal campagnard	On returning from a country ball
S'en allait-elle en robe vague	did she go in her flowing dress
Chercher dans les meules la bague	to seek in the hay stacks the ring
Des fiançailles du hasard?	for the random betrothal?
A-t-elle eu peur, la nuit venue,	Was she afraid, when night fell,
Guettée par les ombres d'hier,	haunted by the ghosts of the past,
Dans son jardin, lorsque l'hiver	in her garden, when winter
Entrait par la grande avenue?	entered by the wide avenue?
Il l'a aimée pour sa couleur,	He loved her for her colour,
Pour sa bonne humeur de Dimanche.	for her Sunday good humour.
Pâlira-t-elle aux feuilles blanches	Will she fade on the white leaves
De son album des temps meilleurs?	of his album of better days?

'La dame d'André' should be sung very simply. André (perhaps one of Louise de Vilmorin's brothers), in a frivolous mood, asks himself if the lady whom he has just met is to be really important in his life, or simply the passing fancy of a day. All the quatrains end with a question mark. The question is posed by poet and musician with similar charm and lightness. This interrogative side must be well brought out.

In my opinion the indicated tempo is a shade too slow— ♩=132 is preferable, with a *ritenuto* at the end of the short piano prelude. The dynamics are well indicated, always in successive planes; observe these scrupulously as they are valuable expressively. For example, after the first *mf*, the *p subito* on 'Et pour le soir a-t-elle une âme?' (implying, would this be true love?) must have expressive value. Note the dynamics indication—*mf* for the piano and always *p* for the voice, on the line, 'A-t-elle eu peur, la nuit venue', (A♭–G♭ in the piano), and 'Dans son jardin lorsque l'hiver' (B♭–A). There is a *mf* for both voice and piano which is omitted in some editions on 'Entrait par la grande avenue'; then *p* for the two following lines and *mf* again with the piano on 'Pâlira-t'elle aux feuilles blanches De son album des temps meilleurs?', a line which could be taken either in its literal sense or figuratively.

The coda for piano should definitely slow down but only where indicated.

2 DANS L'HERBE

2 IN THE GRASS

Je ne peux plus rien dire	I can say nothing more
Ni rien faire pour lui.	nor do anything for him.
Il est mort de sa belle	He died for his beautiful one
Il est mort de sa mort belle	he died a beautiful death*

* He died a natural death.

Dehors	outside
Sous l'arbre de la Loi	under the tree of the Law
En plein silence	in deep silence
En plein paysage	in open countryside
Dans l'herbe.	in the grass.
Il est mort inaperçu	He died unnoticed
En criant son passage	crying out in his passing
En appelant	calling
En m'appelant.	calling me.
Mais comme j'étais loin de lui	But as I was far from him
Et que sa voix ne portait plus	and because his voice no longer carried
Il est mort seul dans les bois	he died alone in the woods
Sous son arbre d'enfance.	beneath the tree of his childhood.
Et je ne peux plus rien dire	And I can say nothing more
Ni rien faire pour lui.	nor do anything for him.

There is infinitely more depth and expression in this second song, which should be deeply moving. Poulenc says: *to be sung very intensely*—assuredly with the total sincerity that inspires the touching poem. It includes some lines that are a little obscure; I have already spoken of 'l'arbre de la Loi' (tree of the Law); as for 'arbre d'enfance' (tree of childhood), is it not probable that the little Vilmorins, like many children brought up in the country, had a familiar tree which they climbed? The poetess also plays, as is her wont, on the words, 'Il est mort de sa belle' (he died for his beautiful one), 'Il est mort de sa mort belle' (an idiomatic French expression meaning he died a natural death).

The excellent tempo ♩ = 56 must be unchanging, with perfect *legato*. All the beginning of the song is *p*, without involuntary changes of dynamics. I suggest two expressive accents on the repeated word 'rien'. The first *mf* is on 'En plein paysage dans l'herbe'. Then continue *mf* and *f* with a *crescendo*. The two interpreters must take a good breath before attacking the *p subito* which is of prime importance on 'Mais comme j'étais loin de lui Et que sa voix ne portait plus'. And then *mf* practically to the end of the song, because the voice descends towards the lower notes. (Always the accents on 'rien'.) There is no *ritenuto* in the piano coda.

3 IL VOLE   3 HE FLIES

En allant se coucher le soleil	As the sun is setting
Se reflète au vernis de ma table	it is reflected in the polished surface of my table
C'est le fromage rond de la fable	it is the round cheese of the fable
Au bec de mes ciseaux de vermeil.	in the beak of my silver scissors.

Mais où est le corbeau? Il vole.

But where is the crow? It flies.

Je voudrais coudre mais un aimant
Attire à lui toutes mes aiguilles.
Sur la place les joueurs de quilles
De belle en belle passent le temps.

I should like to sew but a magnet
attracts all my needles.
On the square the skittle players
pass the time with game after game.

Mais où est mon amant? Il vole.

But where is my lover? He flies.

C'est un voleur que j'ai pour amant,
Le corbeau vole et mon amant vole,
Voleur de cœur manque à sa parole
Et voleur de fromage est absent.

I have a thief for a lover,
the crow flies and my lover steals,
the thief of my heart breaks his word
and the thief of the cheese is not here.

Mais où est le bonheur? Il vole.

But where is happiness? It flies.

Je pleure sous le saule pleureur
Je mêle mes larmes à ses feuilles.
Je pleure car je veux qu'on me veuille
Et je ne plais pas à mon voleur.

I weep under the weeping willow
I mingle my tears with its leaves.
I weep because I want to be desired
and I am not pleasing to my thief.

Mais où donc est l'amour? Il vole.

But where then is love? It flies.

Trouvez la rime à ma déraison
Et par les routes du paysage

Find the rhyme for my lack of reason
and by the roads of the countryside

Ramenez-moi mon amant volage
Qui prend les cœurs | et perd ma
   raison.

bring me back my flighty lover
who takes hearts and drives me mad.

Je veux que mon voleur me vole.

I wish that my thief would steal me.

This poem is entirely based on the double meaning of the word 'vole', meaning to fly or to thieve. It also contains allusions to the fable by La Fontaine, *The Crow and the Fox*. The poet also plays, as she often does, on the words—or rather the expressions—'jouer la belle' (to play the deciding game), 'sans rime ni raison' (without rhyme or reason).

This very brilliant song demands an equal virtuosity from both interpreters. *Dans le style d'une étude pour piano* is Poulenc's indication, and from the singer it demands a rapid articulation, incisive and of great precision, but also of true lyricism. The indicated tempo, ♩ = 120, is in my opinion the minimum of speed, certainly no slower. This tempo is inflexible, the vocal line being often more rhythmic than melodic. But suddenly there are some very important and almost exaggerated contrasts of *legato*, for example on the lines, 'Sur la place les joueurs de quilles De belle en belle passent le temps', and also on the lines, 'C'est un voleur que j'ai pour amant' and 'Et voleur de fromage est absent', and on the whole of the fourth quatrain that begins 'Je pleure sous le saule pleureur' and ends 'Et je ne plais pas à mon voleur'.

To achieve the *legato* effect, it is better to cut out the quaver (1/8) rests in the first three lines of this quatrain—i.e. between: 'Je pleure' and 'sous le saule pleureur'; and between: 'Je mêle' and 'mes larmes à ses feuilles'; and between: 'Je pleure' and 'car je veux qu'on me veuille'. Poulenc said that this last phrase should be sung like *Tosca*! After the big *rallentando* the tempo must be rhythmically and strictly resumed.

The semi-quaver (1/16) rests after 'Trouvez', and after 'Et par' are good because there must be an impression of breathlessness. Resume the *legato* on 'Ramenez-moi mon amant volage', and sing it in one breath, cutting out the quaver (1/8) rest. The indicated dynamics on the last line are impracticable, at least a *mf* is needed for the voice to be able to achieve a nice *diminuendo* on the last 'vole'. As for the *f* indicated for the piano, this should be a maximum of *mf*. The very brilliant coda is without any *ritenuto* at all, but with a *diminuendo*.

Two more remarks for the singer: a liaison must of course be made on 'Mais où est', and the refrain, 'Mais ou est le bonheur', is difficult to make intelligible, but an accent on '<u>bon</u>' will help. In general, the scale of dynamics in this song passes from *mf* to *f*. The several indications of *p* should be used with discretion.

4 MON CADAVRE EST DOUX COMME UN GANT

4 MY CORPSE IS AS LIMP AS A GLOVE

Mon cadavre est doux comme un gant
Doux comme un gant de peau glacée
Et mes prunelles effacées
Font de mes yeux des cailloux blancs.

My corpse is as limp as a glove
limp as a glove of glacé kid
and my two hidden pupils
make two white pebbles of my eyes.

Deux cailloux blancs dans mon visage
Dans le silence deux muets
Ombrés encore d'un secret
Et lourds du poids mort des images.

Two white pebbles in my face
two mutes in the silence
still shadowed by a secret
and heavy with the burden of things
    seen.

Mes doigts tant de fois égarés
Sont joints en attitude sainte

My fingers so often straying
are joined in a saintly pose

Appuyés au creux de mes plaintes	resting on the hollow of my groans
Au nœud de mon cœur arrêté.	at the centre of my arrested heart.
Et mes deux pieds sont les montagnes	And my two feet are the mountains
Les deux derniers monts que j'ai vus	the last two hills I saw
A la minute où j'ai perdu	at the moment when I lost
La course que les années gagnent.	the race that the years win.
Mon souvenir est ressemblant,	I still resemble myself
Enfants | emportez-le bien vite,	children bear away the memory quickly,
Allez, | allez ma vie est dite.	go, go, my life is done.
Mon cadavre est doux comme un gant.	My corpse is as limp as a glove.

This song suggests parallels with 'Dans l'herbe' after the preceding song, but with not at all the same sentiment. In this strange poem of the 'dame déjà morte' (woman already dead), in Louise de Vilmorin's words from 'Aux Officiers de la Garde Blanche', it seems that the person who speaks is already detached from all human contingencies, at least in the first and the last lines in which a sentiment of gravity and simplicity prevails in the intensity. This does not exclude phrases of great lyricism in the middle of the song.

The tempo ♩ = 60 must above all not drag, but should continually maintain its even tranquillity, with perfect *legato*. There are numerous indications of dynamics which should be carefully observed. Nevertheless I advise, on the fifth bar, a reduction of the printed indication to *mp-crescendo, mf-diminuendo*. A definite *f* would be altogether out of place here, more especially after the first bars which are sung *p* without any change of dynamics.

There is a misprint in the seventh bar on the third beat: the note is C ♮ (not C♯) for the piano as it is for the voice. A good breath before the line, 'Et lourd du poids mort des images', which should be almost exaggeratedly phrased with the indicated dynamics reversed: a *crescendo* not a *diminuendo* should be made in descending to the low notes. The line, 'La course que les années gagnent', should be phrased in a similar way. The following *pp* should give the impression of a voice, already far away, saying: bear away the memory of me while I still resemble myself. In the following phrase, the first 'Allez' is *mp*, then a break, and the second 'allez' more *p*. The last phrase should not be too *p* in the lower register. The coda for piano is very *legato* and without *ritenuto*.

5 VIOLON

Couple amoureux aux accents
    méconnus
Le violon | et son joueur me plaisent.
Ah! j'aime ces gémissements tendus

Sur la corde des malaises.
Aux accords sur les cordes des pendus
A l'heure où les Lois se taisent
Le cœur, | en forme de fraise, √
S'offre à l'amour comme un fruit |
    inconnu.

5 VIOLIN

Enamoured couple with the misprized
    accents
the violin and its player please me.
Ah! I love these wailings long drawn
    out
on the cord of uneasiness.
In chords on the cords of the hanged
at the hour when the Laws are silent
the heart, formed like a strawberry,
offers itself to love like an unknown
    fruit.

Of 'Violon', Poulenc says:

> I composed this song with a Hungarian restaurant, on the Champs-Elysées, in my mind, for which Louise's husband, Count Palffy had engaged a tzigane orchestra from Budapest. I have tried to suggest the local colour only very distantly, because the hand that wrote the poem is French. The musician similarly transposes this rhythm of the Danube into our own atmosphere. *Violon* evokes Paris and its listener in a hat from Reboux, just as the fox-trot from *L'Enfant et les Sortilèges* of Ravel is redolent of the Casino de Paris, the rue de Clichy, the rue d'Athènes, where Ravel lived.

Therefore a very elegant woman should be personified in a Hungarian night club: the violinist comes, as is the custom, to play near to her table, and the beautiful listener is not a little affected by the 'couple amoureux' made by the violin and . . . . . . the violinist. This sensuous song demands from its two interpreters a style that is almost exaggerated in expression, but which must always remain within the bounds of good taste! With Poulenc, as I have already said several times, the temptation to overdo his effects must always be resisted. This song must not become a night club song, but should only suggest its atmosphere.

The indicated tempo is clearly too slow, ♩=72 is preferable, at all events it should be supple. The pianist must do his best to suggest the languishing style of the tzigane violinist who so often attacks his sounds from below. The semi-demi quavers (1/32) should be short and a little marked. As for the singer, she need not be afraid of certain *portamenti* . . . and this, moreover, from the first words, 'Couple amoureux' for which an exaggerated *legato* is essential. 'Le vi' is very *staccato*—it must give the impression that the lady is catching her breath—but 'iolon' is very bound. (I asked the publisher to print the letter 'i' twice to obtain the desired effect.) In the following phrase the *legato* must again be exaggerated to the point of *portamento*. Note that the second quaver (1/8) of each beat should be sung with the longest possible value in the phrase, 'j'aime ces gémissements'. An expressive breath can be taken before 'tendus'. 'Sur la corde des malaises', always *portamento*. A *portando* as indicated on 'laises' between the two E♭s beginning on the third beat. Then suddenly no more *portamenti* at all (the poet plays on the word, 'corde'), just a beautiful *legato* on the lines, 'Aux accords sur les cordes des pendus, A l'heure ou les Lois se taisent'. It is important to sing the phrase, 'Le cœur's s'offre à l'amour', at least *mf*, taking care to re-attack 's'offre' with the same intensity, in order to highlight the parenthesis, 'en forme de fraises', which should be *p parlando*, but without *crescendo*. (In fact this is the only *p* in the whole song.) The *portamenti* are resumed on 'comme un fruit inconnue', but always with taste and without vulgarity.

There is no need to comment on the piano coda with its imitation of the violin.

6 FLEURS	6 FLOWERS

Fleurs promises, fleurs tenues dans tes bras,	Promised flowers, flowers held in your arms,
Fleurs sorties des parenthèses d'un pas,	flowers sprung from the parenthesis* of a step,
Qui t'apportait ces fleurs l'hiver	who brought you these flowers in winter
Saupoudrées du sable des mers?	powdered with the sand of the seas?
Sable de tes baisers, fleurs des ‿ amours fanées	Sand of your kisses, flowers of faded loves
Les beaux‿yeux sont de cendre et dans la cheminée	the beautiful eyes are ashes and in the fireplace
Un cœur enrubanné de plaintes	a heart beribboned with sighs
Brûle │ avec ses images √ saintes.	burns with its treasured pictures.

* The shape made by a footprint in the sand.

There must be a long silence before beginning this last song, to emphasize the modulation from *A major* to *D♭ major*. Poulenc writes as follows:

When this song is sung separately always try to precede it with a song in a distant key (*Violon* if possible), or a song in *A*; this will safeguard the impression of *sound that comes from far away*. Attacked on a level, the key of *D♭ major* sounds dull.

The theme of the poem concerns a woman who is burning, in her fireplace, the tokens of a past love. (The flowers are probably the little sea-pinks that grow on the shores of Brittany, in the imprints shaped like parentheses, left by footsteps.)

The indicated tempo ♩ = 56 is excellent and should be unwavering, with perfect equality of the quavers (1/8). The chords of the piano part must be as *legato* as possible 'in a halo of pedals', with the upper melodic line clear and translucent. The singer should begin with a floating tone, and *p* (not *pp*, this effect must be kept for the repeat of the theme), an absolute legato (but here without any *portamento*) and a feeling of nostalgic reverie. Again I quote Poulenc:

> I believe that there is in this song a melancholy so irremediable that the listener will assign to it, after the first bars, its rôle of coda. It must be sung humbly, the lyricism coming from within.

The climax of intensity is on the line, 'Brûle avec ses images saintes'. The 'r' of 'brûle' well rolled, a break before 'avec' and an expressive breath before 'saintes'; the whole line should be continually *mf* so that both performers, after a good breath, can attack truly *pp subito* the reprise of 'Fleurs promises'. From 'Qui t'apportait . . .' it is preferable to sing at least *mp* for all the low *tessitura* of the end. There is no necessity to observe the breath indicated by Poulenc before 'des mers'—it is only a last resource for certain sopranos who are short of breath and lack timbre in the low notes.

*

MÉTAMORPHOSES

Under this general title Poulenc has brought together three other songs on poems by Louise de Vilmorin. Composed during the war, in 1943, they were written, as Henri Hell says, 'as a sign of the friendship of the musician for his poetess friend', who was still so far away from France, as Poulenc mentions in his notes about *Fiançailles pour rire*. The poems were chosen from the same collection. These songs can be performed separately and are equally suitable for a man's voice.

1 REINE DES MOUETTES

Reine des mouettes, mon orpheline,
Je t'ai vue rose, je m'en souviens,
Sous les brumes mousselines
  De ton deuil ancien.

1 QUEEN OF THE SEAGULLS

Queen of the seagulls, my orphan,
I have seen you pink, I remember it,
under the misty muslins
  of your bygone mourning.

Rose d'aimer le baiser qui chagrine

Tu te laissais accorder à mes mains
Sous les brumes mousselines
    Voiles de nos liens.

Rougis, rougis, mon baiser te devine
Mouette prise aux nœuds des grands
    chemins.

Reine des mouettes, mon orpheline,
Tu étais rose accordée à mes mains
Rose sous les mousselines
    Et je m'en souviens.

Pink that you liked the kiss which
    vexes you
you surrendered to my hands
under the misty muslins
    veils of our bond.

Blush, blush, my kiss divines you
seagull captured at the meeting of the
    great highways.

Queen of the seagulls, my orphan,
you were pink surrendered to my hands
pink under the muslins
    and I remember it.

The queen of the seagulls is obviously a charming and elegant young woman, blushing beneath the grey muslin veils 'de son deuil ancien'. Her poetic image is admirably suggested by both poet and musician in a song of palpitating grace. The tempo, $\quad = 108$, is very fast, but perfectly correct. The interpreters will only gradually achieve perfection after many rehearsals. There are constantly opposing rhythmic and melodic phrases which could have been better indicated. The first two bars are rhythmic, and the second two bars melodic and *legato*; this pattern is similar in both the first two quatrains. Thus there are contrasts in each two bars. The four following bars, 'Rougis, rougis . . .', are *f* and very lyrical. Then, 'Reine des mouettes mon orpheline' is *p*, slightly *parlando*, with very precise diction. (Difficult!) 'Tu étais rose accordée à mes mains' is *mf* and *legato*. I insist on perfect equality of the triplets. After a short breath, attack *pp* and very flexibly, 'Rose sous les mousselines'. The last bar for the voice is *mf* with a slight *accelerando* to launch the brilliant and rapid coda for the piano, which has only a very slight *ritenuto* on the last notes with an enchanting *diminuendo*. The palpitation of this song must give no feeling of agitation.

2 C'EST AINSI QUE TU ES

2 IT IS THUS THAT YOU ARE

Ta chair, d'âme mêlée,
Chevelure emmêlée,
Ton pied courant le temps,
Ton ombre qui s'étend
Et murmure à ma tempe.
Voilà, c'est ton portrait,
C'est ainsi que tu es,

Your body imbued with soul,
your tangled hair,
your foot pursuing time,
your shadow which stretches
and whispers close to my temples.
There, that is your portrait,
it is thus that you are,

Et je veux te l'écrire	and I want to write it to you
Pour que la nuit venue,	so that when night comes,
Tu puisses croire et dire,	you may believe and say,
Que je t'ai bien connue.	that I knew you well.

(The literary title of the poem is *Le Portrait*, but Poulenc had already composed a song bearing this title on a poem by Colette. See page 193.)

The lyricism of this very beautiful song is almost romantic, and the two interpreters should not fear to surrender to it. The tempo, ♩ = 60, should be very supple. The important piano part demands playing that is *legato*, fluid and expressive. The appoggiaturas should be unhurried.

The vocal part must be very supply phrased, but without exaggerated *rubato* and 'above all without affectation', says Poulenc. As always in his music the general tempo must be immutable. The voice needs a rich timbre in the lower register and the ability to sing a limpid *pp* on the top notes—unless this can be achieved it is better to abstain from singing the song. For this reason I am inclined to prefer it in a man's voice.

The first four bars of the voice must, in fact, have great warmth in its low *tessitura* and should be sung definitely *mf*, particularly on the lines, 'Ton ombre qui s'étend et murmure à ma tempe'. Then a marvellous contrast can be made with a *p subito*, a clear timbre, floating and *tendrement mélancolique* (tenderly melancholy), on 'Voilà c'est ton portrait c'est ainsi que tu es'. Too often, alas, this effect is lost, the change of *tessitura* obliging the singer to reverse the dynamics. Attack *mf* and *crescendo*, 'Et je veux te l'écrire Pour que'; the low D♯ must be the peak of the *crescendo* in order to have a big *diminuendo* on the words, 'la nuit venue', before the true *pp* on the high phrase, 'Tu puisses croire et dire'. Give a little more voice for the last line, 'Que je t'ai bien connue'. The indicated breath can be made very expressive with the help of the *Cédez un peu* (slow down a little), and can possibly be replaced by a slight break with a held breath.

Poulenc has indicated the important fingering and the pedalling necessary to achieve the *legato* of the coda for piano.

3 PAGANINI

Violon hippocampe et sirène	Violin sea-horse and siren
Berceau des cœurs cœur et berceau	cradle of hearts heart and cradle
Larmes de Marie Madeleine	tears of Mary Magdalen
Soupir d'une Reine	sigh of a queen
Echo	echo
Violon | orgueil des mains légères	Violin pride of agile hands
Départ à cheval sur les eaux	departure on horseback on the water

Amour chevauchant le mystère	love astride mystery
Voleur en prière	thief at prayer
Oiseau	bird
Violon femme morganatique	violin morganatic woman
Chat botté courant la forêt	puss-in-boots ranging the forest
Puit des vérités lunatiques	well of insane truths
Confession publique	public confession
Corset	corset
Violon alcool de l'âme en peine	violin alcohol of the troubled soul
Préférence muscle du soir	preference muscle of the evening
Épaules des saisons soudaines	shoulder of sudden seasons
Feuille de chêne	leaf of the oak
Miroir	mirror
Violon chevalier du silence	violin knight of silence
Jouet | évadé du bonheur	plaything escaped from happiness
Poitrine des mille présences	bosom of a thousand presences
Bateau de plaisance	boat of pleasure
Chasseur.	hunter.

(In the literary edition this poem has the title *Métamorphoses*, which has become the title of the collection of three songs. Louise de Vilmorin suggested *Paganini* as a title for the last of the three, which effectively expresses its virtuosity.)

This song is not a good end to the group. 'It is a "bridging" song,' says Poulenc. Whenever possible it should be followed by a song in a slow tempo which it will show to advantage. It is merely a piece of virtuosity for the singer and the pianist: the poem itself is a kaleidoscope of images, of 'métamorphoses' suggested to the poet by a violin.

The tempo ♩.= 100 must be inflexible from beginning to end. There are few changes of dynamics; even the *pp* on 'Puit des vérités lunatiques . . .' should be relative, especially in this low *tessitura*. The diction must of course be very incisive, but even so it is difficult to make all the words understood. The pianist should take careful account of the directions for performance.

*

In 1949, the singer, Doda Conrad, who is of Polish origin, asked six composers from among his friends to compose a work in homage to the memory of Frederic Chopin, to celebrate the hundredth anniversary of his death. Auric, Français, Milhaud, Poulenc, Preger and Sauguet each wrote a song for bass voice on poems by Louise de Vilmorin, united under the title, *Mouvements du cœur* (The heart's impulse). The song which Poulenc composed is *Mazurka*.

MAZURKA

Les bijoux | ause poitrines,
Les soleils | aux plafonds,
Les robes ⁀opalines,
Miroirs ⁀et violons,

Font ⁀ainsi, font, font, font,

Des mains tomber l'aiguille,
L'aiguille de raison,
Des mains de jeunes filles
Qui s'envolent | et font,

Font ⁀ainsi, font, font, font,

D'un regard qui s'appuie,
D'une ride à leur front,
Le beau temps | ou la pluie.
Et d'un soupir larron,

Font ⁀ainsi, font, font, font,

Du bal une tourmente √
Où sage et vagabond,
D'entendre l'inconstante,
Dire oui, dire non,

Font ⁀ainsi, font, font, font,

Danser l'incertitude
Dont les pas compteront.
Oh! le doux pas des prudes,
Leurs silences profonds,

Font ⁀ainsi, font, font, font,

Du bal une contrée
Où les feux s'uniront.

MAZURKA

The jewels on the breasts,
the suns on the ceiling,
the opaline gowns,
mirrors and violins.

Make thus, make, make, make,

Hands let fall the needle,
the needle of reason,
from hands of young girls
that fly past and make,

Make thus, make, make, make,

Of a stare that is fixed,
of a wrinkle on the brow,
fine weather or rain.
And of a thievish sigh,

Make thus, make, make, make,

A tempest of the ball
where the wise and the flighty,
hear the fickle one,
say yes, say no,

Make thus, make, make, make,

The uncertainty dance
of which the steps will count.
Oh! the soft steps of the prudes,
their profound silences,

Make thus, make, make, make,

A country of the ball
where fires will unite.

Des amours rencontrées	From encountered loves
Ainsi la neige fond.	thus the snow melts.
La neige fond, fond, fond.	The snow melts, melts, melts.

Mazurka moves rather slowly and evokes the pensive mood of young girls at a ball. Poulenc wrote of it to Louise de Vilmorin as follows:

> My sweet Louise, do you know that you have added considerably to the white hairs of your old musician? I thought I should never find the knack of putting to music all your *Font, font, font* and then all at once it came and I like my mazurka very much. The atmosphere is of a ball as in *The Grand Meaulnes**—quite *piano*, melancholy and sensuous. I hope you will be pleased with it. I have not allowed myself any cheating: all the 'font' are there.

As always, Louise de Vilmorin plays with words and rhymes. There is no metronome indication at the beginning, but ♩ = 66 seems good. The *pp* and the recommendation *irréal* (unreal) suggests for the piano introduction a distant sound like a memory, with which the voice should be in accord. The first six bars are *p*, then there is a *mf* for four bars. (The word 'violons' is badly printed under the music; there should be an F♯ on 'vi', an A on 'o'— without the alteration, the line lacks a foot.) After a return of four bars to *p*, 'Des mains . . .' etc should be *mf* and *f* with a nice *diminuendo molto* on the G of 'font', to return to *p*. The dynamics indicated should be made, with the piano, on the lines, 'D'une ride à leur front Le beau temps ou la pluie'. All the following section should be *mf* or *f*, except for the echo effect, 'Dire oui' *mf* and 'dire non' *p*. But an enchanting *pp très doux et très tendre* (very soft and tender), and very well phrased, should be effected on 'Oh le doux pas des prudes Leurs silences profonds'. Resume the dynamics *mf* and *f* before again *p* on 'Des amours rencontrées', but it is good to return once more to *mf* on 'Ainsi la neige fond' and continue *mf* to the end of the voice part.

The coda for the piano must succeed in achieving beautiful effects of sonority, growing more and more *p*, but with no *ritenuto*.

---

* *Le Grand Meaulnes* is the only work of Alain-Fournier, a young writer killed in 1914 in the First World War. It is a real masterpiece, a very poetic novel which seems to be written in a 'waking dream'.

CHAPTER VII

Max Jacob

Max Jacob, poet and novelist, was born at Quimper in 1876. After his arrival in Paris in 1901, he became a friend of Picasso and of Apollinaire. From 1911 onwards he published *La Côte, Les œuvres burlesque et mystique de Frère Matorel*, and the modern prose poem entitled *Le Cornet à dés* (1917), which is a masterpiece.

In 1909 he had a vision of Christ, but he was not baptized into the Christian Church until 1915. Among other works, he published *La Phanérogame* (1918), *Cinématome* (1920) and *Le Laboratoire central* (1921). He then decided to retire close to the monastery of St Benoit-sur-Loire, wishing to 'draw closer to God'. There he divided his time between the exercise of piety and his literary work. Later he published, among other works, *Le cabinet noir* (1922), *Les pénitents en maillots roses* (1925) and *Rivage* (1931).

The war and the German occupation compelled him to be silent, for being born a Jew he could publish nothing at that time. In the end he was arrested by the Gestapo at St Benoit-sur-Loire on the 24th of February 1944, and was taken to the concentration camp at Drancy, where, a few days later, he died.

Andre Billy,* faithful friend of Max Jacob, wrote: 'After *Le cornet à dés*, his thought, his influence, prevailed under the vague name of surrealism, launched by Apollinaire and taken up in a more definite sense by the poets of the subconscious. Max Jacob may be called a great poet if poetry is, before all else, caprice, fantasy, word play and contiguity of mental images; but, pen in hand, he is little of a musician. He does not know the secret of verbal melody, whereas Apollinaire considers it to be of the greatest importance. This factor points the difference between two poets who have often been compared, and about whom research is confused without being able to show if the one had any influence over the other beyond a natural stimulation born of their community of ideas. . . .

'I would like to point out the resemblance which is apparent to me between Max Jacob and Satie, who was likewise a humorist and a mystic, and likewise used parody abundantly. What does Max owe to Satie? What does Dada and its followers owe to Satie through Max? Characteristics common to them all are mockery of derision, of

* André Billy (1882–1924), novelist and biographer, was a close friend of many important writers.

languor, of melancholy, of plaintiveness, of seriousness, and of extreme subtlety. Apollinaire also introduced drollery and gaiety into poetry.'

Max Jacob was a talented painter, in particular of water colours and gouaches. In a letter addressed to Poulenc, September 29th 1922, he writes: 'Painting makes progress too. I am beginning, somewhat late, to become a real painter. . . . Horrible! Something between Corot and Monet—not modest. I am not to blame.'

*   *   *

POULENC CERTAINLY KNEW Max Jacob as early as 1920, to which the following dedication on a copy of *La défense de Tartufe* bears witness: 'This book, a picture of my old heart, to Poulenc, in giving him the real heart.'

It was, however, not until 1931 that Poulenc set to music:

CINQ POÈMES DE MAX JACOB
(Songs from Brittany)

These five poems were chosen from the collection *Chants Bretons* signed Morven le Gaëlique. This is the pseudonym which Max Jacob used when he was 'thinking as a Breton', as Julien Lanoë said, and added:

It is poetry incarnate: monologues, dialogues, songs, which conserve all the inflexions of the human voice, the turn of mind alive and picturesque of the Bretons of Lower Brittany. It was not only a sentimental attachment that bound his thought to these childhood memories, but the conviction that he was drinking at the source of true lyricism.

Towards the end of his life, did not Max Jacob say: 'the pure state of lyricism is found in folk songs and children's stories. . . .' Here is part of a letter of December 1st 1931:

Dear Poulenc, you know that I am truly flattered to have inspired you. This is completely sincere and not said to be polite. Yes, call No V: Souric et Mouric.* I authorize all that your precious fancy dictates, O Master. My sole title to fame will be for my name to appear beside yours.

* In the literary edition the title is 'Chanson'.

In these poems the poet is obviously recalling his childhood in Brittany. An artless, simple-minded little peasant girl sings of her trials and troubles, with sudden poetic moments that Poulenc has brought out admirably. He very much liked these songs, he preferred them to some others that are better known and more often sung. It is true that they are difficult both in their letter and in their spirit, both in performance and in interpretation. I shall, as usual, consider the musical performance in detail, but it is important from the outset to recommend to singers when they interpret these songs not to give the impression of being 'vocalists'. To say so is rather extreme! At the same time this music must be very much sung, for there can be no question of 'speaking' these poems with intelligence and wit; vocal difficulties are not lacking: of *tessitura*, of wide intervals, of rhythms, which must be victoriously surmounted. Since the beginning of this book I have many times insisted on the necessity of 'going far enough but not too far' which is indispensable for the interpretation of certain songs of Poulenc, to give them all their character. For these songs, in order to suggest the little peasant girl, a timbre of voice that is a little childlike and simple should be used, without carrying it too far. The important point is to create a character that is truly touching.

1 CHANSON BRETONNE

J'ai perdu ma poulette
et j'ai perdu mon chat
Je cours à la poudrette
si Dieu me les rendra.

Je vais chez Jean le Coz
et chez Marie Maria.
Va-t'en voir chez Hérode
Peut-être il le saura.

Passant devant la salle
toute la ville était là
à voir danser ma poule
avec mon petit chat.

Tous les oiseaux champêtres
sur les murs | et sur les toits
jouaient de la trompette
pour le banquet du roi.

1 SONG FROM BRITTANY

I have lost my little chicken
and I have lost my cat
I run to the dust hole
if God will give them back to me.

I'll go and see Jean le Coz
and Marie Maria.
Go and see Herode
perhaps he will know.

Passing by the hall
all the town was there
to watch my chicken dancing
with my little cat.

All the birds of the countryside
on the walls and on the roofs
played the trumpet
for the king's banquet.

'This song,' says Poulenc, 'is very difficult to interpret. The scene is the market-place of Guidel, in Brittany,* one summer morning. A peasant girl recounts in a simple way her misfortunes. The last page becomes abruptly poetic and unreal. Birds sing by the wayside.'

The two parts of the song are, in fact, greatly contrasted, but the indicated tempo ♩ = 138 must remain unchanged. The first part should be *non legato*, precisely in order to bring out the *legato* effect *la voix très blanche* (the voice very white) on 'Tous les oiseaux du monde sur les murs et sur les toits', which must not sound sad, but very fresh and full of wonder. (No liaison with the plural of 'murs'—it would be far too refined.) The dynamics of the piano part begin *p* under the word 'chat' and should be maintained despite the indication *mf* which is not good. The attack *mf* is *subito* with the singer, 'Jouaient de la trompette Pour le banquet du Roi', which is again *non legato* and very gay. No *ritenuto* at all on the *mf* coda of the piano.

2 CIMETIÈRE

Si mon marin vous le chassez
au cimetière vous me mettrez,
rose blanche, rose blanche et rose rouge,

Ma tombe, elle est comme un jardin,
comme un jardin rouge et blanche,

Le dimanche vous irez, rose blanche,
vous irez vous promener,
rose blanche et blanc muguet,

Tante Yvonne à la Toussaint
une couronne en fer peint|
elle apporte de son jardin
en fer peint | avec des perles de satin,
rose blanche et blanc muguet.

Si Dieu veut me ressusciter
au Paradis je monterai, rose blanche,
avec un nimbe doré,
rose blanche et blanc muguet.

2 CEMETERY

If you drive my sailor away
you will put me in the cemetery,
white rose, white rose and red rose,

My tomb, it is like a garden,
like a garden red and white,

On Sundays you will go, white rose,
you will go to take a walk,
white rose and white lily,

Aunt Yvonne on All Saints' Day*
a wreath of painted iron
she will bring from her garden
of painted iron with satin pearls,
white rose and white lily.

If God raises me up
I will go to Paradise, white rose,
with a golden halo,
white rose and white lily.

* It is customary in France to visit the cemeteries on All Saints' Day.

* The Jean de Polignacs had their summer home here.

Si mon marin revenait,	If my sailor should return,
rose rouge et rose blanche,	red rose and white rose,
sur ma tombe il vient auprès,	he will come near to my tomb,
rose blanche et blanc muguet.	white rose and white lily.
Souviens-toi de notre enfance, rose	Do you remember our childhood,
blanche,	white rose,
quand nous jouions sur le quai,	when we played on the quay,
rose blanche et blanc muguet.	white rose and white lily.

' "Cimetière",' says Poulenc, 'has the atmosphere of the artificial wreaths of pearls that can be bought at the grocer. The whole is a little like a colour-print. Sing it quite straight.'

Circular wreaths of painted iron, and decorated with satin and pearls, are still seen in small and remote village cemeteries in France.

The tempo *sans lenteur* (not slow) ♩ = 52 is good and the gentle swing of the 6/8 time should be made apparent, which will emphasize the character of a 'plaint'. Each time the little refrain recurs, 'Rose blanche . . .', I think it should be given a certain monotony by placing it (discreetly) in expressive parenthesis. Of the dynamics, the only real *p* begins on 'Souviens-toi de notre enfance' and continues to the end.

The whole song should be sung *molto legato*. (It is not necessary to observe the semi-quaver (1/16) rest in the fourth bar of the voice part.) The most difficult part begins with the line, 'Le dimanche vous irez'. This bar is *mf*, observing the accents. The following bar is *mf* and *legato* for voice and piano. The same effect on the two following bars, with the same accents, and to preserve the *legato*, the semi-quaver (1/16) rest should be omitted—'blanche-et' being linked. The following lines which are not easy to make understood must be clearly articulated. (Of course no liaison between 'peint' and 'elle.) An innocent simplicity must permeate the song which in the second part, from 'Si Dieu veut me ressusciter', is brightened with hope. The refrain that follows should be *mf* in order to reserve the *p* for the repeat of the theme, 'Si mon marin . . .'.

3 LA PETITE SERVANTE   3 THE LITTLE SERVANT

Préservez-nous du feu et du tonnerre,	Keep us safe from fire and thunder,
Le tonnerre court comme un oiseau,	thunder runs like a bird,
Si c'est le Seigneur qui le conduit	if the Lord sends it
Bénis soient les dégats.	blessed be the havoc.
Si c'est le diable qui le conduit	If the devil sends it
Faites-le partir au trot d'ici.	drive it away quickly.

Préservez-nous des dartres_et des boutons
De la peste et de la lèpre.
Si c'est pour ma pénitence que vous l'envoyez,
Seigneur, laissez-la moi, merci.
Si c'est le diable que le conduit
Faites-le partir au trot d'ici.

Keep us from scabs and pimples
from the plague and leprosy.
If you send it to make me penitent,
Lord, let it be, thank you.
If the devil sends it
drive it away quickly.

Goître, goître, sors de ton sac,
Sors de mon cou et de ma tête!
Feu Saint Elme, danse de Saint Guy,
Si c'est le diable qui vous conduit,
Mon Dieu, faites-le sortir d'ici.

Goitre, goitre, out of your pouch,
out of my neck and my head!
St Elmo's Fire, St Vitus's Dance,
if the devil sends you,
dear God, drive him out of here.

Faites que je grandisse vite
Et donnez-moi un bon mari,
Qui ne soit pas trop_ivrogne
Et qui ne me batte pas tous les soirs.

Let me grow up quickly
and give me a good husband,
who is not too much of a drunkard
and will not beat me every evening.

'"*La petite servante*",,' says Poulenc, 'is directly inspired by Moussorgsky. The description of the dreaded maladies must be pronounced strictly and nervously. The end well "bowed".'

This song is difficult and demands very incisive articulation. The indicated tempo is perfect, $\daleth$ = 152. Despite the rapidity of the piano part, the pianist must take care not to drown the singer. From the first verse the singer must make a contrast between the calamities that come from God and those that come from the devil *furioso*. This must be achieved by the diction and the expression, since there is scarcely any change of dynamics. But the line, 'Bénis soient les dégats', can be more *legato*.

It is essential to keep strict time, becoming gradually quicker, as indicated. The second verse is therefore still faster than the first. The indication *amorphe* (toneless) is marvellous for the two first bars of this section, but from the third bar begin to *sing* again as much as possible, and on the whole more *f*, given the piano part as it is. Then a contrast: Poulenc has indicated *sec* (dry), he could have added again *furioso ff*, with as strong articulation as possible. This section, up to the end of the verse, is very difficult. It must again speed up little by little without any *rallentando* at all and above all no *diminuendo*, despite the indication, because of the descent of the voice into the lower register. Considerable relaxation is needed for the last verse: the tempo *plus calme et sans lenteur* (calmer and not slow) must be about $\downarrow$ = 88/92, with, as Poulenc directs, *L'archet à la corde* (well bowed), *mf*, and with the feeling of a very humble prayer.

4 BERCEUSE

Ton père est à la messe,
Ta mère au cabaret,
Tu auras sur les fesses
Si tu vas | encore crier.

Ma mère était pauvresse
Sur la lande à Auray
Et moi je fais des crêpes |
En te berçant du pied.

Si tu mourais du croup
Coliques | ou diarrhées,
Si tu mourais des croutes
Que tu as sur le nez.

Je pêcherais des crevettes
A l'heure de la marée,
Pour faire la soupe aux têtes
Y a pas besoin de crochets.

4 CRADLE SONG

Your father is at mass,
your mother at the cabaret,
you will get your bottom spanked
if you go on crying.

My mother was a beggar woman
on the moor at Auray
and I am making pancakes
while I rock you with my foot.

If you should die of croup
colic or diarrhoea,
if you should die of the scabs
that you have on your nose.

I should go shrimping
at low tide,
to make soup of the heads
there is no need for hooks.

Poulenc's commentary is excellent: 'Everything is topsy-turvy in the poem: the father is at mass, the mother at a cabaret, a waltz rhythm instead of a cradle song. It is redolent of cider and the acrid smell of the thatched cottages.' In the absence of the parents, the poor little girl of Brittany must, while making pancakes, rock a baby whom she detests. She would much rather go shrimping, even the heads make good soup.

The waltz movement, ♩· = 76, is the maximum of speed but indicates that it must not be allowed to drag. The first beat must be well marked. (No liaison 'tu vas encore'). More *legato* and *mp* on 'Ma mère était pauvresse sur la lande à Auray'. Always *legato* but *f*, 'Et moi je fais des crêpes en te bercant du pied'. Then *poco a poco animato* and *crescendo* begins, filled with hate. I am of the opinion that it is best to return to the *tempo primo* on 'Je pêcherais des crevettes' for the whole conclusion, *p et mélancolique* (soft and melancholy), without, of course, any *ritenuto* at the end.

5 SOURIC ET MOURIC

Souric et Mouric
rat blanc, souris noire,
venus dans l'armoire
pour apprendre à l'araignée

5 SOURIC AND MOURIC

Souric and Mouric
white rat, black mouse,
have come into the cupboard
to teach the spider

à tisser sur le métier	to weave on the loom
un beau drap de toile.	a beautiful linen cloth.
Expédiez-le à Paris, à Quimper,	Send it off to Paris, to Quimper,
à Nantes,	to Nantes,
c'est de bonne vente!	it will sell well!
Mettez les sous de côté,	Put the coins aside,
vous achèterez un pré,	you will buy a meadow,
des pommiers pour la saison	some apple trees for the season
et trois belles vaches,	and three fine cows,
un bœuf pour faire étalon.	a bull for stud.
Chantez, les rainettes,	Sing, tree-frogs,
car voici la nuit qui vient,	for night is falling,
la nuit | on les entend bien,	at night you hear them well,
crapauds et grenouilles,	toads and frogs,
écoutez mon merle	listen my blackbird
et ma pie qui parle,	and my magpie who talks,
écoutez toute la journée,	listen all day long,
vous apprendrez | à chanter.	you will learn to sing.

Poulenc's own words are as follows: 'It begins with very rapid delivery, throughout in the style of a counting song (am, stram, gram). If there is not a slight quickening, with suppleness, on the words, 'des pommiers pour la saison', the linking with the conclusion of the song will not come without a shock, and *there must be no shock here*. I confess my predilection for the last two pages which give, I believe, a true impression of night. I composed this at Nogent where I had come to pass two months in 1931 in the house of my childhood, quite empty but full of memories. I cannot play this song without thinking of my dog Mickey, lying under the piano.'

This again is a very difficult song from both the musical and the vocal points of view. I find the indicated tempo, ♩ = 116 a little too fast and can scarcely be achieved on the first page, but it should be approached as nearly as possible. At all events, take care over the rhythmic precision and articulation. But the *tempo primo* is quite attainable from the second page. When Poulenc speaks of quickening the pace on the words, 'des pommiers pour la saison', it is because all singers, in singing a sudden *legato* and *subito p*, which is essential, invariably have the tendency to slow down in tempo. If, in fact, the tempo is strictly maintained it will be exactly right. After the slackening of speed (not too much) of the three bars for the piano which introduce the poetic climate, the *tempo primo* should be resumed, and there also, it seems to me, the maximum of speed. In any case it is best to think in two beats (2/2). The beginning of the conclusion is *mf*, the *p* commencing only with the words, 'écoutez toute la journée', the voice very floating, and above all without *crescendo* up to the end—quite difficult to achieve. A perfect *legato* will help to give this 'impression of night' for which Poulenc asks.

The coda for piano is wholly in *diminuendo*, with the effect of an echo, and without *ritenuto*.

*

In 1932 Poulenc wrote a secular cantata, *Le Bal Masqué* (The Masked Ball), for baritone and chamber orchestra, using four poems by Max Jacob drawn from the collection, *Le Laboratoire central*. Again, choosing two more poems from this collection, he composed two further songs in 1954. The dedication of 1921 in Poulenc's copy of *Le Laboratoire central* reads, 'Here are some flowers, some leaves to scribble. Hurry up.' Max Jacob had to wait 33 years. . . .

PARISIANA

'At the time when I was writing *Le Bal Masqué*,' wrote Poulenc, 'I had thought of introducing into this cantata the poem by Max Jacob, "Jouer du bugle", but I had to give up the idea. Coupled with the absurd "Vous n'écrivez plus", so typically Max Jacob, I gave it, in 1954, the over-all title of *Parisiana* which places them both in the ambience of the streets of Paris.'

I have often spoken of Poulenc's love of Paris. At heart he detested the country and when he was in his house in Touraine, he never left his beautiful terrace with its formal garden in the French style which he had designed himself. A walk in the country gave him the blues. He called Paris 'my town', and I have already quoted his phrase: 'Where Paris is concerned I am often moved to tears and to music.'

JOUER DU BUGLE

Les trois dames qui jouaient du bugle
Tard dans leur salle de bain,
Ont pour maître un certain mufle
Qui n'est là que le matin.

L'enfant blond qui prend des crabes
Des crabes avec la main
Ne dit pas une syllabe
C'est un fils adultérin.

PLAYING THE CORNET

The three ladies who played the cornet
late in their bathroom,
have for master a certain scoundrel
who is there only in the morning.

The blond child who takes some crabs
some crabs with his hand
does not speak a syllable
he is a bastard son.

Trois mères pour cet enfant chauve
Une seule suffisait bien.
Le père est nabab mais pauvre
Il le traite comme un chien.

(SIGNATURE)

Cœur des muses, tu m'aveugles,
C'est moi qu'on voit jouer du
    bugle,
Au pont d'Iéna, le dimanche,
Un écriteau sur la manche.

Three mothers for this bald child
one alone would be quite enough.
The father is nabob but poor
he treats him like a dog.

(SIGNATURE)

Heart of the muses, you blind me,
it is I myself who am seen playing the
    cornet,
by the Pont d'Iéna, of a Sunday,
a placard on my sleeve.

This preposterous poem must, Poulenc explicitly insists, be sung as usual 'without irony' but on the contrary 'very poetically', which is less easy. The irony will of itself be apparent. It must be admitted that the sense and the music of the poem, for the first three stanzas, justify André Billy's assertion that contrary to Apollinaire, Max Jacob is no musician pen in hand, a fact which does not aid interpreters in creating a poetic climate. I think, therefore, that these first three stanzas should be sung without dryness and in a tone of absolute objectivity, being careful to make every word of the unforeseeable text understood (which is not always easy: 'nabab mais pauvre'), while observing carefully the only two dynamic indications, and the short value of certain final notes of phrases. Respect the rests and remain exactly *a tempo*: *Au pas* ♩ = 72, *sans broncher jusqu'à la fin* (with an unflinching step to the end). After this there is a change. Poulenc, in three bars for the piano, introduces a delightful melodic theme which creates a totally different atmosphere for the fourth quatrain, which, in the literary text, is preceded by the word 'signature'.

It is in fact, as at the end of a ballad, a kind of *envoi* to the 'Cœur des muses', which incites the interpreters to sudden poetic nostalgia, *p très doux* (molto dolce). The *mf crescendo molto f* on 'C'est moi qu'on voit jouer du bugle' is important, not only expressively but also to highlight the *pp subito très mélancolique* of the last two lines. The poet imagines himself playing the cornet (like the 'three ladies'), to earn a few sous at the foot of the Eiffel Tower, thanks to the Sunday visitors. A touch of Parisian slang is not out of place on these last two lines (a little stress on 'di' of 'dimanche'), but take care! Without vulgarity! It is always the poetry that must be brought out, and here, a humble melancholy.

VOUS N'ÉCRIVEZ PLUS?

M'as-tu connu marchand d'journaux
A Barbès et sous l'métro
Pour insister vers l'Institut
Il me faudrait de la vertu,
Mes romans n'ont ni rang ni ronds
Et je n'ai pas de caractère.

M'as-tu connu marchand d'marrons
Au coin de la rue Coquillière,
Tablier rendu, l'autre est vert.

M'as-tu connu marchand d'tickets,
Balayeur de double V.C.
Je le dis sans fiel ni malice
Aide à la foire au pain d'épice,
Défenseur au Juge de paix,
Officier, comme on dit | office
Au Richelieu et à la Paix.

YOU DO NOT WRITE ANY LONGER

Did you know me newspaper-seller
at Barbès and under the metro
to persist concerning the Institute
I would have needed courage,
my novels have neither top nor tale
and I have no character.

Did you know me chestnut-seller
at the corner of the rue Coquillière,
I gave my apron back,* the other is
    green.

Did you know me ticket-seller,
latrine-cleaner.
I say it without bitterness or spite
assistant at the gingerbread fair,
defender at the police court,
officer, as it is called office
at Le Richelieu and La Paix.

* I left the job.

The indicated tempo, *A fond de train* (at top speed) ♩ = 176, is practically impossible, and if ♩ = 152 can be managed, it is well enough. At all events the tempo must be implacable. The most important point is, of course, to make every word of this absurd poem understood. There are no indications of dynamics to observe, and the *f* is imperative, except for a *p*, very relative, on 'Défenseur au Juge de paix'.

In this song, too, there can be a slight accent of Parisian slang, and for this I would recommend the following stresses: 'M'as-tu connu marchand d'journaux à Barbès et sous l'métro', 'M'as-tu connu marchand d'marrons', M'as-tu connu marchand d'tickets'. But, once more, take care! This slight accent of the streets must be done with tact and perfect taste. I hope that all I have said on this subject in the chapter devoted to general remarks on the interpretation of Poulenc's songs, and also in the introduction to the songs of Apollinaire, will again be consulted.

On the line, 'Mes romans n'ont ni rang ni ronds', it is not necessary to observe the indicated rest, the pedal on C continues in any case during the whole second half of the bar. For the line, 'Au coin de la rue Coquillière', a big contrast of *legato* is demanded. On the words 'comme on dit office' it is preferable not to make the normal liaison 'dit office' to bring out the joke of the word, 'office', because it refers most certainly to the pantry by the side of the kitchen, where the imagined character rinses out the glasses in one of those two big Parisian cafés *Le Richelieu* and *La Paix*.

I would point out to pianists that although in this song Poulenc indicates *sans pédale* (without pedal), he never played dryly, except when specifically marked, as here, in the introductory bars. In actual fact he always used a little pedal. Apart from the two bars in this song where pedal is indicated, there are several other bars where pianists must use pedal with discretion. Please turn again to the chapter devoted to general remarks on interpretation.

CHAPTER VIII

Maurice Carême

Maurice Carême was born in 1899, at Wavre, in Belgium. He studied at the Teachers' Training College at Tirlemont and took up his first and only teaching post at Anderlecht, near Brussels, a post which he left at the age of 43 to devote his entire time to literature. He has been called 'the poet of joy', the poet of peace', 'the poet of children'. Among the numerous collections of his poems are *La Lanterne magique*, *Mère*, *La cage aux grillons*, *Volière*, *Le Voleur d'étincelles* and *Brabant*. His poems have often been set to music.

*　　　*　　　*

'ON THE CHARMING poems of Maurice Carême, half-way between Francis Jammes and Max Jacob, I have composed seven short songs for Denise Duval* or, more precisely, for Denise Duval to sing to her small son aged six. These melancholy and impish sketches are without pretension. They should be sung with tenderness. That is the most certain way to touch a child's heart.' The songs of which Poulenc speaks in this way are the last he composed. They are dated 1960. After this he was no longer interested in this musical form, and he died two years later. The charming poems are not of the type to inspire great lyrical songs, but these, be they witty or poetic, are a success within their modest pretensions. The most 'impish' of the poems were chosen from *La cage aux grillons* ('Le sommeil', 'Quelle aventure!', 'Ba, be, bi, bo, bu', 'Le carafon'); the most melancholy are from *Le Voleur d'étincelles* ('La reine de cœur', 'Les anges musiciens', 'Lune d'Avril'). Just as Poulenc had often asked of Eluard, he asked Maurice Carême to give him a collective title for these songs. It was:

LA COURTE PAILLE (THE SHORT STRAW)

1 LE SOMMEIL

Le sommeil est en voyage,
Mon Dieu! où est-il parti?

1 SLEEP

Sleep has gone off on a journey,
Gracious me! Where can it have got to?

---

* Denise Duval was the distinguished interpreter and creator of leading rôles in Poulenc's operas.

J'ai beau bercer mon petit,
Il pleure dans son lit-cage,
Il pleure depuis midi.

Où le sommeil a-t'il mis
Son sable et ses rêves sages?
J'ai beau bercer mon petit,
il se tourne tout en nage,
Il sanglote dans son lit.

Ah! reviens, reviens, sommeil,
Sur ton beau cheval de course!
Dans le ciel noir, la Grande Ourse
A enterré le soleil
Et rallumé ses abeilles.

Si l'enfant ne dort pas bien,
Il ne dira pas bonjour,
Il ne dira rien demain
A ses doigts, au lait, au pain
Qui l'accueillent dans le jour.

I have rocked my little one in vain,
he is crying in his cot,
he has been crying ever since noon.

Where has sleep put
its sand and its gentle dreams?
I have rocked my little one in vain,
he tosses and turns perspiring,
he sobs in his bed.

Ah! Come back, come back, sleep,
on your fine race-horse!
In the dark sky, the Great Bear
has buried the sun
and rekindled his bees.

If baby does not sleep well
he will not say good day,
he will have nothing to say
to his fingers, to the milk, to the bread
that greet him in the morning.

A little song that does not demand great subtlety of interpretation but, rather great simplicity, and all the tenderness (a little anxious) of the young mother who does not know how to get her baby to sleep. The tempo, ♩=48, seems very good, and the dynamics are clearly indicated. To break the monotony of taking a breath before each bar line, there can be a breath between 'Dans le ciel noir' and 'la Grande Ourse A enterré le soleil'. Observe carefully the value of all the rests wherever they are seen, and breathe before the bar in 3/4, with a very slight *ritenuto* to highlight the modulation to the final chord in the major.

2 QUELLE AVENTURE!

2 WHAT GOINGS-ON!

Une puce, dans sa voiture,
Tirait un petit éléphant
En regardant les devantures |
Où scintillaient les diamants.

—Mon Dieu! mon Dieu! quelle
  aventure!
Qui va me croire, s'il m'entend?

A flea, in its carriage,
was pulling a little elephant along
gazing at the shop windows
where diamonds were sparkling.

— Good gracious! Good gracious!
  what goings-on!
who will believe me if I tell them?

L'éléphanteau, d'un air absent,
Suçait un pot de confiture.
Mais la puce n'en avait cure,
Elle tirait en souriant.

—Mon Dieu! mon Dieu! que cela
    dure
Et je vais me croire dément!

Soudain, le long d'une clôture,
La puce fondit dans le vent
Et je vis le jeune éléphant
Se sauver | en fendant les murs.

—Mon Dieu! mon Dieu! la chose est
    sûre,
Mais comment la dire à maman?

The little elephant was absent mindedly
sucking a pot of jam.
But the flea took no notice,
and went on pulling with a smile.

— Good gracious! Good gracious! if
    this goes on
I shall really think I am mad!

Suddenly, along by a fence,
the flea disappeared in the wind
and I saw the young elephant
make off, breaking through the walls.

— Good gracious! Good gracious! it is
    perfectly true,
but how shall I tell Mummy?

(In the literary edition the title of the poem is 'The flea and the elephant'.)
First of all I will point out two misprints in the musical edition: in the
second and fourth bar of the song, on the first beat, the rhythm should be,
one quaver (1/8) followed by two semiquavers (1/16).

Despite the rapidity of the tempo, ♩= 138, it is of course essential to make
all the words of this little poem understood. This understanding will be
greatly aided by making the contrasts of dynamics very clear, and also the
variation between phrases that are rhythmic and those that are melodic.
Care should be taken over the short value (quaver (1/8)) of the last note of
many of the phrases: 'éléphant', 'diamants', 'm'entend', 'souriant',
'dément', and particularly 'dans le vent'. All the early part is *f* and rhythmic,
with a sudden *legato* on 'où scintillaient les diamants.' The refrain, each time
it appears, is *ff*: 'Mon Dieu! Mon Dieu! quelle aventure', with a *crescendo* on
the dotted crotchets (1/4) of the high F, to give the effect of a mark of
exclamation! 'L'éléphanteau d'un air absent . . .' is *p subito* and *molto legato*.
The feeling that should be expressed on these two lines is 'd'un air
absent . . .'. Again *f* (not *mf*), and *non legato* on 'Mais la puce n'en avait
cure'. After the refrain, *ff*, return to *p subito* and *legato* on 'Soudain le long
d'une clôture . . .'. The idea which predominates in these two lines is
'fondit dans le vent . . .' (note the very short quaver at the end of the last
word). Then again *f* and *legato* up to the refrain *ff*.

Poulenc has indicated *surtout sans ralentir* (above all no *ritenuto*), but in
reality, to obtain the desired effect, it is better to accelerate these last three
bars. (Twelve bars before the end, in the piano part the G is G♮♭.)

3 LA REINE DE CŒUR   3 THE QUEEN OF HEARTS

Mollement accoudée   Gently leaning on her elbow
A ses vitres de lune,   at her moon windows,
La reine vous salue   the queen waves to you
D'une fleur d'amandier.   with a flower of the almond tree.

C'est la reine de cœur,   She is the queen of hearts,
Elle peut, s'il lui plait,   she can, if she wishes,
Vous mener en secret   lead you in secret
Vers d'étranges demeures.   to strange dwellings.

Où il n'est plus de portes,   Where there are no more doors,
De salles ni de tours   no rooms nor towers
Et | où les jeunes mortes   and where the young who are dead
Viennent parler d'amour.   come to speak of love.

La reine vous salue,   The queen waves to you,
Hâtez-vous de la suivre   hasten to follow her
Dans son château de givre   into her castle of hoar-frost
Aux doux vitraux de lune.   with the lovely moon windows.

(Poulenc has again changed the title from that in the literary edition which is 'Vitres de lune'.)

There should be a long silence before beginning this song, *pp très calme et languide* (very calm and languid) ♩.= 42, extremely *legato* and well phrased to recreate its exquisitely mysterious and poetic atmosphere. The fifth and sixth bars are *mf* and in *crescendo*, but without hurrying towards the very relative *f*. I admit that I do not fully understand the subtlety of the *mf subito* indicated by Poulenc on the seventh bar. In my opinion the ascending and descending curve of the phrase should not be broken, and can be given a slight *diminuendo* in descending, but without anticipating the *pp* of the two following bars, 'Où il n'est plus de portes De salles ni de tours'; *mf* is sufficient on 'Et où les jeunes mortes Viennent parler d'amour'. It is essential to re-attack strictly in time and *pp*, 'La reine vous salue . . .'. Definitely no *crescendo* towards the top E on 'givre', then a slight slowing down to lead into the conclusion in the major.

4 BA, BE, BI, BO, BU . . .   4 BA, BE, BI, BO, BU . . .

Ba, be, bi, bo, bu, bé!   Ba, be, bi, bo, bu, be!
Le chat | a mis ses bottes,   The cat has put on his boots,
Il va de porte en porte   he goes from door to door
Jouer, danser, chanter.   playing, dancing, singing.

Pou, chou, genou, hibou.

'Tu dois apprendre à lire,
A compter, | à écrire',
Lui crie-t'-on de partout.

Mais rikketikketau,
Le chat de s'esclaffer,
En rentrant | au château:
Il est le Chat botté!

Pou, chou, genou, hibou.*

'You must learn to read,
to count, to write',
they cry to him on all sides.

But rikketikketau
the cat bursts out laughing,
as he goes back to the castle:
he is Puss in Boots!

* Words that form their plural with an x.

This little scherzo of 23 seconds obviously does not demand any subtlety. *Très gai, follement vite*, ♩ = 152; *f* or *ff* rhythmic precision in giving all the accents that are indicated and percussive diction, that does the trick.

5 LES ANGES MUSICIENS

5 THE ANGEL MUSICIANS

Sur les fils de la pluie,
Les anges du jeudi
Jouent longtemps de la harpe.

On the threads of the rain
the Thursday* angels
play all day upon the harp.

Et sous leurs doigts, Mozart
Tinte délicieux,
En gouttes de joie bleue.

And beneath their fingers, Mozart
tinkles deliciously
in drops of blue joy.

Car c'est toujours Mozart
Que reprennent sans fin
Les anges musiciens,

For it is always Mozart
that is repeated endlessly
by the angel musicians,

Qui, | au long du jeudi,
Font chanter sur la harpe
La douceur de la pluie.

Who, all day Thursday,
sing on their harps
the sweetness of the rain.

* Traditionally the school half-day holiday in France.

Again a silence is needed before beginning this poetic song. I feel it should have a timbre of voice that is clearer than 'La reine de cœur', *legato* but with less variation in the phrasing, *tendre* (tender) in place of *languide* (languid), very simple and not too *p*. The indicated tempo is good. To avoid taking a breath before every bar, there can be a breath between 'Et sous leurs doigts' and 'Mozart tinte délicieux'. In my opinion a full *f* is excessive on 'Car c'est toujours Mozart . . .'—a *mf* is sufficient. There is no *ritenuto* at the end.

6 LE CARAFON	6 THE BABY CARAFE
'Pourquoi, se plaignait la carafe,	'Why, complained the carafe,
N'aurais-je pas un carafon?	should I not have a baby carafe?
Au zoo, madame la Girafe	At the zoo, Madame the giraffe
N'a-t-elle pas un girafer?'	has she not a baby giraffe?'
Un sorcier qui passait	A sorcerer who happened to be passing
par là,	by
A cheval sur un phonographe,	astride a phonograph,
Enregistra la belle voix	recorded the lovely soprano voice
De soprano de la carafe	of the carafe
Et la fit entendre à Merlin.	and let Merlin hear it.
'Fort bien, dit celui-ci, fort bien!'	'Very good,' said he, 'very good.'
Il frappa trois fois dans les mains	He clapped his hands three times
Et la dame de la maison	and the lady of the house
Se demande encore pourquoi	still asks herself why
Elle trouva, ce matin-là,	she found that very morning
Un joli petit carafon	a pretty little baby carafe
Blotti tout contre la carafe	nestling close to the carafe
Ainsi qu'au zoo, le girafon	just as in the zoo, the baby giraffe
Pose son cou fragile et long	rests its long fragile neck
Sur le flanc clair de la girafe.	against the pale flank of the giraffe.

The title of this poem is 'La carafe et le carafon' (The carafe and the little carafe) which Poulenc has wisely changed, but this being so, it is all the more necessary to take great care to make all the words understood.

This is the most difficult song of the collection. The preliminary indication is very bad, because if the tempo ♩ = 132 is right, it is certainly not *très vite* (very fast). Therefore it is useless to add unnecessary speed to the articulation, which needs to be exaggerated in the very uncomfortable *tessitura* of the opening lines. All the beginning is *f* or *ff*, but without following the indication *très sec* (staccato) which is good for the piano but not for the voice for, if the words are to be understood, the vowel sounds must be well sustained, short of a legato which is not needed.

On the line, 'enregistra la belle voix de soprano de la carafe', the legato should be exaggerated to the point of parodying a bad opera-singer. This of course without slowing down. 'Et la fit entendre à Merlin' is more *p*. 'Fort bien, dit celui-ci, fort bien!' is almost *parlando*, but well on the notes. 'Il frappa trois fois dans les mains' is *mf* and *marcato*.

Then a sudden contrast, with *p legato* which must express the total stupefaction of 'the lady of the house', followed by four bars in the same spirit, but *mf* and without *diminuendo*, with the last quaver (1/8) on 'ce matin-là' very short. A fresh contrast on 'un joli petit carafon', *pp très doux et très tendre* (very soft and tenderly), which lasts until the end of the song, *surtout sans ralentir* (above all no *ritenuto*).

(Piano part, fourth bar, last page, the low C of the bass is C♯.)

<table>
<tr><td>

7 LUNE D'AVRIL

Lune,
Belle lune, lune d'Avril,
Faites-moi voir en mon dormant
Le pêcher | au cœur de safran,
Le poisson qui rit du grésil,
L'oiseau qui, <u>loi</u>ntain comm<u>e</u> un cor,
Doucement réveille les morts
Et surtout, surtout le pays
Où il fait <u>joie</u>, où il fait <u>clair</u>,
Où soleilleux de primevères,
On <u>a</u> brisé tous les fusils.
Belle lune, lune d'Avril,
Lune.

</td><td>

7 APRIL MOON

Moon
beautiful moon, April moon,
let me see in my sleep
the peach tree with the saffron heart,
the fish who laughs at the sleet,
the bird who, distant as a hunting horn,
gently awakens the dead
and above all, above all, the land
where there is joy, where there is light,
where sunny with primroses,
all the guns have been destroyed.
Beautiful moon, April moon,
Moon.

</td></tr>
</table>

Poulenc asks, this time, for a very long silence before beginning the song, the most beautiful and the most intense of the collection. The poem, too, is more substantial that the others.

Très lent et irréal (very slow and unreal) ♩=48, amply suggests the atmosphere that has to be created for this first invocation to the moon. Care must be taken not to make a *crescendo* in going up to the E♭. The three following bars are much more intense and there must be a return to *pp* on 'L'oiseau qui, lointain comme un cor'. The prosody is so good, the value of the notes and the rests so exactly right, that it is possible to succeed in giving a true impression of '<u>loi</u>ntain' (distance) with the stress that I have indicated. The same expression continues for 'Doucement réveille les morts'. Then a big *crescendo* begins where the voice can use its full power. The words 'joie' and 'clair' should be marked. The *molto diminuendo* reaches a *p* which, instead of the indicated *pp*, should continue on the line, 'On a brisé tous les fusils', which is the culmination of the literary phrase. To help the singer to continue the thought and to unite this line with the preceding one, it is important that the pianist should make no *retard* before attacking in strict time the first beat of the bar in 2/4. Thus, after an expressive breath, the *pp* of the second invocation to the moon is achieved, as in the opening of the song.

At the end, the singer, by his attitude, must take especial care to hold the audience during the long coda for piano. The pianist must not feel himself abandoned.

CHAPTER IX

Maurice Fombeure

Maurice Fombeure was born at Jardres (Vienne) in 1906. His poetry, in the style of the native poets of the countryside, is often close to folk song. The principal collections of his poems are: *La rivière aux ores, Arentelle, Grenier des saisons, Achat petit*; and of his prose works, *Les godillots sont lourds* and *La vie aventureuse de M. de Saint-Amam*.

*   *   *

CHANSONS VILLAGEOISES (VILLAGE SONGS)

RAVEL SAID THAT one of Poulenc's virtues was his ability to invent his own folk songs. Understandably, therefore, he was tempted, in 1942, to set to music six poems by Maurice Fombeure, the rustic traditional character of which would allow him to exploit his gift. Henri Hell rightly said:

The poetry of Fombeure, readily lightened with humour and fantasy, evokes, without the slightest hint of pastiche, the old folk songs of France. It has the same graceful simplicity, the same charm, the same rhythm. And the shrewdness of the peasant emerges in a similar way. Touching, quizzical or grave, gay or sad, these songs hide, beneath their nonchalant aspect, beneath their apparent simplicity, a great deal of art: an art that is skilful, subtle, and delicate.

There is no mistaking that these *Chansons Villageoises*, written in the style of *chansons*, are in reality *mélodies* and extremely difficult. Poulenc writes:

These texts evoke for me the Morvan where I have passed such wonderful summers. It is out of nostalgia for the surroundings of Autun that I have composed this collection. I conceived them as a symphonic song turn* for a heavy baritone.

The original version of these *chansons* is, in fact, with orchestral accompaniment, but the piano arrangement, made by Poulenc himself,

* 'Tour-de-chant symphonique.'

is so well done that they can be sung with piano . ... and a good pianist!

The six poems that Poulenc brought together under the title *Chansons Villageoises* are drawn from a small booklet of verse, *Chansons de la grande hune* (Songs of the maintop)—which may seem surprising since he always expressed horror of the sea! Poulenc ignored the first part of the volume, *Chansons de la grande mer*; and it is from the second part, *Chansons de la petite terre*, that he chose the poems that inspired him.

1 CHANSON DU CLAIR-TAMIS	1 SONG OF THE CLEAR SIEVE
Où le bedeau a passé	Where the beadle has gone by
Dans les papavéracées	among the poppies
Où le bedeau a passé	where the beadle has gone by
Passera le marguillier	the churchwarden will go
Notre vidame est mort	Our lord and master is dead
Les jolis yeux l'ont tué	pretty eyes have killed him
Pleurons son heureux sort	Let us weep for his happy lot
En terre et enterré	in earth and buried
Et la croix de Lorraine	and the cross of Lorraine
Sur son pourpoint doré	on his gilded doublet
Ils l'ont couché dans l'herbe	They have laid him in the grass
Son grand sabre dessous	his great sword under him
Un oiseau dans les branches	A bird in the branches
A crié: 'Coucou'	cried: 'Cuckoo'
C'est demain dimanche	It is Sunday tomorrow
C'est fête chez nous	it is the day of our fair
Au son de la clarinette	To the sound of the clarinet
Le piston par en-dessous	the cornet in the lower part
La piquette, la musette	the local wine, the accordion
Les plus vieux sont les plus saoûls	the old folk are the most tipsy
Grand'mère à cloche-lunettes	Grandma with her spectacles askew
Sur ses jambes de vingt ans	on her twenty-year-old legs
Vienne le printemps mignonne	Let the springtime come my sweet
Vienne le printemps	let springtime come
Où la grenouille a passé	Where the frog has gone by
Sous les renonculacées	down among the buttercups
Où la grenouille a passé	where the frog has gone by
Passera le scarabée.	the beetle will go.

This charming and mocking little poem is completely meaningless. The poet plays joyously with words and the composer in turn amuses himself with his musical skill.

Très gai et très vite (very gay and very fast) ♩=84 is an excellent indication, and the range of dynamics remains between *ff* and *mf*, for even the few indications of *p* must not lose resonance (particularly if the songs are sung with orchestra). But it is very important to make a good contrast between the *staccato* phrases, or rather *non legato* phrases, and those that are *legato*. I would like to remark here, that even when singing *staccato*, singers should take great care to remain long enough on the vowels to give them sufficient sonority to allow the words to be intelligible. It is for this reason that I often prefer the expression, *non legato*.

From the *mf* beginning, the first two lines are *non legato* and the next two *legato*. The five following lines are *f* and *non legato*. Do not pay too much attention to the indication *p subito* at [2] in the voice part, but sing the whole quatrain *legato*. The quaver (1/8) rest is not necessary between 'Ils' and 'l'ont', each 'l' should be clearly pronounced. The quaver rest between 'A' and 'crié' is also unnecessary, but that before 'Coucou' is essential, and this last word is *legato* and ironical. At [4] the *non legato* is resumed *follement gai* (madly gay) and *ff*. The indicated accents must be marked; particularly, 'La piquette, la musette, Les plus vieux . . .'

A good breath, with no loss of tempo whatever, before attacking [5] *mf* and *legato* for two bars, and immediately there is a return to *non legato*. An accent on 'Vienne' both times; observe the rest, strictly in time, before attacking the last four lines. The two last lines not too *p*—the expression here must be to establish an obvious fact.

2 LES GARS QUI VONT A LA FÊTE	2 THE LADS GOING TO THE FAIR
Les gars qui vont à la fête	The lads going to the fair
Ont mis la fleur au chapeau	have stuck a flower in their hats
Pour y boire chopinette	To drink a mug there
Y goûter le vin nouveau	to taste the new wine
Y tirer la carabine	to shoot at the rifle range
Y sucer le berlingot	to suck sweets
Les gars qui vont à la fête	The lads going to the fair
Ont mis la fleur au chapeau	have stuck a flower in their hats

Sont rasés | à la cuiller	They have shaved carefully
Sont <u>raclés</u> dessous la peau	have scraped to the under skin
Ont passé la blouse neuve	have put on the new smock
Le faux-col en cellulo	the celluloid collar
Les ga<i>ss</i> qui vont‿à la fête	The lads going to the fair
Ont mis la fleur au chapeau	have stuck a flower in their hats
Y faire danser les filles	They will dance with the girls
Chez Julien le violoneur	at Julian the fiddler's
Des polkas | et des quadrilles |	polkas and quadrilles
Et le pas des patineurs	and the skater's step
Le piston la clarinette √	The cornet the clarinet
Attendrissent les costauds	soften the hearts of the strapping fellows
Les ga<i>ss</i> qui vont‿à la fête	The lads going to the fair
Ont mis la fleur au chapeau	have stuck a flower in their hats
Quand‿ils‿ont bu, se disputent	When they have drunk they quarrel
Et se cognent sur la peau	and go for one another
Puis vont culbuter les filles	then go to tumble the girls
Au fossé sous les‿ormeaux	in the ditch under the elms
Les ga<i>ss</i> qui vont‿à la fête	The lads going to the fair
Ont mis la fleur au chapeau	have stuck a flower in their hats
Reboivent puis se rebattent	They drink again and fight again
Jusqu'au chant du premier jô	until the song of early dawn
Le lendemain | on‿en trouve	the next day some are found
Sont couchés dans le ruisseau	asleep in the ditch
Les gars qui vont‿à la fête	The lads going to the fair
Ont mis la fleur au chapeau.	have stuck a flower in their hats.

The truculence of this song suggests a certain peasant coarseness (quite different from Parisian slang), the wholesome gaiety of country folk out for a spree at the village fair. *Follement animé et gai* (Madly spirited and gay) ♩ = 144. The same remarks as those for the preceding song apply here, the contrasts of *legato* and *non legato* are very important, and the dynamics are between *ff* and *mf*.

The first two bars are *non legato*, the two following bars *legato*. The fifth is *non legato* and the song then remains *legato* until the reprise of the theme. At [7] it is preferable not to make the liaison 'rasés/à la cuiller'. In the following bar there should be a strong accent on 'raclés' with the 'r' very much rolled. In the bar immediately preceding [8], the chromatic scale is very tied with a *rallentando* which unfortunately Poulenc did not mark but which we always made. The *accent faubourien* (common accent) demanded, is achieved by a stress on the syllable 'cellulo' on the A♭. Do not take a breath, but carry the voice on, and at [8] resume *a tempo* and *legato*, until [10], marking well all the indicated accents. Then *ff* and *legato*. The quavers (1/8) not too short on the second bar of [11] on 'se disputent'. 'Et se cognent sur la peau' is very *marcato*, and 'Au fossé sous les ormeaux' is very legato. The last four bars without any *rallentando* and strictly in time. The last 'chapeau' must be exaggeratedly linked, even *portamento* with an accent on 'cha' and the last quaver very short.

3 C'EST LE JOLI PRINTEMPS	3 IT IS PRETTY SPRINGTIME
C'est le joli printemps	It is pretty springtime
Qui fait sortir les filles	bringing the maidens out of doors
C'est le joli printemps	it is pretty springtime
Qui fait briller le temps	making the weather sunshiny
J'y vais à la fontaine	I am going to the fountain
C'est le joli printemps	it is pretty springtime
Trouver celle qui m'aime	to find the one who loves me
Celle que j'aime tant	the one I love so much
C'est dans le mois d'avril	It is in the month of April
Qu'on promet pour longtemps	that a lasting promise is given
C'est le joli printemps	it is pretty springtime
Qui fait sortir les filles	that brings the maidens out of doors
La fille et le galant	The lass and her swain
Pour danser le quadrille	to dance the quadrille
C'est le joli printemps	it is pretty springtime
Qui fait briller le temps	making the weather sunshiny
Aussi profitez-en	So enjoy it while you may
Jeunes gens, jeunes filles	young folk, young maidens

C'est le joli printemps	it is pretty springtime
Qui fait briller le temps	making the weather sunshiny
Car le joli printemps	For pretty springtime
C'est le temps d'une aiguille	is but a point in time
Car le joli printemps	for pretty springtime
Ne dure pas longtemps.	lasts so short a time

Poulenc said that the singing and playing of this song must be as clear and sad as an April day.

The poetic contrast between this song and the last must be well emphasized. The voice needs a timbre of floating clarity with perfect *legato*. All the opening remains *p*, without any involuntary changes in dynamics. I would not even observe the *mf* indicated on 'Trouver celle qui m'aime', and would rather emphasize 'Celle que j'aime <u>tant</u>' which is, after all, more important. . . . Then at [16] *subito mf très chantée* and *très phrasé* (very much sung and phrased). At [17] *f* and *crescendo*. Slightly more softly but not too much on 'Qui fait briller le temps', in order to make at [18] a contrast of *p*, but not *pp*. After four bars, the *mf* must be resumed on 'C'est le joli printemps qui fait briller le temps', in order to have at [19] the new contrast of a real *pp extrèmement doux* (extremely soft) and melancholy. Then the dynamics indication on 'ne dure pas longtemps' must lead to the summit of the *crescendo*, a true *f* on this last syllable, from which there must be a rapid *diminuendo*.

4 LE MENDIANT

4 THE BEGGAR

Jean Martin prit sa besace	Jean Martin took his sack
Vive le passant qui passe	Long live the passer-by
Jean Martin prit sa besace	Jean Martin took his sack
Son bâton de cornouiller	and his dogwood staff
S'en fut au moutier mendier	Went off to the monastery to beg
Vive le passant qui passe	Long live the passer-by
Va't-en dit le père moine	Off with you said the father monk
N'aimons pas les va-nu-pieds	we do not like tramps
S'en fut en ville mendier	Went off to the town to beg
Vive le passant qui passe	Long live the passer-by
Epiciers et taverniers	grocers and innkeepers
Qui mangez la soupe grasse	who eat rich soup

Et qui vous chauffez les pieds	and warm your feet
Puis couchez près de vos femmes	then lie close to your wives
Au clair feu de la veillée	in the light of the evening fire
Jean Martin l'avez chassé	Jean Martin you have driven him away
Vive le passant qui passe	Long live the passer-by
On l'a trouvé sur la glace	he was found on the ice
Jean Martin a trépassé	Jean Martin was dead.
Tremblez les gros et les moines	Tremble over-fed men and monks
Vive le passant qui passe	Long live the passer-by
Tremblez ǀ ah! maudite race	tremble Ah! accursed tribe
Qui n'avez point de pitié	who are without pity
Un jour prenez gardé ǀ ô race	one day, take care O tribe
Les Jean Martin seront en masse	the Jean Martins will become a mob
Aux bâtons de cornouiller	with their dogwood staves
Il vous crè'ront la paillasse	They will stick you through the belly
Puis ils violeront vos garces	then they will ravish your wenches
Et chausseront vos souliers	and be in your shoes
Jean Martin prends ta besace	Jean Martin take your sack
Ton bâton de cornouiller.	your dogwood staff.

In the literary edition the title of the poem is 'Complainte de Jean Martin'. Poulenc modified it for the musical edition, and said that the song was very much influenced by Moussorgsky, a fact which arose *quite naturally* from the subject.

The poem, violently vengeful and vindictive, has indeed inspired the composer to write music that is heavy and violent, and it cannot fail to recall certain passages of the *Songs and Dances of Death* and demands an interpreter capable of similar dramatic intensity with a sufficiently powerful voice and forceful diction.

The preliminary tempo indicated by Poulenc is excellent, ♩ = 66, and *Lent mais allant malgré tout* (Slow but moving on). That means the slowness must not drag. From the entrance of the voice [21], the indications *pesant* (weighty) and *très lié et louré* (very sustained *legato* and *marcato*) are also excellent. For the vocal part, I would be tempted to add a linking and a slight pressure on each note to give the impression of the heavy, tired tread of the beggar. Each time the refrain 'Vive le passant qui passe' occurs, each note should be marked thus.

From [22] to [23] the vocal contour is much broader and the singing must be even more *legato* and must maintain the *mf*. In contrast, at [23] shout the high G very *staccato*, maintaining the *ff*. At the third bar, the semiquaver (1/16) rest between 'Va' and 't'en' must be disregarded—and on the contrary the tone should be well sustained and the indicated accents strongly marked. From [24] there is an effect which was unfortunately not marked by Poulenc but which we always made: begin to accelerate the tempo, but very progressively, for this *accelerando* must continue to [29]. From [24] to [25] remain in the *mf*. (This should also be indicated in the piano part.) Then *f* at [25] and *ff* at [26].

In the bar, 'Jean Martin a trépassé', the quaver (1/8) must be very short on the last syllable to leave room for a silence before attacking [27] *mf* only, to allow for another big *crescendo*. The following accents should be made: 'Tremblez les gros et les moines', 'Tremblez ah maudite race Qui n'avez point de pitié'. Continue to accelerate, giving the whole force of the voice with percussive diction. Accelerate more and more; very strong accents on 'Ils vous crèv'ront la paillasse Puis ils violeront vos garces'. At [29] there must be a return to exactly the slow *tempo primo* ♩ = 66, but with still greater weariness and a kind of despair. Sing only *mf* to reserve the big final *crescendo*, during which the voice is carried down to the C, changing the 'e' of 'cornouiller' into 'a', the last low C being a kind of rattle. In this second bar of [30] fourth beat, in the piano part, the G is an error for G♮.)

5 CHANSON DE LA FILLE FRIVOLE	5 SONG OF THE FLIGHTY GIRL
Ah dit la fille frivole	Ah said the flighty girl
Que le vent | y vire y vole	let the wind blow where it listeth
Mes canards vont sur l'étang	my ducks are swimming on the pond
Belle lune de printemps	lovely moon of springtime
Ah dit la fille frivole	Ah said the flighty girl
Que le vent | y vire y vole	let the wind blow where it listeth
Sous les vergers éclatants	under the full blown orchards
Belle lune de printemps	lovely moon of springtime
Ah dit la fille frivole	Ah said the flighty girl
Que le vent | y vire y vole	let the wind blow where it listeth
Et dans les buissons chantants	in the singing bushes
Belle lune de printemps	lovely moon of springtime
Ah dit la fille frivole	Ah said the flighty girl
Que le vent | y vire y vole	let the wind blow where it listeth

Je vais trouver mes amants	I am going to find my lovers
Sous la lune de printemps	under the springtime moon
Ah dit la fille frivole	Ah said the flighty girl
Que le vent │ y vire y vole	let the wind blow where it listeth
L'âge vient trop vitement	old age comes all too quick
Sous la lune de printemps	under the springtime moon
Ah dit la fille frivole	Ah said the flighty girl
Que le vent │ y vire y vole	let the wind blow where it listeth
Plus tard soucis et tourments	later on cares and torments
Sous la lune de printemps	under the springtime moon
Ah dit la fille frivole	Ah said the flighty girl
Que le vent │ y vire y vole	let the wind blow where it listeth
Aujourd'hui guérissez-m'en	today preserve me from them
Belle lune de printemps	lovely moon of springtime
Ah dit la fille frivole	Ah said the flighty girl
Que le vent │ y vire y vole	let the wind blow where it listeth
Baisez moi bien tendrement	kiss me very tenderly
Sous la lune de printemps.	under the springtime moon.

A piece of virtuosity for the two interpreters who must give the impression of an insouciant volubility. The 'e' mute on the words 'frivole' and 'vole' must never be sung, but articulate the final 'l' clearly. Poulenc has happily left out a line in each verse, 'Belle lune de clair de lune', which would have been almost unpronounceable in the tempo, which must be as quick as possible. ♩ = 168 is an indication. Always observe the quaver (1/8) rest indicated at the end of each bar, even if you breathe only once in each two bars. Maintain the *f* with several *ff*s. Give an effect of *legato* on the third and fourth bar. Take care not to hurry on the seventh and eighth bars of [32]. On the tenth bar of [32] make an accent on the first beat, 'Que', on the E♮. Also an accent on the first beat of [33]. Five bars further in, take a breath before attacking, with an accent on the first beat, 'Ah', and sing more lightly and very airily. Give an effect of *legato* on the two bars before [34]. No slowing down at the end of the song. A small, soothing *diminuendo* on 'Baisez moi bien tendrement', and *crescendo* in the descent of the last phrase, 'Sous la lune de printemps', with a strong accent on 'prin' and the last quaver (1/8), on 'temps', very short.

6 LE RETOUR DU SERGENT

Le sergent s'en revient de guerre
Les pieds gonflés sifflant du nez
Le sergent s'en revient de guerre
Entre les buissons étonnés

A gagné la croix de Saint-Georges
Les pieds gonflés sifflant du nez
A gagné la croix de Saint-Georges
Son pécule a sous son bonnet

Bourre sa pipe en terre rouge
Les pieds gonflés sifflant du nez
Bourre sa pipe en terre rouge
Puis soudain se met à pleurer

Il revoit tous ses copains morts
Les pieds gonflés sifflant du nez
Il revoit tous ses copains morts
Qui sont pourris dans les guérets

Ils ne verront plus leur village
Les pieds gonflés sifflant du nez
Ils ne verront plus leur village
Ni le calme bleu des fumées

Les fiancées va marche ou crève
Les pieds gonflés sifflant du nez
Envolées comme dans un rêve
Les copains s'les sont envoyées

Et le sergent verse une larme
Les pieds gonflés sifflant du nez
Et le sergent verse une larme
Le long des buissons étonnés.

6 THE RETURN OF THE SERGEANT

The sergeant is returning from the war
swollen feet sniffling nose
the sergeant is returning from the war
between the astonished thorn bushes

He has won the St George Cross
swollen feet sniffling nose
he has won the St George Cross
has his gratuity under his cap

Fills his red clay pipe
swollen feet sniffling nose
fills his red clay pipe
then suddenly begins to weep

He sees again all his dead chums
swollen feet sniffling nose
he sees again all his dead chums
who have rotted in the fields

They will see their village no more
swollen feet sniffling nose
they will see their village no more
nor the calm blue of smoking chimneys

Their sweethearts go on or die
swollen feet sniffling nose
scattered as in a dream
the chums have ravished them

And the sergeant sheds a tear
swollen feet sniffling nose
and the sergeant sheds a tear
along by the astonished thorn bushes.

Everything is admirably indicated by Poulenc for the interpretation of this song and all must be minutely observed. It is unnecessary, I think, for me to repeat all the instructions regarding dynamics, accents, *legato* and *non legato*. Certain indications of *legato* are nevertheless missing from [37] to [39], but they are self-evident. The nostalgia and the poetry of these passages must be emphasized, to intensify the violent contrast of [39]. Note that the bar before [40] in the voice part needs to be modified: the two quaver (1/8) rests must be disregarded and a *portamento* made, not without coarseness, on 'envoyées', with an accent on the B♭. The listener must be made sensible of the refrain-like character of 'Les pieds gonflés sifflant du nez', always *non legato*. The tempo of *marche enleveée* (march *con brio*) ♩ = 138, must not waver from beginning to end, despite all the contrasts which <u>must</u> be made.

CHAPTER X

Jean Cocteau—Raymond Radiguet

Jean Cocteau was born in 1889, into a well-to-do middle class family. He was gifted with lively intelligence and a brilliant mind, named sometimes 'magician of modern wit', and from his youth he had great influence on the artists of his period. He has been reproached for a certain superficiality and worldliness, which he none the less developed into something that was truly poetic in all its forms. His bibliography is considerable, the following may be mentioned: Poems, *Plain-Chant*, *Romans*, *Le Grand Ecart*; Essays, *La difficulté d'être*; Drama, *Les parents terrible; La voix humaine* (set to music by Poulenc); Film Poetry, *Le sang dun poète*, *Orphée*, Poetic graphs (for Cocteau had great talent as a designer), as well as numerous drawings, illustrations and frescoes.

He died in 1963.

*   *   *

As I SAID in Chapter I, Jean Cocteau had always been a friend of Francis Poulenc. After 1919 he became the spokesman of *Les Six*. In an article in the style of a manifesto, he reacted partly against the 'Russian snare', in other words, the music of Moussorgsky and Rimsky-Korsakov, but also against Debussy and above all the Debussyists and the 'impressionist mists'.

The reaction of the composer Erik Satie was equally positive and consisted of a return to simplicity. Cocteau maintained that it was the only possible reaction during an epoch of extreme refinement.

It is this epoch that must be recalled in speaking of the only three songs composed by Poulenc on texts by Cocteau, and it is particularly by reason of their character, which is representative of the aesthetic of this period, that they are interesting. Curiously enough, Poulenc wrote no other songs on texts by Cocteau. When speaking of *Tel jour telle nuit* I mentioned that he had destroyed a collection of songs. These were on poems taken from the collection *Plain-Chant*, by Cocteau, and it was not until 1958, with the play, *La Voix Humaine*, that they collaborated again. Later, in 1961 he wrote a monologue for soprano and orchestra, *La Dame de Monte Carlo*.

COCARDES (COCKADES)

MIEL DE NARBONNE

Use ton cœur. Les clowns fleurissent du
    crottin d'or.
Dormir! Un coup d'orteil: on vole.
Volez-vous jouer | avec moi?
Moabite, dame de la croix bleue.
    Caravane.
Vanille. Poivre. Confiture de tamarin.
Marin, cou, le pompon, moustaches,
    mandoline.
Linoléum en trompe-l'œil. Merci.
Cinéma, nouvelle muse.

HONEY OF NARBONNE

Use your heart. The clowns flourish on
    golden manure.
To sleep! A kick with the toe; one flies.
Will you play with me?
Moabite, lady of the blue cross.
    Caravan
Vanilla. Pepper. Tamarind jam.
Sailor, neck, pompon, moustaches,
    mandoline.
Deceptive linoleum. Thanks.
Cinema, new muse.

BONNE D'ENFANT

Técla: notre âge d'or. Pipe, Carnot,
    Joffre.
J'offre à toute personne ayant des
    névralgies . . .
Girafe. Noce. Un bonjour de
    Gustave.
Ave Maria de Gounod,
    Rosière,
Air de Mayol, Touring-Club,
    Phonographe.
Affiche, crime en couleurs. Piano
    mécanique,
Nick Carter; c'est du joli!
Liberté, Egalité, Fraternité.

CHILDREN'S NURSE

Tecla: our golden age. Pipe, Carnot,
    Joffre.
I offer to everybody who has
    neuralgia . . .
Giraffe. Wedding. A good day from
    Gustave.
Ave Maria by Gounod,
    Queen of the village,
Air by Mayol, Touring-Club,
    Phonograph.
Poster, crime in colours. Mechanical
    piano,
Nick Carter; that's a nice thing!
Liberty, Equality, Fraternity.

ENFANT DE TROUPE

Morceau pour piston seul, polka.
Caramels mous, bonbons | acidulés,
    pastilles de menthe.
ENTR'ACTE. L'odeur en sabots.
Beau gibier de satin tué par le
    tambour.
Hambourg, Bock, Sirop de
    framboise
Oiseleur de ses propres mains.
Intermède; uniforme bleu.
La trapèze encense la mort.

CHILD OF THE TROUPE

Piece for solo cornet, polka.
Soft caramels, acid drops, mint
    pastilles.
ENTR'ACTE. The smell in sabots.
Fine game bird of satin killed by the
    drum.
Hamburg, beer glass, syrup of
    raspberries
Bird-catcher by his own hands.
Interlude; blue uniform.
The trapeze incenses death.

The date of the three songs is 1919, and the first performance was given at the Comédie des Champs-Elysées on February 25th 1920, at one of the concerts organized by Cocteau. In the same programme there were first performances of works by Satie and Auric, as well as *Le Bœuf sur le Toit* by Darius Milhaud. Referring to this concert Raymond Radiguet wrote:

> Too often it is to the detriment of the words that the music is heard. That of Poulenc does not smother, but underlines these poems which, in some thirty lines, summarize what might be called the patriotism of Paris, the love of a Parisian for his city. A tri-coloured flag awakens in us the idea of our country far better than speaking the word 'country'. Similarly Cocteau's lines do not name Paris. They do better—they evoke it. At café concerts, refreshments can be taken without leaving the seats. Poulenc's music seems to me a musical refreshment.

The accompaniment, as in *Le Bestiaire* of the same period, is played by a group of instruments: violin, cornet, trombone, bass-drum and triangle. This version is greatly preferable. 'It accords perfectly,' says Poulenc, 'with the itinerant player style that Cocteau wished for.' But I admit that I myself prefer *Le Bestiaire* with piano.

The full title is *Cocardes, folk songs on poems by Jean Cocteau*, but neither the songs nor the music suggest folk songs. The texts (I scarcely dare to say the poems), are a kind of word 'puzzle', repeating one or several of the last syllables of each line to begin the following word. As, for instance, the titles of the three songs: 'Miel de Narbonne', 'Bonne d'enfant', 'Enfant de troupe'.

Here is Poulenc's commentary:

> *Cocardes* were written under the orchestral influence of Stravinsky, even though that is less visible here than elsewhere, and under the aesthetic influence, tricoloured, of Roger de la Fresnaye.* The cycle must be sung without irony. The essential point is to believe in the words which fly like a bird, from one branch to another. Medrano† of 1920, Paris before 1914, Marseilles in 1918, are evoked here. It is a matter of divining them, like those views that you look at in a pen-holder. I class *Cocardes* among my 'Nogent works' with the smell of French fried, the accordion, Piver perfume. In a word, all that I loved at that age and that I still love. Why not?

---

*The portrait of Poulenc at this period, by Roger de la Fresnaye, is reproduced on the cover of *Journal de mes Mélodies*.

† A well known circus.

Henri Hell very perceptively writes:

> Rather than Stravinsky's influence, that of Erik Satie is disclosed here.
> *Parade* comes to mind. The source of inspiration is the same: the music-
> hall, the circus, the travelling fairs, with their poetry, tender, mechanical
> and droll.

These songs were written for a light tenor voice. I will not enlarge on their
interpretation, for I hope to have suggested their atmosphere sufficiently,
and they are without complexity. It is enough to follow with precision all
the indications for performance which are numerous and very clearly
explained: *tempi*, dynamics, expression, etc. . . . Sing with absolute
simplicity, without seeking for subtlety or comic effects. That which the
poet and musician have written is sufficient to recreate the atmosphere they
desired.

*   *   *

Raymond Radiguet was born at Saint-Maur, in the nearby suburbs of
Paris, to a family of very modest means. His father was a newspaper
cartoonist. After a few years at the public elementary school, he
entered the Lycée Charlemagne in Paris, but when he was fourteen he
gradually broke away from his family and his studies and, with the
assistance of André Salmon,* introduced himself into the literary life
of Paris. He met Max Jacob and Jean Cocteau. The latter had a
determining influence on him.

At the age of sixteen he began to write his first novel, *Le Diable au
Corps*, which was published in 1923, the year of his death. At that time
he was correcting the proofs of his second novel, *Le Bal du Comte
d'Orgel*. His poems are collected under the title, *Les Joues en feu*.

*   *   *

In 1946 Poulenc wrote a short song on words by Radiguet. His commentary
follows.

PAUL ET VIRGINIE	PAUL AND VIRGINIA
Ciel! les colonies.	Heavens! The colonies.
Dénicheur de nids,	Bird-nester,
Un oiseau sans ailes,	a bird without wings,
Que fait Paul sans elle?	what is Paul doing without her?
Où est Virginie?	Where is Virginia?

* André Salmon (1881–1969). Poet, novelist, memorialist. Companion of all the great painters at the
beginning of the century.

Elle rajeunit.	She grows younger.
Ciel des colonies,	Heaven of the colonies,
Paul et Virginie:	Paul and Virginia:
Pour lui et pour elle	for him and for her
C'était une ombrelle.	it was an umbrella.

These few lines by Radiguet have always had a magic savour for me. In 1920 I set them to music, I do not know in what manner. As far as I can remember, I found the curve of the first line and, very nearly, the launching of the following four, but at this period, lacking authority, I began to get into difficulties; whereas I now believe I have found the means to progress, without any real motivation, until this sudden stop, this silence, which makes the ultimate unprepared modulation into C♯ unexpected and as though perched on the top of a tree. . . .

I took a good look at this time at the other poems in *Joues en feu*. Only 'Paul et Virginie' seemed to me possible to set to music. One rainy day, a feeling of great melancholy helped me to find the sound which I believe to be right. I think it is useful to bear in mind carefully how modern poetry is placed on the page. It is this that gave me the idea to respect the blank space in the letter-press before 'elle rajeunit'. If the tempo is not maintained strictly the same, this little song, made of a little music, of much tenderness and one silence, will be destroyed.

This poem evokes the novel of Bernardin de Saint-Pierre (1737–1814), which bears the same title. The innocent idyll of two children on Maurice Island, which inaugurated the 'exotic' trend in France, had an immense success at the dawn of romanticism. 'Ciel!' is a typically romantic exclamation. Try to give expression to the dream contained in this phrase: 'Ciel, les colonies': the long voyages in a sailing ship, the 'good savages', the fairy tale isles. . . . In the very calm tempo, ♩ = 50, sing *mp* with a slight accent on 'Ciel'. Then the first quatrain is *mf* in a faster tempo, ♩ = 76, but always with similar feeling. Take care to pronounce clearly the very short 'le' of 'ombrelle' exactly with the piano part. The bar rest that follows remains in the same tempo and the last exclamation resumes the slow tempo, *pp* and even more expressive than the first.

In addition to the obvious small mistake (a quaver (1/8), not a crotchet (1/4), on the syllable 'oiseau'), I would point out that in the second bar of the introduction in the piano part, Poulenc always sounded again *pp* with both hands, the whole chord including the two Es which are indicated as tied, but intended as a linking of expression. At the end of the song, the G♯ and the E♯, under the last exclamation, should be given the same treatment.

CHAPTER XI

Louis Aragon—Robert Desnos

Poulenc set two poems from each of these two poets, and the poems which he chose evoke, each in a different way, the dark period of the German invasion and the French Resistance during the war of 1940.

> Louis Aragon was born in Paris in 1897. He was one of the creators of the surrealist movement. From 1927 he was a member of the Communist Party, and often used his works to further his political ideas. During the occupation he encouraged the intellectual Resistance together with his wife, Elsa Triolet, herself a remarkable writer. Aragon is not only a poet, but a politician, an essayist and novelist.
>
> Among his poems let us cite *Les yeux d'Elsa*, *Les yeux et la mémoire*, *Le fou d'Elsa*; and among his novels, *Les cloches de Bale*, *La semaine sainte* and *La mise à mort*. His work is considerable.

* * *

DEUX POÈMES DE LOUIS ARAGON

During the German occupation, in September and October 1942, Poulenc wrote these two songs on poems that were clandestinely published. They both allude, in completely contrasting ways, to the events of the time.

C	C
J'ai traversé les ponts de Cé	I have crossed the bridges of Cé
C'est là que tout a commencé	it is there that it all began
Une chanson des temps passés	a song of bygone days
Parle d'un chevalier blessé	tells of a wounded knight
D'une rose sur la chaussée	of a rose on the carriage-way
Et d'un corsage délacé	and an unlaced bodice
Du château d'un duc insensé	of the castle of a mad duke
Et des cygnes dans les fossés	and swans on the moats

De la prairie où vient danser
Une éternelle fiancée
Et j'ai bu comme un lait glacé
Le long lai des gloires faussées

La Loire emporte mes pensées
Avec les voitures versées
Et les armes désamorcées
Et les larmes mal effacées

O ma France ô ma délaissée
J'ai traversé les ponts de Cé.

of the meadow where comes dancing
an eternal betrothed
and I drank like iced milk
the long lay of false glories

the Loire carries my thoughts away
with the overturned cars
and the unprimed weapons
and the ill-dried tears

O my France O my forsaken France
I have crossed the bridges of Cé

The poem was given this title because all the rhymes end in 'cé'. Aragon wrote the following dedication on my copy of the song:

Et tout l'étonnement d'entendre mes pensées
Par la voix dépécées, depensées, depassées.
O le joli <u>dessin</u> qui va de c en c.

Je rêvais à <u>des seins</u> quand j'étais au lycée
<u>Carnot car nos</u> amours d'enfance, elles ont beau passer,
Deviennent la chanson qui nous revient bercer.

And all the astonishment of hearing my thoughts
by the voice torn, spent, transcended.
O the pretty pattern that goes from c to c.

I was dreaming of breasts when I was at Carnot school,
for the loves of our childhood, though they are passed,
become the song that returns to soothe us.

The poem, 'C', evokes the tragic days of May 1940, when a great part of the French population fled before the invading armies. In this horrible exodus, the poet himself, at the Bridges of Cé close to Angers, had crossed the Loire, crowded with overturned vehicles and discarded weapons, in the total confusion of a forsaken France. The poet recalls his memories in a style that is extremely melancholy and poetically touching, like an old ballad. It has inspired the musician to write a song, the harmonic climate and the melodic line of which have made it one of his most deeply moving and successful works.

It is essential that both singer and pianist should achieve a perfect *legato*. Poulenc emphasizes that the piano part 'is very difficult, owing to the play of pedals and the quick succession of quaver chords which should be veiled'. Even the four bars of piano introduction, which represent the curve of a bridge, are not easy to achieve successfully. To the *très calme* (very calm) ♩=54, I would add: above all no faster; and to the indication *très librement* (very freely), which suggests the idea of an improvisation, I would add: do not vary the equality of the quavers. The whole curve must, of course, be played with the left hand. As always it is of prime importance to observe with the greatest care the indications of dynamics. The two first lines are *pp*, the two following lines *mf*, then again *pp* and without any *crescendo* for the two following lines. If the singer cannot succeed in singing the high A♭ *pp*, it is better not to attempt this song. . . .

In the following four lines, a *crescendo* which increases to a *f* diminishes, with a slight slowing down, on the line, 'Et des cygnes dans les fossés'. A long breath must then be taken and the tempo resumed with *pp infiniment doux* (infinitely gentle), 'De la prairie ou vient danser Une éternelle fiancée', which allows the contrasting *mf* and *f* on the next two lines.

It is preferable, in order not to anticipate the *p* dynamics, to sing *mp* and *crescendo* on the following four bars. Then *p*, not *pp*, on 'Et les armes désamorcées', which should not be too expressive, in order to reserve the *pp* for 'Et les larmes mal effacées' which, with *cédez un peu* (slight *rallentando*). should be, on the contrary, full of feeling. 'O ma France' must be attacked *mf*, but the indicated *crescendo* is not good. After an expressive breath, attack *mf* 'O ma délaissée', with a *diminuendo* (not a *subito p*!) which leads to the high A♭ *pp*. The pause must be short and the *portando*, certainly not *molto*, done with good taste. It is very important for the pianist not to wait too long before beginning the first beat of the following bar, which must be *a tempo*, the *cédez* exactly where it is indicated. The short piano coda, after a breath, must slow down very freely. The essential point, as Poulenc says, is 'to interpret the song poetically. That is the whole secret'.

FÊTES GALANTES	FÊTES GALANTES*
On voit des marquis sur des bicyclettes	You see fops on bicycles
On voit des marlous | en cheval jupon	You see pimps in kilts
On voit des morveux | avec des voilettes	You see brats with veils
On voit des pompiers brûler les pompons	You see firemen burning their pompons
On voit des mots jetés_à la voirie	you see words thrown on the rubbish heap
On voit des mots | élevés_au pavois	You see words extolled to the skies

* This title is here used as a parody of the poetic *Fêtes galantes* of Watteau and Verlaine. This poem consists of many idioms, and words which are occasionally used as much for their sound as for their sense. It is difficult to translate it adequately, but an attempt is made to give an idea of the meaning.

On voit les pieds des enfants de Marie	You see the feet of Mary's children
On voit le dos des diseuses à voix	You see the backs of cabaret singers
On voit des voitures à gazogène	You see motor cars run on gasogene
On voit aussi des voitures à bras	You see also handcarts
On voit des lascars que les longs neez gênent	You see wily fellows whose long noses hinder them
On voit des coïons de dix huit carats	You see fools of the first water
On voit ici ce que l'on voit ailleurs	You see what you see elsewhere
On voit des demoiselles dévoyées	You see girls who are led astray
On voit des voyous on voit des voyeurs	You see gutter-snipes you see perverts
On voit sous les ponts passer les noyés	You see drowned folk floating under the bridges
On voit chômer les marchands de chaussures	You see out of work shoemakers
On voit mourir d'ennui les mireurs d'œufs	You see egg candlers bored to death
On voit péricliter les valeurs sûres	You see true values in jeopardy
Et fuir la vie à la six quatre deux.	And life whirling by in a slap-dash way.

Even the most tragic periods are not without their absurdities. This ludicrous and cynical poem recalls, in the form of parody, the hard days of the occupation—the many kinds of restrictions, the deterioration of certain expressions and certain true values. Is it not typically French 'to be ready to laugh at everything for fear of being obliged to weep'?

Poulenc has set this text to music 'in the style of a catchy cabaret song' with, as he says himself, 'commonplace harmonies and the rhythms of the bazaar.' Its buffoonery is given free reign, and interpreters can enjoy themselves with it, on condition that they maintain the tempo: 'Incroyablement vite ♩ = 152 au moins'. (Unbelievably fast ♩ = 152 at least.) I will not give a detailed study of this song (if I dare call it so!) as all the dynamics are precisely indicated, and also the contrasts of *staccato* and *legato*. The voice must have plenty of timbre in the phrases marked *p*, the more so as they lie in a low register. Impeccable diction and the imagination of the interpreters will do the rest.

* * *

Robert Desnos was born in Paris in 1900. Initially he was a member of the surrealist group, but afterwards left it. His pronounced taste for the language of the people gives a very personal character to his poetry. During the war of 1940, he took an active part in the Resistance and was arrested by the Gestapo. Sent into exile, he died of typhus in the concentration camp of Terezin in Czechoslavakia, in 1945. A collected edition of his poems appeared under the title, *Domaine public.*

*   *   *

LE DISPARU	THE ONE WHO DISAPPEARED
Je n'aime plus la rue St Martin	I no longer like the Rue St Martin
Depuis qu'André Platard l'a quittée.	since André Platard left it.
Je n'aime plus la rue St Martin,	I no longer like the Rue St Martin,
Je n'aime rien pas même le vin.	I like nothing not even wine.
Je n'aime plus la rue St Martin	I no longer like the Rue St Martin
Depuis qu'André Platard l'a quittée.	since André Platard left it.
C'est mon ami, c'est mon copain,	He is my friend, he is my pal,
Nous partagions la chambre et le pain.	we shared a room and bread.
Je n'aime plus la rue St Martin.	I no longer like the Rue St Martin.
C'est mon ami c'est mon copain,	He is my friend, he is my pal,
Il a disparu un matin,	he disappeared one morning,
Ils l'ont emmené, on ne sait plus rien,	they took him away nothing more is known,
On ne l'a plus revu dans la rue St Martin.	he was seen no more in the Rue St Martin.
Pas la peine d'implorer les saints	No use to implore the saints,
Saint Merry, Jacques, Gervais | et Martin,	Saint Merry, Jacques, Gervais and Martin,
Pas même Valérien qui se cache sur la colline.	not even Valérien who hides on the hill
Le temps passe, on ne sait rien,	Time passes, nothing is known,
André Platard a quitté la rue St Martin.	André Platard has left the Rue St Martin.

This little poem recalls the Parisian Resistance with its daily tragedies. Like Robert Desnos himself (possibly only a few days after writing these lines), 'André Platard' has disappeared, arrested by the Gestapo. His friend, his chum speaks in the most simple words of his great distress. A distress that is essentially virile, and, of course, this song is suitable only for a man's voice. As I have already remarked concerning *L'Anguille* and *Voyage de Paris,* when Poulenc wishes to evoke a certain Parisian atmosphere—even Parisian slang—he uses the rhythm of the *valse-musette,* as it would be played on the accordion. 'Here,' he says, 'the immutable rhythm progresses through three colours: the *bal-musette* (a dance with accordion band), the peal of bells, the funeral march.' With this procedure which gives unity to the song, the musician succeeds, without the least sentimentality, in expressing the piercing sorrow, then the mood of rebellion, and finally the despair and resignation suggested by the poem, which touched Poulenc deeply. It inspired him to express musically, with all the sincerity of his heart, his attitude of mind during the war.

I have already advised the manner in which interpreters must approach this type of 'Parisian' song, and I hope that readers will refer back to my former remarks, therefore I will not labour the point. Poulenc writes: 'If the pianist does not respect the preliminary indication—bathed in pedals, the chords scarcely touched, the dotted minims a little brought out—the game is lost.'

Tempo de valse à 1 temps (waltz tempo one beat in the bar), $\dot{} = 76$, seems exactly right, as also the indications of dynamics which must be carefully observed. The numerous modulations and changes of colour must always be made without altering the tempo. Nevertheless, allow a very short pause before beginning, on the last line of page 2, 'C'est mon ami, c'est mon copain'. Then an *accelerando* begins which continues until *Céder un peu* (slow down a little). The bar of silence before: 'Le temps passe . . .' allows a complete change of atmosphere. The tempo, a little slower, gives the rhythm of the funeral march. I suggest an accent of pressure on the word 'rien'. The last phrase, 'André Platard a quitté la rue St Martin', must be sung in one breath. The piano coda remains *p*, except the short *mf* which suggests the crack of a rifle shot.

DERNIER POÈME

J'ai rêvé tellement fort de toi,
J'ai tellement marché, tellement parlé,
Tellement aimé ton ombre,
qu'il ne me reste plus rien de toi.
Il me reste d'être l'ombre parmi les
    ombres
D'être cent fois plus ombre que
    l'ombre
D'être l'ombre qui viendra et
    reviendra
           dans ta vie ensoleillée.

LAST POEM

I dreamed so intensely of you,
I walked so much, talked so much,
so much loved your shadow,
that nothing more is left for me of you.
It is left for me to be the shadow among
    shadows
to be a hundred times more shadow
    than the shadow
to be the shadow that will come and
    come again
        into your sun-filled life.

It is said that Desnos sent this disturbing little poem to his wife (to whom

Poulenc's song is dedicated), written on a cigarette-paper, a few days before his death in the concentration camp. However that may be, it is certainly the expression of the profound weariness of a being who has reached the depths of human suffering, and foresees that before long only his shade will be left to haunt the memory of her whom he loves.

An emotion of equal sincerity must therefore be given to this song, which if not one of the most musically supreme is at least one of the most moving of all Poulenc's songs. Like the former song it is suitable only for a baritone, who must essentially have the ability to sing a high E *pp*.

Bien lent et mélancolique (quite slow and melancholy), ♩ = 52. From the first bars there is a feeling of tragedy in the counter-melody of the piano part, quite *marcato*. The *mf* then the *f* are essential, with accents on 'tellement', in order to contrast with the *p subito* in the sixth bar. Above all no *crescendo* whatever on the octave leap, 'ton ombre'. Then there is a return to the *mf* to prepare the effect of *pp*. *Très doux* (very gentle) and very *legato* at the modulation into the major. Then carefully observe the *crescendo* in the fourth bar of page 2, *mf* then *f*, until the repeat of the first lines *mf* with the same accents, and two bars of *f* leading to the moving effect which must be made with *ppp subito*, before ending the poem *mf* with an accent of despair on the word, 'rien'. The lashing character of the piano coda must make a truly tragic impression.

CHAPTER XII

Colette—Laurence de Beylié—Jean Anouilh

Colette (Gabrielle, Sidonie) was born at Saint-Sauveur-en-Puisaye (Yonne) in 1873. Her numerous novels were written in a very personal style, full of accurate observation and poetry. Among the best known are *La maison de Claudine, Sido, La blé en herbe, La naissance du jour, La vagabonde, Chéri* and *Gigi*. The victim of a cruel illness, she was bedridden for the last years of her life.

LE PORTRAIT	THE PORTRAIT
Belle, méchante, menteuse, injuste, plus changeante que le vent d'Avril, tu pleures de joie, tu ris de colère, tu m'aimes quand je te fais mal, tu te moques de moi quand je suis bon. Tu m'as à peine dit merci lorsque je t'ai donné le beau collier, mais tu as rougi de plaisir, comme une petite fille, le jour où je t'ai fait cadeau de ce mouchoir et tous disent de toi: 'C'est à n'y rien comprendre!' Mais je t'ai, un jour, volé ce mouchoir que tu venais de presser sur ta bouche fardée. Et, avant que to ne me l'aies enlevé d'un coup de griffe, j'ai eu le temps de voir que ta bouche venait d'y peindre, rouge, naïf, dessiné à ravir, simple et pur, le portrait même de ton cœur.	Beautiful, wicked, lying, unjust, more changeable than the April wind, you weep for joy, you laugh in anger, you like me when I treat you badly, you mock me when I am kind. You scarcely thanked me when I gave you the beautiful necklace, but you blushed with pleasure, like a little girl, when I gave you this handkerchief as a present and everyone said of you: 'It is beyond me!' But one day I stole this handkerchief when you had just pressed it against your rouged lips. And, before you snatched it away as a cat with its claws, I had time to see that your mouth had just painted upon it, red, naïve, designed to delight, simple and pure, the very portrait of your heart.

Poulenc writes:

For years Colette promised me some poems. One day sitting next to her bed, with Thérèse Dorny* and Helen Joudan-Morhange.† I begged her

---

* A renowned actress.   † A music critic who was a great friend of Ravel.

for some. 'Here, take this,' she said to me, laughing as she threw me a large gauze handkerchief on which was reproduced in facsimile a charming poem. I must confess that my music expresses very inadequately my admiration for Colette.

This poem in prose purports to be masculine, but perhaps only a woman could write it, in fact only Colette herself could have created such a character as a woman-cat. No doubt the song is not one of Poulenc's most beautiful works, but he has captured to perfection the impulse suitable to the text and its poetic fall.

Strangely enough a metronomic indication is missing, but given the character *très violent et emporté* (very violent and passionate) of the music, and taking into account also the pattern of the piano part, about ♩ = 88 seems a good tempo. As always in Poulenc's music, this must be maintained, despite the modulations and changes of atmosphere, with, none the less, some moments of suppleness which I shall indicate.

The attack is *f* or *ff*, very vehement and with strong articulation. The *legato* begins on 'Tu m'as à peine dit merci' which is *mf*. The indication *mp* seems to me insufficient in this low *tessitura*, and there is a *crescendo* of six bars leading to the high G of the voice part. After that the *f* must continue. The phrase, 'C'est à n'y rien comprendre', is without rigidity, without dragging, and almost spoken on the notes. Resume exactly the tempo *mf* in *crescendo* until 'griffe', then *p subito*, but without any *rallentando*. (The beats in the piano part must remain immutable.) But the *cédez* (slower) on 'que ta bouche' can be considerable and without any *crescendo*, the whole phrase being *pp*. Rapid *crescendo*, 'rouge, naït, dessiné à ravir' being definitely *mf*. 'Simple et pur' is *p* and a little slower and affecting, but *a tempo* on 'le portrait même', *p* with a *crescendo* in descending towards the lower notes and a *diminuendo* in reascending, slowing the tempo a little, with an expression of wonder. The piano coda resumes the *tempo primo*, retaining the same expression.

*   *   *

Laurence de Beylié, whose maiden name was Laurence de Ferry, was born on December 24th 1893. She lived in Marseilles. A booklet of her verses, *Lueurs*, was published in 1968, after her death.

NUAGE	CLOUD
J'ai vu reluire en un coin de mes âges,	I saw shining in a corner of my past life,
un souvenir qui n'était plus à moi.	a memory that was no longer mine.

Son père était le temps	Its father was time
sa mère une guitare	its mother a guitar
qui jouait sur des rêves errants.	that played on wandering dreams.
Leur enfant tomba dans mes mains	Their child fell into my hands
et je le posai sur un chêne.	and I put him in an oak tree.
Un oiseau en prit soin,	A bird took care of him
maintenant | il chante.	now he sings.
Comment retrouver son père,	How to find his father again,
voilé de vent,	veiled with wind,
et comment recueillir les larmes de sa	and how to gather the tears of his
mère	mother
pour lui donner un nom.	to give him a name.
Dans le passage d'un nuage	In the passing of a cloud
nous verrons poindre l'éternité	we shall see eternity appear
chassant le temps.	pursuing time.
En ce point tout est écrit.	At this point all is written.

Poulenc wrote in 1956:

When, a year ago, a friend* sent me this anonymous, typewritten poem, I at once put it aside in case. . . . It is with real pleasure that today I have set it to music, for it has delicate and manifold overtones. The cascade of modulations which are underlying:

> Comment retrouver son père
> voilé de vent
> et comment recueillir
> les larmes de sa mère
> pour lui donner un nom

is not without reminiscence of the *Valse oubliée* of Liszt, no doubt because during these last few days I listened to the old recording, divine, of Horowitz. Two years ago I thought I would never write any more songs, I am decidedly incorrigible. I am told that the taste for this musical form is passing. So much the worse. Long live Schubert, Schumann, Moussorgsky, Chabrier, Debussy, etc. . . . etc. . . .

This charming and rather mysterious poem inspired Poulenc to write a song *doucement mélancolique* (sweetly melancholy) which progresses by successive planes, thus throwing differing lights on the diverse parts of the poem. These different planes are clearly indicated. The poetic imagination of the two interpreters must give them all their meaning. The metronomic

---

* Countess Pastré.

tempo, ♩=76, seems a little too fast to ensure the quiet mood of the song.
♩=72 is more advisable.

   The beginning of the song is marked *p* and this must be maintained until
the *mf*, 'son père était le temps sa mère une guitare qui jouait sur des rêves
errants'. The following four bars are again *p*, as indicated in the piano part,
but omitted in the voice part. Then comes a *f subito*, while the piano plays a
descending pattern so much favoured by Poulenc. (Look at the end of
'Souric et mouric' in the poems of Max Jacob and also, from the same poet,
the end of 'Jouer du bugle'.) A *pp très doux* (very gentle) and poetic is found
under the lines quoted above, then *f* is resumed for the whole end of the
song, with a *ritenuto* to lead into the last bars of 3/4. The indications of small
diminuendi in the voice part are not advisable, if the sense of fatality
expressed by the poem is to be given full effect.

                    *   *   *

   Jean Anouilh was born in Bordeaux in 1910. He has written a great
   number of plays—light comedy and black comedy, with a humour
   that is often caustic—which have made him one of the most
   celebrated playwrights of our time.

LES CHEMINS DE L'AMOUR

Les chemins qui vont à la mer
Ont gardé de notre passage,
Des fleurs effeuillées |
Et l'écho sous leurs arbres,
De nos deux rires clairs.
Hélas! des jours de bonheur,
Radieuses joies envolées,
Je vais sans retrouver traces
Dans mon cœur.

Chemins de mon amour,
Je vous cherche toujours,
Chemins perdus, vous n'êtes plus
Et vos échos sont sourds.
Chemins du désespoir,
Chemins du souvenir,
Chemins du premier jour,
Divins chemins d'amour.

Si je dois l'oublier un jour,
La vie effaçant toute chose,

THE PATHS OF LOVE

The paths that lead to the sea
have kept from our passing,
flowers with fallen petals
and the echo beneath their trees
of our clear laughter.
Alas! of our days of happiness,
radiant joys now flown,
no trace can be found again
in my heart.

Paths of my love,
I seek you for ever,
lost paths, you are there no more
and your echoes are mute.
Paths of despair,
paths of memory,
paths of the first day,
divine paths of love.

If one day I must forget,
life effacing all remembrance

Je veux, dans mon cœur, qu'un souvenir repose,	I would, in my heart, that one memory remains,
Plus fort que l'autre amour.	stronger than the former love.
Le souvenir du chemin,	The memory of the path,
Où tremblante et toute éperdue,	where trembling and utterly bewildered,
Un jour j'ai senti sur moi	one day I felt upon me
Brûler tes mains.	your burning hands.
Chemins de mon amour,	Paths of my love,
etc. . . .	etc. . . .

In this book devoted to the 'mélodies' of Poulenc, I did not at first intend to speak of a waltz song that he wrote in 1940, which was part of the incidental music for a play by Jean Anouilh called *Léocadia*. This pseudo Viennese waltz, as it is described in the text of the play, had an important place in the development of the plot, for it is the *leitmotiv*. It was sung by the celebrated actress-singer Yvonne Printemps.

Five years before this, Poulenc wrote a song for Yvonne Printemps which is found in Chapter XV that analyses the songs written on poems by Ronsard. She sang it in a play by Edouard Bourdet, *Margot*.

I shall not give detailed indications of interpretation for this waltz. It should be sung with a kind of nonchalant elegance, in a style which is in itself pseudo Viennese, as if accompanied by a gypsy orchestra. The important point is to give the character of this charming light music, without ever bordering on bad taste.

CHAPTER XIII

Federico Garcia-Lorca

Federico Garcia-Lorca was born in 1898 at Fuente Vaqueres, a village in the province of Granada, where his father was a landowner. He passed his childhood among the country people and became for ever imbued with the soul of Andalusia. After finishing his studies of Literature and Law at Granada, he left for Madrid, where the Students' Residence was a centre of exalted spirituality. He formed friendships with the painter Salvador Dali, the cinema scenario writer Buñuel, and the most eminent writers of his time. Among his poetical works let us mention *Romancero Gitano* (1928—celebrated the world over and translated into twenty languages), *Poema del cante jondo* (1931), *Oda a Walt Whitman*, *Llanto por Sanchez Mejias* (1935), etc. . . . ; and among his theatrical works, *Yerma* (1934), *Bodas de Sangre* (1933) and *La casa de Bernada Alba* (1936).

Solely because his liberal opinions were known, though he had never taken part in politics, Garcia-Lorca was shot by Franco's Falangists in 1936.

*   *   *

IN 1937, POULENC set to music the French translation, by P. Dermangeat, of three poems of Lorca which were published under the title:

TROIS CHANSONS DE F. GARCIA-LORCA

Poulenc's commentary on this work is rather severe: 'It is of little importance in my vocal work.' Nevertheless, in a rough draft which I possess of the *Diary of my Songs*, he repented some years later of this severity. But it cannot be denied that these songs have a very special savour, although it may be better to forget a little that the poet is Spanish. 'The last song,' says Poulenc, 'has the drawback of being "nobly French", whereas it should have been "gravely Spanish".' In spite of all his fondness for Lorca, Poulenc could never adopt a foreign accent, neither in speaking (!) nor in composing. He was too typically French.

L'ENFANT MUET

L'enfant cherche sa voix.
C'est le roi des grillons qui l'a.
Dans une goutte d'eau, l'enfant
    cherchait sa voix.
Je ne la veux pas pour parler, j'en ferais
    une bague
Que mon silence portera à son plus petit
    doigt.
Dans une goutte d'eau l'enfant
    cherchait sa voix
(La voix captive, loin de là, met un
    costume de grillon).

THE DUMB CHILD

The child searches for his voice.
It is the king of the crickets who has it.
In a drop of water, the child looked
    for his voice.
I do not want it to speak with,
I should make a ring of it
that my silence will carry to his
    smallest finger.
In a drop of water the child looked
    for his voice
(The captive voice, far from there,
    put on a cricket's costume).

The interpreters must succeed in recreating all the mystery and all the poetry of these words and the music which they have inspired. The indications for performance are precisely stated in their entirety with the greatest care; they must be followed exactly. Once again it can be seen that the metronomic speed, $\downarrow = 66$, must be rigorously maintained, and that the few indications of dynamics go from *p* to *pp*, with only a small *crescendo* when the voice descends towards the lower notes in the penultimate bar of the first page. The two lines, 'Dans une goutte d'eau l'enfant cherchait sa voix', should preferably be *p* rather than *pp* in this low *tessitura*, in order to conserve the effect of *pp* for the last two lines, which are an octave higher, and in parenthesis in the literary text.

During the whole song the very least involuntary change of dynamics must be strictly avoided. It is only with absolute vocal mastery and infinite poetic imagination that there can be an attempt to suggest, to make apparent the strange mystery of this work. (In the second bar of the second page, in the left hand of the piano part, C♯ on the third beat should be played one octave lower.)

ADELINA À LA PROMENADE

La mer n'a pas d'oranges | et Séville n'a
    pas d'amour,
Brune, quelle lumière brûlante!
Prête-moi ton parasol.
Il rendra vert mon visage
— Jus de citron | et de limon —

ADELINA OUT WALKING

The sea has no oranges and Seville
    has no love.
Brunette, what a burning light!
lend me your parasol
it makes my face look green—
juice of lemon and of lime—

Et tes mots — petits poissons —	and your words—little fishes—
Nageront tout‿à l'entour.	Will swim all round about.
La mer n'a pas d'oranges	The sea has no oranges
Ay amour	Alas love
Et Séville n'a pas d'amour.	and Seville has no love.

This song which lasts only a few seconds can be extremely effective if it is performed at the tempo indicated, *Follement vite* (madly fast) ♩· = 138, without any *rallentando* at all (except on the last two bars of the piano part) and with incisive and forceful diction. Only the second quatrain is, in contrast, very *legato* but in exactly the same tempo. The *p* on 'nageront tout à l'entour' is relative, as also that of the last line in preparing the big *crescendo* on the last note, which must cease exactly in time. This literary and musical sketch needs a great deal of 'chic' and airiness.

CHANSON DE L'ORANGER SEC	SONG OF THE DRIED UP ORANGE TREE
Bûcheron	Woodman
Abat mon ombre	cut down my shadow
Délivre-moi du supplice	deliver me from the anguish
De me voir sans‿oranges.	of seeing myself without oranges
Pourquoi suis-je né entre des miroirs?	why was I born between mirrors
Le jour me fait tourner	day turns me round
Et la nuit me copie dans toutes ses‿ étoiles.	and night imitates me in all its stars
Je veux vivre sans me voir	I want to live without seeing myself
Les fourmis │ et les liserons,	the ants and the lizards
Je rêverai que ce sont mes feuilles‿et mes oiseaux.	I will dream that they are my leaves and my birds
Bûcheron	woodman
Abat mon ombre	cut down my shadow
Délivre-moi du supplice	deliver me from the anguish
De me voir sans‿oranges.	of seeing myself without oranges.

A difficult song, perhaps because it is not completely successful. In the introduction to these *Trois Poèmes*, you will have read that Poulenc says that he finds there is more French nobility than Spanish gravity in this last song. Such as it is, it can be given great style. For both interpreters the opening is *f* or *ff* and very *marcato*, with broad declamation from the singer. Two bars lead to *pp*, very *legato* in a halo of pedals, very gentle, very clear—all this is precisely indicated. The line, 'Je veux vivre sans me voir', alone resumes some intensity. The repeat of 'Bûcheron' is, of course, like the opening, *ff* and *marcato*. The following bar, *subito p*, must all the same remain *marcato*, like the following *f* and the following *p* which must be only relative, because of the low *tessitura*. (In the last bar of the second page, in the piano part, on the first beat, the high G is in error for G♭.)

CHAPTER XIV

Jean Moréas

Jean Moréas (born Jean Papadiamantopoulos), a Greek poet who wrote in French, was born in Athens (1856–1910). Not wishing to be parnassian or symbolist, he founded the *École Romane*, of which the one pride was his own collection, *Stances* (1899).

*　　　*　　　*

THE POETS WHO inspired the songs which have been studied so far, were all more or less contemporary with Poulenc and, with the exception of Laurence Beylié, were all personally known to him. Jean Moréas, on the other hand, was chronologically and aesthetically of another generation, and it is perhaps surprising that these mediocre poems inspired this musician, so enamoured of contemporary poetry. Poulenc also confessed that he only felt musically at ease with poets whom he knew personally.

AIRS CHANTÉS (SUNG AIRS)

Poulenc writes:

> I perpetrated in 1927 four *Airs Chantés* on poems by Jean Moréas. I do not admire this poet, but for fun, to tease my publisher and friend François Hepp, who adored his work, I decided to set four of his poems to music, promising myself every possible sacrilege. . . . I, who am so little gifted for paradox, it needs the mastery of a Ravel for that, I am always astonished at myself for having been able to write these songs.

As Henri Hell writes:

> It is obvious that the pseudo-classicism of the poetry of Moréas, melodious according to rule and cold as an imitation of the antique in the style of Louis Quatorze: 'l'aquilon', 'le noble océan', 'la source déesse'—all pompous vocables devoid of sense, could scarcely inspire Poulenc.

And yet, although these songs may not be among the best from their composer, they certainly have a charm and a vocal line infinitely attractive to interpreters. *Air Grave* is the one exception, and can scarcely be justified. 'Air Romantique' is suitable for a mezzo soprano; 'Air Champêtre' and 'Air Vif' for a soprano.

AIR ROMANTIQUE

J'allais dans la campagne avec le vent
   d'orage,
Sous le pâle matin, sous les nuages bas,

Un corbeau ténébreux | escortait mon
   voyage
Et dans les flaques d'eau retentissaient
   mes pas.

La foudre à l'horizon faisait courir sa
   flamme
Et l'Aquilon doublait ses longs
   gémissements;
Mais la tempête était trop faible pour
   mon âme,
Qui couvrait le tonnerre avec ses
   battements.

De la dépouille d'or du frêne et de
   l'érable
L'Automne composait son éclatant
   butin,
Et le corbeau toujours, d'un vol
   inexorable,
M'accompagnait sans rien changer à
   mon destin.

ROMANTIC AIR

I walked in the countryside with the
   storm wind,
beneath the pallid morning, under
   the low clouds,
a sinister raven followed me on my
   way
and my steps splashed in the
   puddles.

The lightning on the horizon forked
   its flame
and the North Wind redoubled its
   long wailing;
but the tempest was too weak for my
   soul,
which drowned the thunder with its
   throbbing

From the golden spoils of the ash and
   the maple
Autumn amassed her brilliant
   booty,
and the raven still, with inexorable
   flight,
bore me company changing nothing
   towards my fate.

The 'corbeau ténébreux et inexorable' is obviously reminiscent of 'Krähe, wunderliches Tier' of Schubert. But instead of the deathly lassitude expressed in Schubert's song, Poulenc's song evokes a romanticized storm. His commentary is as follows: 'The first song should be sung very fast, the wind in one's face. The tempo must be implacable.'

This tempo is ♩ = 152 and, after the second quatrain, still faster. Eight bars of piano gradually slowing down with a *diminuendo* lead to a more peaceful section of eight bars in 2/2. But do not be mistaken here, it is important to conserve the crotchet equal to the crotchet (1/4) of the initial tempo. Thus the linking with the repeat of the original 2/4 is made without altering the speed. (In fact, the whole song is counted in one beat to the bar, except the section in 2/2 which is counted in two.) All the first part of the song is *f* or *ff*. Certain accents can be made, for example: 'Et dans les flaques d'eau retentissaient mes pas'; 'qui couvrait le tonnerre avec ses battements'. A great gust of wind, very *legato*, on 'Et l'Aquilon doublait ses longs gémissements', then, *mf* (rather than *p*) is suitable for the description of autumn, also with a good *legato*. The last part is *f*. Another impression of a gust of wind can be given, by a slight *diminuendo* on the words 'Sans rien changer à mon destin' and by making a big *crescendo-diminuendo* on the last E, which can be prolonged *ad libitum*. The squall of the piano coda is at its maximum two bars before the end; observe carefully the use of the pedals.

AIR CHAMPÊTRE

Belle source, je veux me rappeler sans
    cesse,
  Qu'un jour guidé par l'amitié
Ravi, j'ai contemplé ton visage, ô
    déesse,
  Perdu sous la mousse à moitié.

Que n'est-il demeuré, cet ami que je
    pleure,
  O nymphe, à ton culte attaché,
Pour se mêler encore au souffle qui
    t'effleure
  Et répondre à ton flot caché.

PASTORAL AIR

Lovely spring, I will never cease to
    remember,
  that on a day, guided by friendship
entranced, I gazed upon your face, O
    goddess,
  half hidden beneath the moss.

Had he but remained, this friend for
    whom I weep,
  O nymph, a devotee of your cult,
to mingle once again with the breeze
    that caresses you
  and to respond to your hidden
    waters.

Poulenc writes:

> In the Air Champêtre, I have actually permitted, 'sous la mou, sous la mousse à moitié'. Have I been punished for my vandalism? I am afraid so because this song is said to be 'a success'.

And this can be understood, for Poulenc, not having considered the words or the meaning of the poem, has used his marvellous melodic gift.

The tempo *Vite* (fast) ♩ = 144 seems good. Poulenc always insisted on metronomic precision from beginning to end of the song, and clear, precise diction which must never prevent *legato* and great charm of phrasing in the vocal line. The marking *mf* is essential, and the whole song does not ask for big changes in dynamics. The final 'e' mute of the word 'source' should not be vocalized. The quaver (1/8) rest between 'demeuré' and 'cet ami' should be disregarded. Phrase gracefully the contour of 'Pour se mêler encore au souffle qui t'effleure'. The F♯ must be very 'major' on 'à ton flot caché'. The syncopations should be well marked in the piano part just before the repeat of the first phrase. The quaver (1/8) rest should be disregarded between 'je veux' and 'me rappeler', both in the first phrase and also in the repeat. The high B♮ can on occasion be *staccato* for certain voices; at all events sing frankly 'O', the one essential is to make a pretty sound. It is preferable to disregard the quaver (1/8) rest between 'contempler' and 'ton visage', and to breathe or break before 'O déesse'.

The end of the coda for piano should be very transparent in the high phrases and above all without *rallentando*.

AIR GRAVE	GRAVE AIR
Ah! fuyez à présent,	Ah! begone now,
malheureuses pensées!	unhappy thoughts!
O! colère, ô remords!	O! anger, O remorse!
Souvenirs qui m'avez	Memories that beset
les deux tempes pressées,	my two temples
de l'étreinte des morts.	with the grip of the dead.
Sentiers de mousse pleins,	Moss-grown paths,
vaporeuses fontaines,	vaporous fountains,
grottes profondes, voix	deep grottoes, voices
des oiseaux et du vent	of birds and of the wind,
lumières incertaines	fitful lights
des sauvages sous-bois.	of the wild undergrowth.
Insectes, | animaux,	Insects, animals,
Beauté future,	beauty to come,
Ne me repousse pas	do not repulse me
Oh divine nature,	O divine nature,
Je suis ton suppliant	I am your suppliant
Ah! fuyez à présent,	Ah! begone now,
colère, remords!	anger, remorse!

Air grave 'has indefensible lack of originality' according to Poulenc. Therefore I will not try to defend this song. It is the duty of all interpreters to do their best with all works, for unfortunately they cannot expect to sing only masterpieces. But here it is not easy, for in addition to lack of musical interest, there is great clumsiness in the vocal writing, and that is exceptional with Poulenc.

I advise a *f* for the whole of the first page. Then *p* and very *legato* from 'Sentiers de mousse pleins, vaporeuses fontaines . . .' etc. (It must be admitted that this is a charming phrase!) There is a *crescendo* from 'Insectes, animaux, . . .' etc. to return to *f* for all the end of the song.

<table>
<tr><td align="center">AIR VIF</td><td align="center">LIVELY AIR</td></tr>
</table>

Le trésor du verger et le jardin
    en fête,
	The riches of the orchard and the
	    festive garden,

Les fleurs des champs, des bois |
    éclatent de plaisir
	the flowers of the fields, of the woods
	    burst forth with delight

Hélas! | et sur leur tête le vent | enfle sa
    voix.
	Alas! and above their head the wind's
	    voice is rising.

Mais toi, noble océan que l'assaut des
    tourmentes
	But you, noble ocean whom the
	    assault of tempests

Ne saurait ravager,	cannot ravage,

Certes plus dignement lorsque tu te
    lamentes |
	most certainly with more dignity,
	    when you lament

Tu te prends à songer.	you lose yourself in dreams.

'To be sung very fast, in an explosion of joy. It is typical of a spurious success.' I do not altogether agree with this comment of Poulenc. Moreover, twenty years after he had written these songs he admitted that he was exaggeratedly severe about 'Air champêtre' and 'Air vif'. In my opinion this song is a true success. As for the 'explosion of joy', this applies particularly to the first four lines, for it is good to contrast them with 'Hélas, le vent enfle sa voix'—the wailing and roaring of the wind. The tempo, ♩ = 192, may at first seem very difficult, especially for the pianist! But it is excellent and must be assumed at once and maintained without slackening. It is, of course, counted one beat in the bar. Observe all the indicated accents. From 'hélas. . . .' exaggerate the *legato*.

The E♭ which begins the central section is very low for some sopranos, and Poulenc allowed an alternative of an octave higher. The *ff* for the piano is, in any case, impossible. For the last vocalize, the groups of three notes must be clearly marked. For high sopranos who wish to end with a C in alt, Poulenc gave the following alternative: after the indicated breath, which should obviously not be taken, replace G C A with high F E A, and the three last groups an octave higher.

CHAPTER XV

Ronsard

Pierre Ronsard was born in 1524 at Couture-en-Vendômois. He was one of the group of the *Pléiade* with Antoine de Baïf, Joachim du Bellay, etc. . . . He wrote, among other works, *Odes, Les Amours* (sonnets à Cassandre) and *Sonnets à Hélène*. He died at St Cosme-les-Tours in 1585.

*   *   *

POÈMES DE RONSARD

In his commentary, Poulenc is extremely hard on these songs for which Picasso designed a cover, he says:

That is the best thing about this work! These songs (written in 1924/25), after *Les Biches*,* with all possible carelessness, except, thank goodness, in the prosody. The first poem is quite successful, greatly influenced by *Mavra*.† Some of my colleagues sang the praises of this collection when it appeared. Doubtless because, not liking my music much, they were glad to find me less absolutely myself. Auric was not mistaken about it. I remember a night in March, in the station at Meudon. We were coming back from a visit to a friend.‡ Waiting for the train he proved to me in two seconds that my true nature was not in these songs, despite the last pages of 'A son page' and certain places in 'Ballet'.

Poulenc, who had been self-taught, was studying counterpoint at this time with Charles Koechlin, which caused him to seek a more complicated style; but also caused the loss of that beautiful spontaneity which was so characteristic of him. I will, therefore, not dwell at length on these songs. The beauty of the poems and the perfection of the prosody will allow

---

* Ballet created by the Russian Ballet of Serge Diaghilev at the Théâtre de Monte Carlo, January 6th 1924.

† Opera by Stravinsky.

‡ Louis Laloy.

interpreters to turn them to best account, even though the music is not fully satisfying.

All the dynamics are clearly indicated, also the accents and the several changes of *tempi*. Poulenc himself insisted that the metronomic speeds of these songs must be strictly respected: 'The singing of "Attributs" must be imperturbable, without any *rubato*. The interpretation of the other songs is without surprise . . . like the music.' Poulenc thus confirmed here, what he has stressed from his very first works, that he demands above all else precision of *tempi* and absence of *rubato*, and on which I, also, have never ceased to insist throughout this book.

However, I have recently verified the metronomic speeds of these five songs, and I am bound to acknowledge that they are <u>all</u> a little too fast. Could it be that Poulenc had a lazy metronome at that time? I think a more likely reason is that he had in his youth, as I have already mentioned, a tendency to play all his works at too fast a tempo. It is good, therefore, to bear this in mind, but, of course, without exaggeration.

1 ATTRIBUTS

Les épis sont à Cérès,
Aux dieux bouquins les forêts,
A Chlore l'herbe nouvelle,
A Phoebus le vert laurier,
A Minerve l'olivier
Et le beau pin | à Cybèle;

Aux Zéphires le doux bruit,
A Pomone le doux fruit,
L'onde aux Nymphes | est sacrée,
A Flore les belles fleurs;
Mais les soucis et les pleurs
Sont sacrés à Cythérée.

1 ATTRIBUTES

The corn belongs to Ceres,
to the satyrs the forests,
to Chloris the fresh grass,
to Phoebus the laurel,
to Minerva the olive tree,
and the lovely pine to Cybele;

to Zephyrus sweet sound,
to Pomona sweet fruit,
the waters are sacred to the nymphs,
to Flora the beautiful flowers;
but cares and tears
are sacred to Cytherea.

This enchanting poem without doubt inspired the composer to write the best song of the collection. It has more unity and freshness than the rest.

2 LE TOMBEAU

Quand le ciel et mon heure
Jugeront que je meure,
Ravi du beau séjour
　　Du commun jour,

2 THE TOMB

When heaven and my hour
decree that I should die,
torn away from the beauty
　　Of everyday existence,

Je défend qu'on ne rompe	I forbid that they should break
Le marbre pour la pompe	marble for display
De vouloir mon tombeau	with the wish
Bâtir plus beau,	to beautify my tomb,
Mais bien je veux qu'un arbre	but my dearest wish is that a tree
M'ombrage en lieu d'un marbre	should shade me rather than marble
Arbre qui soit couvert	a tree which will be covered
Toujours de vert.	always with green.
De moi puisse la terre	May the earth
Engendrer un lierre	make of me an ivy
M'embrassant en maint tour	to twine round about me
Tout à l'entour;	in many a coil;
Et la vigne tortisse	and may the twisted chain of the vine
Mon sépulcre embellisse,	embellish my sepulchre,
Faisant de toutes parts	spreading on all sides
Un ombre épars.	a scattered shade.

Le tombeau is the most laboriously and artificially elaborate of the set. Observe carefully the tempo *plus animato et marcato* of the central section.

3 BALLET	3 BALLET
Le soir qu'Amour vous fit en la salle descendre	The evening when Eros brought you down into the hall
Pour danser d'artifice un beau ballet d'Amour,	to dance designedly a beautiful ballet of love,
Vos yeux, bien qu'il fut nuit, ramenèrent le jour,	your eyes, although it was night, brought back the day,
Tant ils surent d'éclairs par la place répandre.	so well did they know how to spread brilliance around them.
Le ballet fut divin, qui se soulait reprendre,	The ballet was divine, it was wont to revive anew,
Se rompre, se refaire et, tour dessus retour,	to break away, to join again, to twist and turn,
Se mêler, s'écarter, se tourner à l'entour,	to mingle, to separate, to circle round and round,
Contre imitant le cours du fleuve de Méandre.	as though to simulate the winding course of the river Meander.
Ores il était rond, ores long, or' étroit,	Now in a ring, now in a line, now close together,
Or' en pointe, en triangle, en la façon qu'on voit	now tapering, triangular, in the manner
L'escadron de la grue évitant la froidure.	of a flight of cranes fleeing from the cold.

Je faux, tu ne dansais, mais ton pied voletait	I am wrong, you were not dancing, but rather did your foot soar
Sur le haut de la terre; aussi ton corps s'était	above the ground; your body too was
Transformé pour ce soir, en divine nature.	transformed for this one evening, into divinity.

Ballet is more genuine Poulenc. Take well into account the three different *tempi* which become less and less fast. The *legato* begins with the first part of the second tempo, ♩=144, the second part being, on the contrary, very rhythmic. The *legato* is resumed for the whole end of the song with the third tempo, ♩=120.

4 JE N'AI PLUS QUE LES OS . . .	4 I AM NOTHING BUT BONES
Je n'ai plus que les os, un squelette je semble,	I am nothing but bones, I seem but a skeleton,
Décharné, dénervé, démusclé, dépoulpé,	emaciated, feeble, without muscles, without flesh,
Que le trait de la mort sans pardon │ a frappé.	such that the stroke of death has knocked without leave,
Je n'ose voir mes bras que de peur je ne tremble.	I dare not look at my arms for I should tremble with fear.
Apollon │ et son fils, deux grands maîtres ensemble	Apollo and his son, two great masters together
Ne me sauraient guérir; leur métier m'a trompé.	could not cure me; their skill has deceived me.
Adieu, plaisant soleil; mon œil est étoupé.	Farewell, pleasant sun; my eyes are obscured.
Mon corps s'en va descendre où tout se désassemble.	my body will descend where all come to dust.
Quel ami, me voyant │ en ce point dépouillé	What friend, seeing me reduced to this extremity
Ne remporte au logis un œil triste et mouillé,	would not return to the dwelling with sad and tearful eye,
Me consolant au lit et me baisant la face,	consoling me on my couch and bathing my face,
En essuyant mes yeux, par la mort endormis?	wiping my eyes already lulled to sleep by death?

Adieu, chers compagnons, adieu, mes
    chers amis,
Je m'en vais le premier vous préparer
    la place.

Farewell, dear companions, farewell
    my dear friends,
I go before to prepare a place
    for you.

This song begins well and is then lost in pointless complications.

5 A SON PAGE

5 TO HIS PAGE

Fais rafraîchir mon vin de sorte
Qu'il passe en froideur un glaçon;
Fais venir Jeanne, qu'elle apporte
Son luth pour dire une chanson;

Cool my wine until
it is colder than an icicle;
tell Jeanne to come, and bring
her lute to give us a song;

Nous ballerons tous trois au son,
Et dis à Barbe qu'elle vienne
Les cheveux tors à la façon
D'une folâtre italienne.

We will all three dance to the tune,
and tell Barbe she should come
her locks twisted like
a sprightly Italian girl.

Ne vois-tu que le jour se passe?
Je ne vis point au lendemain;
Page, reverse dans ma tasse,
Que ce grand verre soit tout plein.

Do you not see that day is ending?
I never give a thought to the morrow;
page, fill my cup
until this great glass be quite full.

Maudit soit qui languit en vain!
Ces vieux médecins je n'appreuve;
Mon cerveau n'est jamais bien sain
Si beaucoup de vin ne l'abreuve.

A plague on those who languish in vain!
I disapprove of these old doctors;
my brain is never quite sane
if it be not soaked in plenty of wine.

A son page rediscovers for a moment Poulenc's true verve. The conclusion, scarcely any slower, has a melancholy lyricism that intoxicates.

*

A SA GUITARE

TO HER GUITAR

Ma guitare, je te chante,
Par qui seule je déçois,
Je déçois, je romps, j'enchante
Les amours que je reçois.

My guitar, I sing to you,
through whom alone I deceive,
I deceive, I break off, I enchant
the loves that I receive.

Au son de ton harmonie
Je rafraîchis ma chaleur,
Ma chaleur flamme infinie
Naissante d'un beau malheur.

At the sound of your harmony
I refresh my ardour,
the infinite flame of my ardour
born of a beautiful sorrow.

In 1935, the playwright Edouard Bourdet wrote a play *La Reine Margot*, on the loves of Marguerite de Valois who married the King, Henri IV, but was later repudiated. Bourdet asked Poulenc to write the incidental music. A work of this same period, the *Livre des Danceries* (*Book of Dances*) by Claude Gervaise (about 1550), freely inspired Poulenc to write a suite of pieces now often played, either on the piano, or in the instrumental version, under the title, *Suite Française*.

The rôle of Marguerite was taken by the well known actress-singer Yvonne Printemps, and Poulenc wrote a song for her on some lines of Ronsard. She sang it accompanied by a harp.

These two pages are imbued with elegant, nonchalant and melancholy poetry, which interpreters must enrich with *legato* and beautiful phrasing. The indicated tempo, ♩ =60, is good, The rhythm: can be stressed by a slight pressure on each first beat. It is effective (but not imperative) to sing the first four bars in one breath. I consider that it is better not to observe the *mf* of the fifth bar, but to attack *f*, 'Au son de ton harmonie'. Firmly establish the A (on <u>chaleur</u>) which is against the A♯ in the piano part. In this bar, and without changing the tempo, Poulenc played the semiquavers (1/16) almost like demi-semiquavers (1/32) and did not observe the '*subito dolce*' of the following bar, the vocal line remaining *f* with a *p subito* on 'Naissante d'un beau malheur'. The repeat is *pp* instead of the *p* at the beginning of the song. Continue the dynamics *pp* until the repetition of the last line, 'Les amours que je reçois', which I advise should be *mp* to make it possible to sing, on the last note, a long F♯ with plenty of timbre.

The introduction and the coda for piano must be well established and played very freely, like an improvisation. Carefully observe the *staccato*, then the *legato* of the two ascending scales. The arpeggio of the last chord of all should be played very slowly. Poulenc played it as four crotchets (1/4).

CHAPTER XVI

Anonymous Texts of the Seventeenth Century

A YEAR AFTER having composed the *Poèmes de Ronsard*, Poulenc wrote a collection of eight songs which he entitled:

CHANSONS GAILLARDES (RIBALD SONGS)

Here Poulenc is fully himself. The spontaneity of his inspiration and his melodic invention are again ascendant in these most authentic songs. He found the texts in an old edition of seventeenth-century songs. Henri Hell writes perceptively:

> Not a suspicion of pastiche or archaism in the style. It is the seriousness of these songs that is striking: no insinuation, no permissiveness into which an interpreter might be drawn, tempted by the broad texts; not the least trace of musical coarseness. Poulenc says in music the most audacious things with the greatest seriousness, almost with gravity.

Poulenc said, moreover, that he detested smutty stories but liked obscenity. His conversation and the tone of certain of his letters often indicate this by their Gallic pungency. He has a similar blunt frankness in his *Chansons gaillardes* of which the texts are always very spicy, either in playing on the double sense of the words, or in calling a spade a spade. The interpreters, therefore, must play the game straightforwardly. Speaking of *Le Bal Masqué*, his secular cantata on texts by Max Jacob, Poulenc writes the following, which can apply equally well to the *Chansons Gaillardes*: 'No reticence, no false air of awareness, no knowing looks.' It is precisely by their naturalness and their unashamed candour that interpreters can make audacity of language acceptable. The piano part is at times extremely difficult; great virtuosity is demanded in the fast-moving songs, and in the slower songs a wide variety of tone colours is essential.

These songs are, of course, only suitable for a baritone voice.

1 LA MAÎTRESSE VOLAGE

Ma maîtresse est volage,
Mon rival est heureux;
S'il a son pucelage,
C'est qu'elle en avait deux.

Et vogue la galère,
Tant qu'elle pourra voguer.

1 THE FICKLE MISTRESS

My mistress is fickle,
my rival is fortunate;
if he has her virginity,
she must have had two.

Let's chance our luck
as long as it will last.

The singer could scarcely show greater unconcern and off-handedness about the infidelity of his mistress! *Rondement* (briskly) ♩=176, is excellent, and except for a brief passage, the dynamics are *f* and *ff*, with <u>all</u> the indicated accents <u>very</u> strongly marked. For the vocal line, take care to sing *non legato* rather than *staccato*, in order to give good resonance to the vowels. In the one bar in 3/4, a *portamento* should be made not only between 'deux' and 'et', but also between 'et' and 'vogue'. The beginning of the second verse is only *mf*, and the very *legato* effect and *p subito* must not be missed on the phrases, 'S'il a son pucelage, C'est qu'elle en avait deux'. The accents on 'lala' should be very stressed. I suggest: <u>la</u>la lall<u>a</u>la <u>la</u>ll<u>a</u>la la lall<u>a</u>la', doubling the 'l' as indicated. The last note of the song is *ff* without any *diminuendo* and should be sharply cut off exactly in time.

2 CHANSON À BOIRE

Les rois d'Egypte | et de Syrie,
Voulaient qu'on embaumât leurs
        corps,
Pour durer plus longtemps morts.
    Quelle folie!

Buvons donc selon notre envie,
Il faut boire et reboire encore.
Buvons donc toute notre vie,
Embaumons-nous | avant la mort.
    Embaumons-nous;
    Que ce baume est doux.

2 DRINKING SONG

The kings of Egypt and Syria,
wished to have their bodies embalmed,

to last for a longer time dead.
    What folly!

Let us drink then as we will,
we must drink and drink again.
Let us drink our whole life long,
embalm ourselves before death.
    Embalm ourselves;
    since this balm is sweet.

The singer has <u>already</u> been drinking a little too much. . . . *Adagio* ♩=60. Without any forcing in this low *tessitura*, an ample, sonorous tone is needed with very marked diction. The *legato* begins with *mf* on 'Quelle folie!' and continues for the whole of the following quatrain. On 'Buvons donc', do not pronounce the 'c'. There should be an accent on 'Boire et <u>re</u>boire encore'. No liaison: 'Embaumons-nous/avant la mort'. 'Les Rois d'Egypte/et de Syrie' should have a break similar to the first verse. All the end is *ff* and very *marcato*.

3 MADRIGAL

Vous‿êtes belle comme un‿ange,
Douce comme un petit mouton;
Il n'est point de cœur, Jeanneton,
Qui sous votre loi ne se range.
Mais‿une fille sans têtons
Est‿une perdrix sans‿orange.

3 MADRIGAL

You are as beautiful as an angel,
sweet as a little lamb;
there is not a heart, Jeanneton,
that has not fallen beneath your spell.
But a girl without tits
is a partridge without orange.

A little musical sketch that cannot fail if it is sung at the correct speed of '♩ = 152/160', while observing all the indications of interpretation for the voice and the piano. Nevertheless, I will warn singers that the marking *très sec* (very *staccato*) at the opening and in the repeat, seems dangerous for the clarity of the diction. It is always necessary to sonorise the vowels well. For example, 'Vous' and 'mais' must have the full value of their quavers (1/8) *non staccato*. There should be an indication of *legato* on the *mf* (or better *p*) *subito*, 'douce comme un petit mouton'. The *mf* is then resumed with continual *legato*, *avec charme* (with charm), 'Il n'est point de cœur, Jeanneton', and *f*, 'qui sous votre loi ne se range'. The end is obvious.

4 INVOCATION AUX PARQUES

Je jure, tant que je vivrai,
De vous‿aimer, Sylvie.
Parques, qui dans vos mains tenez
Le fil de notre vie,
Allongez, tant que vous pourrez,
Le mien, je vous‿en prie.

4 INVOCATION TO THE FATES

I swear, as long as I shall live,
to love you, Sylvie.
Fates, who hold in your hands
the thread of our life,
extend, as long as you can,
mine, I beg you.

This poem, full of gravity and nobility, might almost be attributed to Racine—except for the scandalous double meaning!

According to my experience, Poulenc did not take the indicated tempo, ♩ = 56, until the entrance of the voice *tendrement—sans lenteur* (tenderly—without dragging). He always played the piano prelude with its contrasts of *sombre* (dark) and of *très clair* (very clear) in a noticeably slower tempo (about ♩ = 50). The short rests after each two bars were always observed, very restfully, to allow for the change of colour. The little notes in the bar *pp très clair* were played on the beat, but still shorter than the demi-semiquavers (1/32). The voice sings a good *legato mf* with rich timbre. To aid the comprehension of the text, give a little stress on 'Sylvie' and on 'tenez'. In the following bar establish the B♯ and also the F♮ firmly. Then comes the last phrase which should be exaggeratedly bound in the singing. It can be seen here that the composer has expressed very well the double meaning of the poem in his music.

5 COUPLETS BACHIQUES

Je suis tant que dure le jour
Et grave et badin tour à tour.
Quand je vois un flacon sans vin,
Je suis grave, je suis grave,
Est-il tout plein, je suis badin.

Je suis tant que dure le jour
Et grave et badin tour à tour.

Quand ma femme me tient au lit,
Je suis sage, je suis sage,
Quand ma femme me tient au lit
Je suis sage toute la nuit.

Si catin | au lit me tient
Alors je suis badin
Ah! belle hôtesse, versez-moi du vin
Je suis badin, badin, badin.

5 BACCHIC COUPLETS

As long as day lasts I am
serious and merry by turns.
When I see a wine bottle empty
I am serious, I am serious,
when it is full, I am merry.

As long as day lasts
I am serious and merry by turns.

When I am in bed with my wife,
I am serious, I am serious,
when I am in bed with my wife
I behave well all night long.

If I am in bed with a wench
then I am merry
Ah! fair hostess, pour me some wine
I am merry, merry, merry,

A piece of great virtuosity for both interpreters, especially for the pianist, because the indicated tempo, ♩ = 152, is exact and must be implacable. For the singer, who must show the greatest possible effrontery, there are also some difficulties of articulation, for example, it is not easy to make the word 'flacon' understood, and the very rapid contrasts of dynamics and expression are difficult. Then again, the sombre gravity of 'Je suis grave, je suis grave' must be exaggerated, and from the word 'est', of 'est-il tout plein, je suis badin', the bright timbre of the jocosity must ring out at once. In contrast, with 'Quand ma femme me tient au lit', which is very *marcato*, the phrases 'Je suis sage, je suis sage' should be *mp* with a sudden *legato*, as should be indicated. The whole of the third page of the song is *ff* with very strong accents—no matter if they are not vocally beautiful. It is difficult to make the word 'catin' understood. These same remarks apply to the repeat. Observe all up-beat accents on the 'la, la' at the end of the song.

6 L'OFFRANDE	6 THE OFFERING
Au dieu d'Amour une pucelle	To the god of Love a virgin
Offrit un jour une chandelle,	offered one day a candle
Pour en obtenir un amant.	thus to gain a lover.
Le dieu sourit de sa demande	The god smiled at her request
Et lui dit: Belle en attendant	and said to her: Fair one while you wait
Servez-vous toujours de l'offrande.	the offering always has its uses.

This is, without doubt, the text which is the most difficult to find admissible. The only solution is to sing the song in a manner that is very poetic and charming, as in fact the music already is, without apparently understanding the obscenity of the text.

The indicated tempo, ♩=92/96, can seem on the fast side, but Poulenc liked it so. The voice must be clear and floating, and the phrasing graceful. I advise that the *mf* should be maintained for the whole of the first page, and the effect of *p* reserved for the god of Love's reply. Poulenc altered the dynamics on my copy in this way. For the final 'Ha', a little *sforzando* on the E♮, and the D very short, but not loud. I must again insist that these few bars must be sung in all innocence and very seriously. It is a wanton little picture, but charming and poetic.

7 LA BELLE JEUNESSE	7 THE BEAUTY OF YOUTH
Il faut s'aimer toujours	You should love always
Et ne s'épouser guère.	and seldom marry.
Il faut faire l'amour	You should make love
Sans curé ni notaire.	without priest or notary.
Cessez, messieurs, d'être épouseurs,	Cease, good Sirs, to be marrying men,
Ne visez qu'aux tirelires,	only aim at the tirelires,
Ne visez qu'aux tourelours,	only aim at the tourelours,
Cessez, messieurs, d'être épouseurs,	cease, good Sirs, to be marrying men,
Ne visez qu'aux cœurs.	only aim at the hearts.
Cessez, messieurs, d'être épouseurs,	Cease, good Sirs, to be marrying men,
Holà, messieurs, ne visez plus qu'aux	enough, good Sirs, only aim at the
cœurs.	hearts.
Pourquoi se marier,	Why marry,
Quand les femmes des autres	when the wives of others
Ne se font pas prier	need no persuasion
Pour devenir les nôtres.	to become ours.

Quand leurs ardeurs,	When their ardours,
Quand leurs faveurs,	when their favours,
Cherchent nos tirelires,	seek our tirelires,
Cherchent nos tourelours,	seek our tourelours,
Cherchent nos cœurs.	seek our hearts.

Again this is a piece of virtuosity for both interpreters, who must achieve the greatest possible precision. The tempo, ♩ = 176, is a minimum of speed and must be implacable. It expresses the joy of life when you are young and wanton.

The two bars, 'ne visez qu'aux tirelires, ne visez qu'aux tourelours', must be *subito p*, very well articulated and without hurrying; thus they make an excellent contrast. The 'la, la' are *legato*, but all the rest *non legato*. The third and fourth pages of the song must be exactly *in tempo*, but very *legato*, except the two bars, 'cherchent nos tirelires, cherchent nos tourelours', which are *ff* and *non legato*. There should be a big *crescendo* in descending on 'Ne se font pas prier pour devenir les nôtres', with good resonance on the low B♭. Similar indications for the repeat. The last note must be held *ff* until the last chord of the piano (not the bar before, which is indicated by mistake), and sharply cut off.

8 SÉRÉNADE   8 SERENADE

Avec une si belle main,	With so fair a hand,
Que servent tant de charmes,	possessed of so many charms,
Que vous devez du dieu malin,	that you must indeed
Bien manier les armes.	handle Cupid's darts.
Et quand cet Enfant est chagrin	And when this child is troubled
Bien essuyer ses larmes.	wipe away his tears.

This enchanting pastorale can be sung to any kind of audience, providing there is no apparent awareness of the scandalous double meaning of the poem. To draw the interpreters' attention to it is enough for it to become obvious, but above all, they must not try to bring it out. As in 'Invocation aux Parques', it can be seen that the composer was conscious of it by the music and by the marks of expression indicated at the end of the song. It is a real piece of *bel canto* that must be performed with perfect *legato* and phrasing.

Take care to lengthen the third and the sixth quavers (1/8). The tempo, ♩. = 56, is the maximum of speed. In the line, 'Et quand cet Enfant est chagrin', the liaison between 'Enfant' and 'est' is impossible according to the rules; but nevertheless Poulenc insisted on it! It should therefore be done, gently. It is essential that the semiquaver (1/16) rest between the E and the F# of the first 'la, la' should <u>not</u> be observed. This phrase must be sung *legato* with precise rhythm. Then there should be a breath before the two 'la, la,'—'la, la,' that follow and which continue *mf*, but the last two 'la, la,'—'la, la' are *p* with a *rubato* to emphasize the modulation.

The second verse is on the whole more *f* than the first. On the last 'bien essuyer ses larmes', the indicated dynamics should be followed exactly, the *portamenti* being made without exaggeration and with good taste. On the last note the final 'e' mute of 'larmes' is not pronounced, but only a very clear 'rm'.

CHAPTER XVII

Malherbe—Racine—Charles d'Orléans

THE SONGS WHICH Poulenc wrote on poems by these three poets are gravely serious or inspired by religious feeling.

> François de Malherbe. Poet born at Caen (1555–1628), who was favoured by Henri IV and Louis XIII. He was the author of works for court occasions, of odes and of sonnets. He opened the way to classicism.

<table>
<tr><td align="center">ÉPITAPHE</td><td align="center">EPITAPH</td></tr>
<tr><td>

Belle âme qui fus mon flambeau,
Reçois l'honneur qu'en ce tombeau
Le devoir m'oblige à te rendre;
Ce que je fais te sert de peu,
Mais au moins tu vois en la cendre
Que j'en aime encore le feu.

</td><td>

Beautiful soul that was my torch
receive the homage that in this tomb
duty obliges me to render you;
that which I do serve you but little,
but at least you see in the mortal ashes
that I still love their fire.

</td></tr>
</table>

Six beautiful lines inspire Poulenc to write a short song of noble gravity. He says:

> While writing it I had in mind the architecture of Louis XIII. It should be sung without bombast, because Raymonde Linossier in whose memory I composed these two pages, detested bombast more than anything.

Poulenc always remained devoted to the memory of this friend of his youth, who died prematurely, and had a determining influence on his literary culture, as I said in Chapter I. Therefore these few bars must be sung with sincerity and simplicity.

The metronomic tempo is not indicated, but ♩ = 52 seems appropriate. In this song with its low *tessitura* there is no occasion to sing really *p*, the timbre of the voice must be rich and full. Disregard the quaver (1/8) rest between 'ce que je fais' and 'te sert de peu' which should be sung in one breath. Both executants must maintain a beautiful *legato*. Poulenc, with his big hands, did not spread any of the chords in the piano part.

* * *

Jean Racine, poet and dramatist, born at La Ferté Milon in 1639. He was educated by the Jansenists at Port Royal but left them to devote himself to the theatre. He reached the acme of classic tragedy. (*Andromaque*, *Bérénice*, *Phèdre*, etc . . .) He was reconciled with the Jansenists and died in 1699.

HYMNE

Traduit du Bréviaire Romain

Sombre nuit, aveugles ténèbres, √
Fuyez, √ le jour s'approche | et
    l'Olympe blanchit;
Et vous, démons, rentrez dans vos
    prisons funèbres;
De votre empire affreux, un Dieu nous
    affranchit.

Le soleil perce l'ombre obscure,

Et les traits éclatants qu'il lance dans les
    airs,
Rompant le voile épais qui couvrait la
    nature,
Redonnent la couleur et l'âme à
    l'univers.

O Christ, √ notre unique lumière, √
Nous ne reconnaissons que tes saintes
    clartés,
Notre esprit t'est soumis, entends notre
    prière,
Et sous ton divin joug, range nos
    volontés.

Souvent notre âme criminelle √
Sur sa fausse vertu, | téméraire,
    s'endort;

HYMN

Translated from the Roman Breviary

Dark night, blind shadow,
fly away, day approaches and Olympus
    pales;
and you, demons, go back to your
    gloomy prisons;
a God releases us from your dreadful
    power.

The sun penetrates the obscure
    shadow,
and the glittering arrows that it shoots
    into the air
breaking through the thick veil that
    covered nature,
give colour once again to the soul and
    the universe.

O Christ, our only light,
we acknowledge only your holy
    clarity,
our spirit is in submission to you,
    hear our prayer,
and beneath your divine yoke, subject
    our will.

Often our guilty soul
with false courage, recklessly sleeps;

Hâte-toi d'éclairer, | ô lumière   hasten to enlighten, O eternal light,
    éternelle,
Des malheureux assis dans l'ombre de   the wretched ones crouched in the
    la mort.   shadow of death.

    Gloire à toi, Trinité profonde,   Hail to thee, profound Trinity,
Père, Fils, | Esprit Saint: qu'on t'adore   Father, Son, Holy Ghost; let us ever
    toujours,   adore you,
Tant que l'astre des temps | éclairera le   as long as the sun illuminates the
    monde,   world,
Et quand les siècles même | auront fini   and even when the centuries end their
    leur cours.   course.

This song is written for a bass voice. Its exact title is 'Hymne, traduit du bréviaire Romain'. Poulenc's commentary is as follows:

> There are parts of this hymn which satisfy me well enough, others where I would have liked more suppleness. It is impossible to set alexandrines to music when the rhythm is not felt in a live way. This is my position.

This poem comprises five stanzas, each consisting of a line of eight feet and of three alexandrines. Curiously enough, Poulenc begins each stanza of his musical setting *pp* (except the last which is only *p*). It is of prime importance to observe these dynamics which then allow a big *crescendo* leading without hesitation to a broad *f*. Each time the opening of these stanzas gives an opportunity for a change of light and colour in the voice, which must not be lacking. I am sure there is no need for me to stress that the declamation must be broad like that of a Racine tragedy, and the vocal line perfectly *legato*. The indicated tempo, 'Largo— ♩ = 60' seems right and authentic.

*   *   *

> Charles d'Orléans was born in Paris in 1391. He had a sad life, which, with 25 years of captivity in England, gave his poetry a melodious melancholy. He ended his life in the Castle of Blois surrounded by a court of poets and artists. He died in 1465.

During the terror of war that threatened the world in 1938, Poulenc found in *Le Figaro* of September 28th, some admirable lines of Charles d'Orléans in the form of a prayer for peace addressed to the Virgin Mary. He set them to music immediately. Here are his own words which are the best possible commentary that could be made on this work. It gives the spirit and the tone:

I tried to give here a feeling of fervour and above all of humility (for me the most beautiful quality of prayer). It is a prayer for a country church. My conception of religious music is essentially direct and often intimate.

Humility, simplicity, fervour, sweetness, confidence. . . .

<table>
<tr><td>

PRIEZ POUR PAIX

</td><td>

PRAY FOR PEACE

</td></tr>
<tr><td>

Priez pour paix, douce Vierge Marie,
Reine des cieux | et du monde
    maîtresse,
Faites prier, par votre courtoisie,
Saints et saintes, √ et prenez votre
    adresse
Vers votre Fils, √ requérant sa Hautesse.
Qu'il lui plaise son peuple regarder, √

Que de son sang a voulu racheter,

En déboutant guerre qui tout dévoie.
De prières ne vous veuillez lasser.
Priez pour paix, priez pour paix,
Le vrai trésor de joie.

</td><td>

Pray for peace, gentle Virgin Mary,
Queen of the skies and Mistress of the
    world,
of your courtesy, ask for the prayers
of all the saints, and make your
    address
to your Son, beseeching his Majesty
that he may please to look upon his
    people,
whom he wished to redeem with his
    blood,
banishing war which disrupts all.
Do not cease your prayers.
Pray for peace, pray for peace,
and true treasure of joy.

</td></tr>
</table>

This song is published in two keys: in C minor for low voice (original key), and F minor for medium voice.

The tempo, *très lent et très calme* (very slow and calm) is ♩=60, which should have been so indicated. It is very important for the pianist to have the courage to play the four bars of introduction exactly in this tempo, in order to remain absolutely unchanged when the voice enters. The first three lines are *p*; 'Saints et Saintes' is *mf*. Breathe after these words and sing in one breath 'et prenez votre adresse, Vers votre Fils, Requérant sa Hautesse', with a *p subito* on 'Vers votre Fils'. (Note that in the edition for medium voice there is an unfortunate misprint: *f* is indicated instead of *p*.) From the second page the dynamics are *mf* for the voice, with a *crescendo* to *f*. The two bars, 'En déboutant guerre qui tout devoie', should be even and a little *marcato*, with a line over each note. (In the edition for medium voice, there is obviously a ♭ missing on the G in the right hand (G|♭|).) 'De prières ne vous veuillez lasser' is *legato* (disregard the semiquaver (1/16) rest after 'prières'), and *mp* in order to reserve the *p* for the repeat. There should, of course, be a breath between the two phrases of, 'Priez pour paix', and before 'de joie', because this last word must be marked a little and held for the full length of the value indicated. This song is very beautiful accompanied by the organ.

BIBLIOGRAPHICAL NOTE

Francis Poulenc: *Entretiens avec Claude Rostand*, Julliard, 1954
Francis Poulenc: *Entretiens avec Stéphane Audel*: 'Moi et mes amis', La Palatine, 1963
Francis Poulenc: *Journal de mes mélodies*, Grasset, 1964
Francis Poulenc: *Correspondence 1915–1963*, Seuil, 1967
Francis Poulenc: *Emmanuel Chabrier*, La Palatine, 1961

*

Henri Hell: *Francis Poulenc*, Plon, 1958
Jean Roy: *Francis Poulenc*, Seghers, 1964

Index of Titles

A son page (Poèmes de Ronsard), 211

A sa guitare, 211

A toutes brides (Tel jour telle nuit), 102

Adelina à la promenade (Trois chansons de F. Garcia-Lorca), 199

Airs chantés, 202

Air champêtre (Airs chantés), 204

Air grave (Airs chantés), 205

Air romantique (Airs chantés), 203

Air vif (Airs chantés), 206

Allons plus vite, 64

Amoureuses (Cinq poèmes—Paul Eluard), 96

Anges musiciens, Les (La courte paille), 167

Anguille, L' (Quatre poèmes—G. Apollinaire), 57

Attributs (Poèmes de Ronsard), 208

Au-delà (Trois poèmes de Louise de Vilmorin), 133

Aux officiers de la Garde Blanche (Trois poèmes de Louise de Vilmorin), 135

Aussi bien que les cigales (Calligrammes), 87

Avant le cinéma (Quatre poèmes—G. Apollinaire), 59

Ba, be, bi, bo, bu (La courte paille), 166

Ballet (Poèmes de Ronsard), 209

Banalités, 69

Belle jeunesse, La (Chansons gaillardes), 217

Berceuse (Cinq poèmes de Max Jacob), 157

Bestiaire, Le, 51

Bonne d'enfant (Cocardes), 182

Bonne journée (Tel jour telle nuit), 98

Bleuet, 68

Calligrammes, 83

'C' (Deux poèmes de Louis Aragon), 186

Carafon, Le (La courte paille), 168

Carpe, La (Le Bestiaire), 53

Carte postale (Quatre poèmes—G. Apollinaire), 58

Ce doux petit visage, 124

C'est ainsi que tu es (Métamorphoses), 146

C'est le joli printemps (Chansons villageoises), 174

Chanson (Trois poèmes de Louise Lalanne), 56

Chanson à boire (Chanson gaillardes), 214

Chanson bretonne (Cinq poèmes de Max Jacob), 153

Chanson de la fille frivole (Chanson villageoises), 177

Chanson d'Orkenise (Banalités), 70

Chanson de l'oranger sec (Trois chansons de F. Garcia-Lorca), 200

Chanson du clair tamis (Chansons villageoises), 171

Chansons gaillardes, 213

Chansons villageoises, 170

Chemins de l'amour, Les, 196

Chèvre du Thibet, La (Le Bestiaire), 52

Cimetière, Le (Cinq poèmes de Max Jacob), 154

Cinq poèmes (Eluard), 94
Cinq poèmes de Max Jacob, 152
Cocardes, 182
Couplets bachiques (Chansons
　gaillardes), 216
Courte paille, La, 163

Dame d'André, La (Fiançailles pour
　rire), 137
Dans l'herbe (Fiançailles pour rire),
　138
Dans le jardin d'Anna, 61
Dernier, poème, 191
Deux mélodies, 1956, 54, 194
Deux poèmes de Louis Aragon, 186
Disparu, Le, 190
Dromadaire, Le (Le Bestiaire), 52
Dauphin, Le (Le Bestiaire), 53

Ecrevisse, L' (Le Bestiaire), 53
Enfant de troupe (Cocardes), 182
Enfant muet, L' (Trois chansons de F.
　Garcia-Lorca), 198
Epitaphe, 220
Espionne, L' (Calligrammes), 83

Fagnes de Wallonie (Banalités), 72
Fêtes galantes (Deux poèmes—Louis
　Aragon), 188
Fiançailles pour rire, 137
Figure de force brûlante et farouche
　(Tel jour telle nuit), 104
Fleurs (Fiançailles pour rire), 144
Fraîcheur et le feu, La, 112
Front comme un drapeau perdu, Le
　(Tel jour telle nuit), 101

Garçon de Liège, Le (Trois poèmes de
　Louise de Vilmorin), 132
Gars qui vont a la fête, Les (Chansons
　villageoises), 172
Georges Braque (Le travail du peintre),
　119
Grace exilé, La (Calligrammes), 86
Grenouillère, La, 66

Hier (Trois poèmes de Louise Lalanne),
　56
Hôtel (Banalités), 72
Hymne, 221
Hyde Park, 79

Invocation aux Parques (Chansons
　gaillardes), 215
Il la prend dans ses bras (Cinq
　poèmes—Paul Eluard), 95
Il pleut (Calligrammes), 86
Il vole (Fiançailles pour rire), 139

Jacques Villon (Le travail du peintre),
　123
Je n'ai plus que les os (Poèmes de
　Ronsard), 210
Je nommerai ton front (Miroirs
　brûlants), 110
Joan Mirò (Le travail du peintre),
　122
Jouer du bugle (Parisiana), 159
Juan Gris (Le travail du peintre), 120

Madrigal (Chansons gaillardes), 215
Main dominée par le cœur, 126
Maîtress volage, La (Chansons
　gaillardes), 214
Mais mourir, 125
Mazurka, 149
Mendiant, Le (Chansons villageoises),
　175
Métamorphoses, 145
Miel de Narbonne (Cocardes), 182
Miroirs brûlants, 107
Mon cadavre est doux comme un gant
　(Fiançailles pour rire), 141
Montparnasse, 77
Mutation (Calligrammes), 84
Marc Chagall (Le travail du peintre),
　118

1904 (Quatre poèmes—G. Apollinaire),
　60
Nuage (Deux mélodies 1956), 194

Nous avons fait la nuit (Tel jour telle nuit), 105

Offrande, L' (Chansons gaillardes), 217

Pablo Picasso (Le travail du peintre), 116
Paganini (Métamorphoses), 147
Parisiana, 159
Paul et Virginie, 185
Paul Klee (Le travail du peintre), 121
Petite servante, La (Cinq poèmes de Max Jacob), 155
Peut-il se reposer (Cinq poèmes—Eluard), 94
Poème, Un, 82
Poèmes de Ronsard, 207
Pont, Le, 80
Plume d'eau clair (Cinq Poèmes—Eluard), 95
Portrait, Le, 193
Présent, Le (Trois poèmes de Louise Lalanne), 55
Priez pour paix, 223

Quatre poèmes de G. Apollinaire, 57
Quelle aventure! (La courte paille), 164

Rayon des yeux (La Fraicheur et le Feu), 112
Reine des mouettes (Métamorphoses), 145
Reine de cœur, La (La courte paille), 166

Retour du sergent, Le (Chansons villageoises), 179
Rôdeuse au front de verre (Cinq poèmes de Paul Eluard), 95
Rosemonde, 90

Sanglots, (Banalités), 75
Sauterelle, La (Le Bestiare), 52
Sérénade (Chansons gaillardes), 218
Sommeil, Le (La Courte Paille), 163
Souric et Mouric (Cinq poèmes de Max Jacob), 157
Souris, La (Deux mélodies 1956), 54

Tel jour telle nuit, 97
Tombeau, Le (Poèmes de Ronsard), 208
Travail du peintre, Le, 116
Trois chansons de F. Garcia-Lorca, 198
Trois poèmes de Louise Lalanne, 54
Trois poèmes de Louise de Vilmorin, 131
Tu vois le feu du soir (Miroirs brûlants), 108

Une chanson de porcelaine, 127
Une herbe pauvre (Tel jour telle nuit), 103
Une roulotte couverte en tuiles (Tel jour telle nuit), 101
Une ruine coquille vide (Tel jour telle nuit), 99

Vers le sud (Calligrammes), 85
Violon (Fiançailles pour rire), 143
Voyage (Calligrammes), 88
Voyage à Paris (Banalités), 74
Vous n'écrivez plus? (Parisiana), 161

Index of First Lines

Adieu, Amour, nuage qui fuit
   (Calligrammes), 88
Ah dit la fille frivole (Chansons
   villageoises), 177
Ah! la charmante chose (Banalités),
   74
Ah! fuyez à present (Airs chantés), 205
Ane ou vache coq ou cheval (Le travail
   du peintre), 118
André ne connait pas la dame
   (Fiançailles pour rire), 137
A Strasbourg en dix-neuf-cent-quatre
   (Quatre poèmes de Guillaume
   Apollinaire), 60
A toutes brides toi dont le fantôme (Tel
   jour telle nuit), 102
Au bord de l'île on voit, 66
Au dieu d'Amour, une pucelle
   (Chansons gaillardes), 217
Avec ses quatre dromadaires (Le
   Bestiaire), 52
Avec une si belle main (Chansons
   gaillardes), 218

Ba, be, bi, bo, bu, bé! (La courte
   paille), 166
Belle âme qui fut mon flambeau, 220
Belles journées souris du temps, 54
Belle, méchante, menteuse, 193
Belle source, je veux me rappeler sans
   cesse (Airs chantés), 204
Bijoux aux poitrines, Les, 149
Bonne journée j'ai revu qui je n'oublie
   pas (Tel jour telle nuit), 98
Bûcheron, abats mon ombre (Trois
   chansons de F. Garcia-Lorca), 200

Certes si nous avions vecu (Deux
   poèmes de G. Apollinaire), 61
C'est le joli printemps (Chansons
   villageoises), 174
Chemins qui vont à la mer, Les,
   196
Ciel! les colonies, 184
Couples amoureux aux accents
   méconnu, 143

Dans vos viviers dans vos étangs (Le
   Bestiare), 53
Dauphins vous jouez dans la mer (Le
   Bestiare), 53
De jour merci de nuit prends garde (Le
   travail du peintre), 120
Deux dames le long du fleuve, 80

Eau-de-vie! Au-delà! (Trois poèmes de
   Louise de Vilmorin), 133
Elles ont les épaules hautes (Cinq
   poèmes—Eluard), 96
En allant se coucher le soleil (Fiançailles
   pour rire), 139
Enfant cherche sa voix, L' (Trois
   chansons de F. Garcia-Lorca), 199
Entoure ce citron de blanc d'œuf
   informe (Le travail du peintre), 116
Epis sont à Cérès, Les (Poèmes de
   Ronsard), 208
Et puis ce soir on s'en ira (Quatre
   poèmes de G. Apollinaire), 59
Et le soir vient et les lys meurent (Deux
   poèmes de G. Apollinaire), 64

Fais rafraîchir mon vin (Poèmes de
  Ronsard), 211
Faiseurs de religions, Les, 79
Figure de force brûlante et farouche
  (Tel jour telle nuit), 104
Fleurs promises, fleurs tenues dans tes
  bras (Fiançailles pour rire), 144
Front comme un drapeau perdu, Le
  (Tel jour telle nuit), 101

Gars qui vont a la fête, Les (Chansons
  villageoises), 172
Gens du midi, gens du midi
  (Calligrammes), 87

Hier, c'est ce chapeau fané (Trois
  poèmes de Louise Lalanne), 56

Il est entré, 82
Il faut s'aimer toujours (Chansons
  gaillardes), 217
Il la prend dans ses bras (Cinq poèmes
  de Paul Eluard), 95
Il pleut des voix de femmes
  (Calligrammes), 86
Irrémédiable vie (Le travail du peintre),
  123

J'ai perdu ma poulette (Cinq poèmes de
  Max Jacob), 153
J'ai rêvé tellement fort de toi, 191
J'ai traversé les ponts de Cé (Deux
  poèmes de Louis Aragon), 186
J'ai vu reluire, en un coin de mes âges,
  194
J'allais dans la campagne (Airs chantés),
  203
Jeanne Houhou la très gentille (Quatre
  poèmes de G. Apollinaire), 57
Jean Martin prit sa besace (Chansons
  villageoises), 186
Je n'ai plus que les os (Poèmes de
  Ronsard), 210

Je n'ai envie que de t'aimer (Tel jour
  telle nuit), 103
Je n'aime plus la rue St Martin, 190
Je ne peux plus rien dire (Fiançailles
  pour rire), 138
Je nommerai to front (Miroirs
  brûlants), 110
Jeune homme de vingt ans, 68
Je jure, tant que je vivrai (Chansons
  gaillardes), 215
Je suis tant que dure le jour (Chansons
  gaillardes), 216

Longtemps au pied du perron, 90
Lune, belle lune, lune d'Avril (La
  courte paille), 169

Ma chambre a la forme d'une cage
  (Banalités), 72
Ma guitare, je te chante, 211
Ma maîtresse est volage (Chansons
  gaillardes), 214
Main dominée par le cœur, 126
Mains agitée, aux grimaces nouées,
  125
M'as tu connu marchand d'journaux
  (Parisiana), 161
Mer n'a pas d'oranges, La (Trois
  chansons de F. Garcia-Lorca), 199
Mollement accoudée (La courte paille),
  166
Mon cadavre est doux comme un gant
  (Fiançailles pour rire), 141
Morceau pour piston seul (Cocardes),
  182
Myrtilles sont pour la dame, Les (Trois
  poèmes de Louise Lalanne), 56

Nous avons fait la nuit (Tel jour telle
  nuit), 105
Notre amour est reglé par les calmes
  étoiles (Banalités), 75

Officiers de la Garde Blanche (Trois
  poèmes de Louise de Vilmorin), 135

Ombre de la très douce, L' (Quatre
  poèmes de G. Apollinaire), 58
On voit des marquis sur des bicyclettes
  (Deux poèmes de Louis Aragon), 188
O porte de l'hôtel, 77
Où le bedeau a passé (Chansons
  villageoises), 171

Pâle espionne de l'Amour
  (Calligrammes), 83
Par la porte d'Orkenise (Banalités), 70
Peut-il se reposer celui qui dort (Cinq
  poèmes de Paul Eluard), 94
Plume d'eau claire, pluie fragile (Cinq
  poèmes de Paul Eluard), 95
Poils de cette chèvre, Les (Le Bestiaire),
  52
Pourquoi, se plaignait la carafe (La
  courte paille), 168
Préservez-nous du feu et du tonnerre
  (Cinq poèmes de Max Jacob), 155
Priez pour paix, 223

Quand le ciel et mon heure (Poèmes de
  Ronsard), 208

Rayons des yeux et des soleils (La
  fraicheur et le feu), 113
Reine des mouettes, mon orpheline
  (Métamorphoses), 145
Rien que ce doux petit visage, 124
Rôdeuse au front de verre (Cinq
  poèmes de Paul Eluard), 95
Rois d'Egypte, Les (Chansons
  gaillardes), 214

Sergent s'en revient de guerre, Le
  (Chansons villageoises), 179
Si mon marin vous le chassez (Cinq
  poèmes de Max Jacob), 154
Si tu veux je te donnerai (Trois poèmes
  de Louise Lalanne), 55
Soir qu'amour vous fit en la salle
  descendre (Poèmes de Ronsard),
  209

Soleil de proie prisonnier de ma tête (Le
  travail du peintre), 122
Sombre nuit, aveugles ténèbres, 221
Sommeil est en voyage, Le (La courte
  paille), 163
Souric et Mouric, rat blanc, souris noire
  (Cinq poèmes de Max Jacob), 157
Sur la pente fatale (Le travail du
  peintre), 121
Sur les fils de la pluie (La courte paille),
  167

Ta chair d'âme mêlée
  (Métamorphoses), 146
Tant de tristesse pleinières (Banalités),
  72
Técla: notre age d'or (Cocardes),
  182
Ton père est à la messe (Cinq poèmes de
  Max Jacob), 157
Trésor du verger et le jardin en fête, La
  (Airs chantés), 206
Trois dames qui jouaient du bugle, Les
  (Parisiana), 159
Tu vois le feu du soir (Miroirs brûlants),
  108

Une chanson de porcelaine bat des
  mains, 127
Une femme qui pleurait
  (Calligrammes), 84
Une herbe pauvre (Tel jour telle nuit),
  103
Une puce dans sa voiture (La courte
  paille), 164
Une roulotte couverte en tuiles (Tel
  jour telle nuit), 101
Une ruine coquille vide (Tel jour telle
  nuit), 99
Un garçon de conte de fée (Trois
  poèmes de Louise de Vilmorin),
  132
Un oiseau s'envole (Le travail du
  peintre), 119
Use ton cœur (Cocardes), 182

Va-t'en, va-t'en mon arc en ciel
  (Calligrammes), 86
Violon, hippocampe et serène
  (Métamorphoses), 147
Voici la fine sauterelle (Le Bestiaire), 52

Vous êtes belle comme un ange
  (Chanson gaillardes), 215

Zénith, Tous ces regrets
  (Calligrammes), 85